全国高职高专规划教材·机械设计制造系列

机械工程专业英语

管俊杰　王素艳　主编

内容简介

本书由科普篇、基础篇、专业篇及附录等四部分组成。主要包括机器人、计算机、公差、机械原理及零件、金属材料等科普和机械类专业基础方面的内容，机械加工工艺、机床夹具、数控、机电产品说明书等机械类专业课内容，科技英语的特点、英文机械图样用语、机械工程常用词汇等附录。

本书适合作为机械类高职学生的专业英语教材，也可供机械类中职学生、本科学生及机械工程专业技术人员学习参考。

图书在版编目(CIP)数据

机械工程专业英语/管俊杰，王素艳主编．—北京：北京大学出版社，2010.7

（全国高职高专规划教材·机械设计制造系列）

ISBN 978-7-301-16897-4

Ⅰ.机… Ⅱ.①管…②王… Ⅲ.机械工程—英语—高等学校：技术学校—教材 Ⅳ.H31

中国版本图书馆CIP数据核字（2010）第017512号

书　　名：机械工程专业英语
著作责任者：管俊杰　王素艳　主编
策 划 编 辑：温丹丹
责 任 编 辑：成　淼
标 准 书 号：ISBN 978-7-301-16897-4/TH·0177
出　版　者：北京大学出版社
地　　址：北京市海淀区成府路205号　100871
网　　址：http://www.pup.cn
电　　话：邮购部62752015　发行部62750672　编辑部62765126　出版部62754962
电 子 信 箱：zyjy@pup.cn
印　刷　者：三河市北燕印装有限公司
发　行　者：北京大学出版社
经　销　者：新华书店
787毫米×980毫米　16开本　14.5印张　345千字
2010年7月第1版　2010年7月第1次印刷
定　　价：29.00元

前 言

高职院校机械类专业英语教学以提高学生职业综合能力为目标，其主要任务是：通过本门课程的学习，使学生能够掌握机械工程常用专业词汇及术语，能够借助专业词典阅读、理解本专业英文资料、设备（产品）说明书，初步具备专业英语的翻译能力。这本教材就是为适应高职院校机械类专业英语教学，满足教师和学生的教学、学习需要而编写的。

全书共 24 课 48 篇文章，由科普篇、基础篇、专业篇及附录四部分组成。科普篇 5 课共 10 篇文章，其中包括：物理学、机器人、计算机辅助设计基础、多媒体技术等内容；基础篇 5 课共 10 篇文章，其中包括：公差与技术测量、机械原理及零件、力学、金属材料热处理、金属材料热加工等内容；专业篇 14 课共 28 篇文章，其中包括：机械加工工艺、金属切削机床、金属切削原理与刀具、机床的液压传动、机床夹具、计算机辅助设计与制造、数控机床与编程、机床的控制元件与 PLC、计算机集成制造系统、机电产品说明书、谈判、合同等内容；附录包括：科技英语的特点、英语应用文的特点、英汉科技翻译基础知识、英文机械图样用语、机械工程常用词汇、总词汇表、参考译文等，供学生和专业技术人员进行本课程学习、机械类专业资料学习和翻译时参考。为了扩大学生专业英语阅读量，了解更多的专业词汇，每课除一篇课文之外，还有一篇与课文内容相关的阅读材料。

本书与基础英语有较好的衔接，文章内容覆盖面比较宽，阅读材料丰富，专业词汇比较全面，难度适当，又具有较强的实用性，适合作为机械类高职学生的专业英语教材。本书也可供机械类中职学生、本科学生及机械工程专业技术人员学习参考。

本书的教学时数推荐为 60 学时。其中，阅读材料可由教师讲授，也可由学生自学。凡在阅读材料中出现的生词均可在总词汇表中查到。教师还可根据实际教学情况，选讲部分附录。

本书由沈阳职业技术学院管俊杰教授和王素艳副教授共同编写。

由于水平所限，编写时间又很仓促，书中如有疏漏或错误之处，恳请广大读者批评指正。

编　者

2010 年 6 月

目　录

Part I Science

Lesson 1 Forces Have both Magnitude and Direction

Probably the simplest way to define a force is to say that it is a push or a pull. However, when we speak of a force being responsible for motion, it is not enough for us to tell only its magnitude if we want to know what result it will cause. So if there are two pulling forces of equal magnitude, the result they bring about will have to depend upon the direction in which they are applied. Pulling directly upwards on an object with a force of 10 kilograms can change the position of the object in a completely different way than if the same object is pulled from one side with an equal force. Force is what is known as a vector quantity, that is, it has both magnitude and direction. In order to explain the effect of any force. Both its magnitude and direction must be known.

Very often two forces act on an object at the same time. In such cases it is often helpful to know the resultant of these two forces, that is, the effect the combination of the forces produces. If two separate forces are applied in the same direction, it is easy to find out the resultant. The magnitudes of the two forces added determine the magnitude of the resultant force.

There are also cases in which two forces acting on an object are opposite in direction. If two people want the same object at the same time and are pulling on it in opposite directions, the motion of the object is always in the direction of the person applying the larger force. A tug-of-war is an example of two such forces. To determine the magnitude of the resulant force, the smaller force must be subtracted from the larger in this case.

Sometimes there may be more than two forces acting on a body simultaneously. In such cases the result they bring about will be known only through analyzing concretely the magnitude of each of them and the angles at which they act. So magnitude and direction are the two indispensable criterion in determining the effect a force will cause.

New Words

1. define	[di'fain]	*vt.*	解释，给……下定义
2. responsible	[ri'spɔnsəbl]	*a.*	有责任的，（应）负责任的
3. magnitude	['mægnitju:d]	*n.*	大小，量
4. apply	[ə'plai]	*vt.*	应用，施加

5. vector	['vektə]	*n.*	矢量，向量
6. resultant	[ri'zʌltənt]	*n.*	合力；
		v.	组合的，合成的
7. determine	[di'tə:min]	*vt.*	决定，确定
8. simultaneously	[ˌsiməl'teinjəsli]	*ad.*	同时发生（或存在）地
9. analyze	['ænəlaiz]	*vt.*	分析，分解
10. angle	['æŋgl]	*n.*	角，角度
11. Indispensable	[ˌindis'pensəbl]	*a.*	不可缺少的，必需的
12. criterion	[krai'tiəriən]	*n.*	依据，准则
13. concretely	['kɔnkri:tli]	*ad.*	具体地

Phrases and Expressions

1. to speak of	提到，谈到
2. (be) responsible for	对……负责任，担负
3. to bring about	引起，产生，导致
4. (be) known as	被称为
5. to act on	作用于
6. a tug of war	拔河比赛
7. (be) subtracted from	从……减去

Notes

1. Probably the simplest way to define a force is to say that it is a push or a pull.
   解释一个力的最简单的方法大概就是说它是推或拉。
   * 动词不定式 to define a force 作定语修饰 way，动词不定式 to say 作表语。
2. So if there are two pulling forces of equal magnitude, the result they bring about will have to depend upon the direction in which they are applied.
   所以，如果有两个大小相等的拉力，其合力则取决于这两个力的方向。
   * 定语从句 they bring about 中省略了关系代词 which（或 that）。
3. In such cases it is often helpful to know the resultant of these two forces, that is, the effect the combination of the forces produces.
   在这种情况下，弄清这两个力的合力，即这两个力合成而产生的作用，往往是有益的。
   * 句中 it 为形式主语，动词不定式 to know the resultant 为真正主语。
4. So magnitude and direction are the two indispensable criterion in determining the effect a force will cause.
   因此，大小和方向是确定力所产生的作用的两个不可分割的依据。

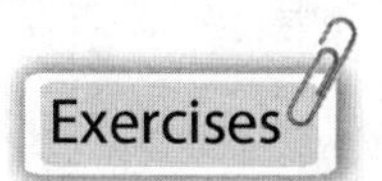

1. Why is a force known as a vector quantity?

2. How can we find out the resultant of two separate forces which are applied in the same direction?

3. How can we find out the resultant of two forces which are acting on an object at the same time and pulling on it in opposite direction?

4. Are magnitude and direction the two indispensable criterion in determining the effect a force will cause? Why or why not?

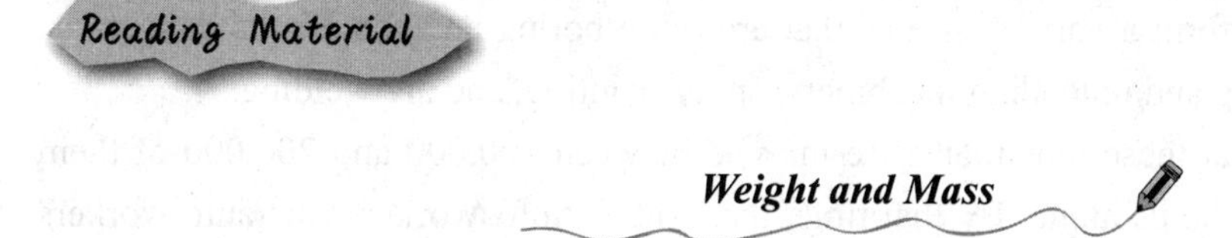

Weight and Mass

Do you remember what weight is? Weight is the gravitational pull on an object. If, somehow, the pull of gravitation changes, then the weight of the object changes. The mass of the object, the amount of matter it is made of, does not change.

If a bag of sugar weighs 6 kilograms on earth, what will it weigh on the moon? It will weigh one kilogram on the moon, 1/6 of its weight on the earth.

Here on the earth we usually talk as if weight and mass were the same thing. We use weight as a way of measuring mass. On the earth this is very convenient. A mass of sugar that weighs 6 kilograms in California will weigh about 6 kilograms in Hawaii or Canada or Germany because the force of gravitation in each place is practically the same.

As long as we stay on earth, using weight to measure mass works pretty well. Now, however, men have left the earth. Suddenly we realize that weight and mass are not the same thing! Away from the earth, the force of gravitation changes. As the pull of gravitation changes, weight changes, but the mass of an object ways the same anywhere in the universe whether it is on earth, on the moon, in a spaceship, or on Mars.

Have you wondered why the pull of gravitation on the moon is only 1/6 of the pull on the earth? Here is a reason. When the mass of an object is greater, its gravitational pull is greater, when the mass is less, gravitation is less. The moon has less mass than the earth. Since the moon has much less mass than the earth, it has much less gravitational force than the earth.

It is important to remember the difference between mass and weight. Mass is a basic physical concept having to do with the amount of matter involved, while weight is a more complicated concept than mass in that it involves not only the amount of matter, but also the gravitational attraction of the earth.

Lesson 2 Robots

Not long ago, the only time you'd see a robot is when you were reading a comic book or watching a science fiction movie such as Star Wars. Today, however, science fiction is fast becoming science fact. Robots are starting to make their presence felt in our everyday lives. These robots come in all sizes, shapes and colors. They all have the same type of "brain"-tiny silicon chips imbedded with thousands of electronic pathways. These kinds of chips also serve as brains for microcomputers.

Factory robots: But robots do more than microcomputers. They not only "think", but they also sense, respond to, and, alter their surroundings.

Industrial robots perform a variety of jobs that are often boring and sometimes dangerous. These jobs include loading and unloading machinery, spray-painting, and arc welding.

Robots are so good at these jobs that there may be between 100,000 and 200,000 of them hard at work by 1990 in the us alone. By that time, the United Auto Workers (the auto workers union) predicts that assembly line work performed by human beings will be cut in half.

Home robots: Robots are also coming to American homes, though not as quickly as they are invading factories. These robots aren't as friendly and bright as those of Star Wars. But, their makers claim that today's home robots can walk (actually roll), sense objects in their way (and sometimes crash into them), and even carry objects (which they sometimes drop). Well, Nobody's perfect.

We may joke about home robots today, but someday they may see and hear better than humans do. We humans can only see certain wave lengths of light, and hear certain frequencies of sound. That's because our eyes and ears have limitations. Robots, however, need not have the same limitations we have. Robots may also be equipped with sensors that pick up information human can't-such as radio waves, or ultraviolet light.

New Words

1. robot	[ˈrəubɔt]	*n.*	机器人
2. comic	[ˈkɔmik]	*n.*	连环漫画；喜剧的
3. fiction	[ˈfikʃən]	*n.*	虚构，杜撰
4. science fiction			科学幻想
5. silicon	[ˈsilikən]	*n.*	[化] 硅
6. chip	[tʃip]	*n.*	片，板，切屑
7. imbed	[imˈbed]	*vt.*	埋置，把……嵌入
8. perform	[pəˈfɔːm]	*vt.*	完成，执行
9. alter	[ˈɔːltə]	*vt.*	改变，改动

10. microcomputer	[ˈmaikrəukəmˈpjuːtə]	*n.*	微机
11. load	[ləud]	*vt.*	装载；负荷，负载
12. unload	[ˌʌnˈləud]	*v.*	卸载
13. predict	[priˈdikt]	*v.*	预言
14. spray-painting			喷漆
15. welding	[ˈweldiŋ]	*n.*	焊接，熔接
16. arc	[ɑːˈk]	*n.*	电弧，弧
17. invade	[inˈveid]	*vt.*	拥入，占领
18. frequence	[ˈfriːkəns]	*n.*	频率
19. sensor	[ˈsensə]	*n.*	传感器
20. ultraviolet	[ˈʌltrəˈvaiəlet]	*a.*	紫外（线）的

Phrases and Expressions

1. crash into	撞上，闯入
2. be equipped with	装备……
3. pick up	探测出
4. arc welding	电弧焊
5. electronic pathway	电子线路

Notes

1. Not long ago, the only time you'd see a robot is when you were reading a comic book or watching a science fiction movie such as Star Wars.
   不久前，我们只是在看一本连环画或一部像“星球大战”这样的电影时，才能看到机器人。
   *（1）you'd see a robot 是定语从句，修饰 time。
   （2）从 when you were 到最后是表语从句。
   （3）Star Wars 是电影名，译为“星球大战”。
2. By that time, the United Auto Workers (the auto workers union)predicts that assembly line work performed by human being will be cut in half.
   美国汽车工人联合会预言，到那时装配线上的工人数将会减少一半。
   *（1）that assembly line…in half 为宾语从句。其中 performed by human beings 为过去分词短语作后置定语，修饰 work。
   （2）the United Auto Worker：美国汽车工人联合会。
3. These robots aren't as friendly and bright as those of Star Wars.
   这些机器人不如“星球大战”中的那些机器人那么使人称心和能干。
   * 这句中的 friendly 直译为“便利的”，bright 直译为“聪明的、伶俐的”，转译为“称心和能干”。

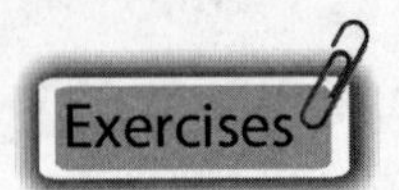

1. What jobs can factory robots perform?
2. Are home robots as friendly and bright as those of Star Wars?
3. Can today's home robots walk the same way as a man?
4. Can home robots see and hear better than humans do? Why?
5. Have you seen a robot? When and where?

Applications of Industrial Robots

Industrial robots are general-purpose, programmable machines possessing certain anthr-opomorphic characteristics. They are most likely to be economical and practical in applications with the following characteristics.

1. Hazardous working conditions. In job situations where there are potential dangers to a human operator or where the workplace is hot and uncomfortable, industrial robots are likely candidates for the job.

2. The job is repetitive. Even if the cycle is long and involves a sequence of many separate moves, an industrial robot may be feasible. One requirement is that the sequence of actions must not change from one cycle to the next.

3. The workpiece to be moved is heavy. Some industrial robots are capable of lifting items as heavy as several hundred kilograms.

The tasks performed by industrial robots would include the following more typical applications:

Part handling: A large variety of pick-and-placer jobs , moving workpieces from one location and repositioning them at another location.

Machine loading and unloading: The types of production equipment involved include stamping presses, forge presses, die-casting machines, and most types of metal-cutting machine tools.

Spray painting: The spray paint nozzle is attached to the robot's arm. The arm is programmed to move through a sequence of continuous-path motions to complete the painting operation.

Welding: Both spot welding and continuous welding.

Assembly: In simple mechanical assembly, robots perform operations which are basically an extension of their pick-and-place motions.

Lesson 3 CAD's Benefits

The benefits of computer use in drafting and design tasks are impressive：increased speed, greater accuracy, reduction of hardcopy storage space as well as better recall, enhanced communication capabilities, improved quality and easier modification.

Speed

A personal computer used in industry can perform a task at an average rate of 33 million operations per second；newer computers are even faster.This is an important feat when using it to calculate the amount of deflection of a component, when theoretical physical forces are applied to it, through finite element analysis (FEA) or when displaying an entire city plan on a monitor, both of which are time-consuming and calculation-intensive tasks. AutoCAD software can duplicate any geometry as many times as required and can also perform crosshatching and dimensioning automatically and equally as fast.

Accuracy

The AutoCAD program has an accuracy of 14 significant digits of precision for each point, depending on the operating system and computer platform. This extremely important when the program must round off numbers during mathematical calculations such as segmenting a circle.

Storage

The computer can store thousands of drawings in the physical space that it would take to store hundreds of manual drawings. Also, the computer can search and find a drawing with ease, as long as the operator possesses the correct file name.

Communication

Because the computer's data is stored in an electronic form, it can be sent to a variety of locations. The first obvious location is the monitor. The computer can display the data on the screen in different forms such as graphics, easily converting the data into readable drawings. The data can also be sent to a plotter to produce the familiar paper drawing, via a direct link to a computer-aided manufacturing (CAM) machine or via telephone to anywhere around the globe. You no longer have to mail drawings, risking damage and loss；they can now be at their destination instantly via the telecommunications network.

Quality

The computer always retains the data in the form in which it was first created. It can repeat the same output of data continuously without regard to fatigue. Lines will always be crisp and clear, with uniform line weight, and text will always be legible. The computer doesn't alter its output quality because of a wild weekend or a late night watching the game.

Modification

The computer data is stored in a format that allows easy modification to any facet of a drawing and gives instant feedback to the user. When something is drawn once, it never has to be drawn again because the object in question can be duplicated, stretched, sized, and changed in many ways without having to be redrawn.

Except for the initial cost to purchase a CAD workstation, CAD's only disadvantage is a small one because it can be so easily overcome. Because the drawing is stored in an electronic format and not a paper format, it is possible to erase a drawing file easily. That's why it is essential to train yourself in good CAD practices to avoid an accidental erasure.

New Words

1. draft	[drɑ:ft]	*n.*	草稿，草案，草图；汇票
2. hardcopy	[ˈhɑ:dkɔpi]	*n.*	硬拷贝
3. feat	[fi:t]	*n.*	功绩，伟业；技艺
		a.	漂亮的；整洁的；合适的，合身的（衣服）
4. deflection	[diˈflekʃən]	*n.*	（尤指击中某物后）突然转向，偏斜，偏离
5. calculate	[ˈkælkjuleit]	*vt./vi.*	计算，估计；打算，旨在
6. facet	[ˈfæsit]	*n.*	（宝石或首饰的）小平面，面；（事物的）面，方面；磨光面
7. monitor	[ˈmɔnitə]	*n.*	监视器，监听器；检测器
		vt.	监听，监视；监测，检测
8. duplicate	[ˈdju:plikət]	*n.*	完全一样的东西，复制品
		a.	完全一样的，复制的
		vt.	复制
9. crosshatching	[ˈkrɔshætʃiŋ]	*n.*	交叉排线（法）；十字晕滃；双向影线
10. segment	[ˈsegmənt]	*n.*	部分，片段；瓣；[机]扇形体；[电]整流子片；[计]程序段
11. plotter	[ˈplɔtə]	*n.*	密谋策划者；搞阴谋的人；描绘器，图形显示器，绘图器
12. retain	[riˈtein]	*vt.*	保持；保留；止住；容纳；雇用，聘请（律师等）
13. fatigue	[fəˈti:g]	*n.*	疲劳，劳累[物]（金属材料等）疲劳
14. crisp	[krisp]	*a.*	脆的，鲜脆的；新奇的，整洁的
		n.	〈英〉炸马铃薯片
15. uniform	[ˈju:nifɔ:m]	*n.*	制服
		a.	全都相同的，一律的，清一色的
16. legible	[ˈledʒəbl]	*a.*	清晰的，易读的

Phrases and Expressions

1. finite element analysis(FEA)	有限元分析
2. except for	除……之外

Notes

1. The benefit of computer use in drafting & design tasks are impressive increased speed. Greater accuracy, reduction of hardcopy storage space as well as beaer recall, enhanced communication capabilities, improved quality and easier modification.
   * 本句为简单句，impressive increased speed 及后面均为并列成分。
2. This is an important feat when using it to calculate the amount of defection of a component, when theoretical physical faces are applied to it, through finite element analysis(FEA)or when displaying an entire city plan on a monitor, both of which are time-and-calculation-intensive tasks.
   * when using…和 when displaying…为并列时间状语从句。both 指 calculate the amount of defection of a component 及 plan an entire city。

Exercises

1. Describe the CAD's benefits.
2. Is it possible that the CAD data can be transmitted by network?
3. List the main fields of CAD application in recent years.
4. When something is drawn once, it never has to be drawn again, why?
5. Why is it possible to erase a drawing file easily.

Reading Material

Computer Aided Design

Computer aided design gives the designer the ability to experiment with several possible solutions. Usually some forms of design, analysis calculations need to be done and many programs have been written for this task. The computer provides the designer with a powerful tool for analyzing proposed designs and for preparing formal drawings of the final design.

Two-dimensional drawing is one area in which computer methods can offer significant, quantifiable cost advantages over traditional paper and pen methods, but a CAD system is not just an electronic drawing board. Computer drawing systems enable designers to produce fast accurate drawings and easily modify them. Draught productivity rises dramatically when repetitive work is involved, since standard shapes are constructed only once and can be retrieved from a library. Cut and paste techniques are used as labor-saving aids. When several detail designers are working on the same project a central database is established so that details drawn by one person can be easily incorporated into different assembly drawings. The central database also serves as a library of standard preferred components.

Finite element is a sophisticated stress analysis technique much used by civil and mechanical engineers. It consists of dividing a structure into small, but finite, components and calculating the force between each element. If the elements are small enough, a good estimate of the internal stresses in a structure or solid body can be obtained. These computer techniques are routinely used in the design of large structures such as ship hulls, bridges, aircraft fuselages and offshore oil rig. The motor car industry also uses similar methods for design and manufacture of car bodies.

Lesson 4 Water as a Cutting Tool

Ever thought of water, whose versatility has never been in question, being used as a liquid knife?

A recent experiment has proved that indeed water jets can cut metals - aluminum, granite and just about any other material-the same way as an electrically-operated sawing machine .

The discovery of this technique goes to an Indian scientist, Dr. Mohan Vijay of National Research Council of Canada, who works with water jet cutting, tools whose blade is a high pressure stream of water. It generates as powerful as 150kw of power. The water jet is capable of quickly slicing through most materials without much mess, waste, or disturbance to surrounding material.

"The industrial applications for water jet cutters are enormous," says Vijay, "And though they have been around for more than a decade, recent developments in high pressure pumps have made these cutters more reliable, and thus more economically feasible, than ever", he said.

They are already widely used for tough cleaning jobs (like knocking marine growth from offshore oilrigs) and are starting to be used in the mining industry. Jet cutters, which are working in several countries, can slice through concrete and could be of use in the construction industry, especially for disposing of the debris left when a building is torn down.

But jet cutters can also handle jobs requiring more finesse. A precision instrument capable of accurately cutting fur, aluminum, siding, rubber, and other materials has been developed, he says. The nozzle of the instrument is made of artificial sapphire, looks like a tiny glass bead, and measures less than 0.076 mm in diameter.

Dr. Vijay says the stream of water shooting out of this nozzle can cut most material as well as a knife can, but without many of the problems encountered in mechanical cutting. There are no blades to dull in waterjets, he says.

There is a growing demand for this type of precision instrument in the manufacturing sector, Vijay says. "The prospects are good, and already they have quite a few customers, specially from the cleaning industry," he adds.

New words

1. versatility ['vɜ:sə'tiləti] *n.* 多功能性，多才多艺
2. technique [tek'ni:k] *n.* 技巧，手法
3. granite ['grænit] *n.* 花岗岩，花岗石
4. sapphire ['sæfaiə] *n.* 蓝宝石，蔚蓝色
5. disturbance [dis'tə:bəns] *n.* 动乱；干扰；侵犯
6. debris ['deibri:] *n.* 废墟，残骸
7. nozzle ['nɔzl] *n.* 管嘴，喷嘴

8. just about 几乎

9. pump [pʌmp] *n.* 泵
vt. 用泵抽吸，间歇地喷出

10. marine [mə'riːn] *a.* 海生的
n. 海军陆战队士兵

11. bead [biːd] *n.* 水珠；[机]卷边；车轮圆缘
vt. 用珠装饰；把……连成一串
vi. 起泡；瞄准

1. Ever thought of water.
   * 这是省略句，ever 前省略了 Have you。
2. The water jet is capable of quickly slicing through most materials without much mess, waste, or disturbance to surrounding material.
   喷射的水流能迅速地切割大多数材料而不留下任何残留物，对被切割物没有任何影响。
3. Dr. Vijay says the stream of water shooting out of this nozzle can cut most material as well as a knife can, but without many of the problems encountered in mechanical cutting.
   Dr. Vijay 说，从这种喷嘴喷射的水流能够像刀一样切削大多数材料，但是没有机械加工中遇到的很多问题。

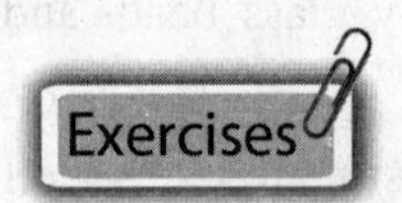

1. How many years have water jet cutters been around for more than a decade?
2. Who discovered the water jet cutters technique?
3. How many kilowatt does the water jet cutters generate?
4. What is the nozzle of the jet cutter made of ?

Switches and Fuses

An electric switch is often on a wall near the door of a room. Two wires lead to the lamp in the room. The switch is fixed in one of them. The switch can cause a break in this wire, and then the light goes out. The switch can also join the two parts of the wire again, then we get a light.

Switches can control many different things. Small switches control lamps and radio sets because these do not take a large current. Larger switches control electric furnace. Other switches can control electric motors.

Good switches move quickly. They have to stop the current suddenly. If they move slowly, an electric spark appears. It jumps across the space between the two ends of the wire. This is unsafe and it heats the switch. Very big switches are sometimes placed in oil. Sparks do not easily jump through oil, and so the oil makes the switch safer.

A large current makes a wire hot. If the wire is very thin, even a small current makes it hot. This happens in an electric lamp.

The electric wires in a house are covered with some kind of insulation. No current can flow through the insulation； so the current can never flow straight from one wire to the other. But the insulation on old wires is often broken； then the copper of the two wires can touch. A large current may flow, and if this happens, the wires will get very hot. Then the house may catch fire.

Fuses can stop this trouble. A fuse is only a thin wire which easily melts. It is fixed in a fuse-holder. The fuse-holder is made of some material which cannot burn. A large current makes the fuse hot and then it melts away. We say that the fuse"blows". The wire is broken, and no current can flow. So the house does not catch fire； but all the lights and electric fires go out because there is no current.

When a fuse blows, something is wrong. We must find the fault first. Perhaps two wires are touching. We must cover them with new insulation of some kind. Then we must find the blown fuse and repair it.

Some people get angry when a fuse blows. So they put a thick copper wire in the fuse-holder! Of course this does not easily melt, if the current rises suddenly, nothing stops it. The thick wire easily carries it. Then the wires of the house may get very hot, and the house may catch fire. Some of the people in it may not be able to escape. They may lose their lives. So it is always best to use proper fuse-wire. This will keep everyone and everything in the house safe.

Lesson 5 Multimedia in Our Time (I)

Despite its tremendous potential, today's revolutionary machine for multimedia, the Internet, bears an unfortunate resemblance to that aborted project. And other types of communication channels, such as mobile phones, are hardly in the picture. But this time, the great opportunity will not go unexplored, courtesy of MPFEG-4, the name given to a revolutionary communications standard released this month (the acronym is pronounced"M-Peg") .

The standard, developed over five years by the Moving Picture Experts Group 2 (MPEG)of the Geneva-based International Organization for Standardization (ISO), explores every possibility of the digital environment. Recorded images and sounds co-exist with their computer-generated counterparts; a new language for sound promises compact-disk quality at extremely low data rates; and the multimedia content could even adjust itself to suit the transmission rate and quality.

Possibly the greatest of the advances made by MPEG-4 is that viewers and listeners need no longer be passive. The height of "interactivity" in audiovisual systems today is the user's ability merely to stop or start a video in progress. MPEG-4 is completely different: it allows the user to interact with objects within the scene, whether they derive from so-called real sources, such as moving video, or from synthetic sources, such as computer-aided design output or computer-generated cartoons. Authors of content can give users the power to modify scenes by deleting, adding, or repositioning objects, or to alter the behavior of the objects; for example, a click on a box could set it spinning.

Perhaps the most immediate need for MPEG-4 is defensive. It supplies tools with which to create uniform (and top-quality) audio and video encoders and decoders on the Internet, preempting what may become an unmanageable tangle of proprietary formats. For example, users must choose among video formats such as QuickTime (from Apple Corp., Cupertino, Calif.), AVI (from Microsoft Corp. , Redmond, Wash.), and Real Video (from Real Networks Inc. , Seattle, Wash.) as well as a bewildering number of formats for audio.

New Words

1. multimedia ['mʌlti'mi:djə] *n.* 多媒体
2. tremendous [tri'mendəs] *a.* 惊人的，非常的
3. opportunity ['ɔpə'tju:niti] *n.* 机会
4. unexplored ['ʌnliks'plɔ:id] *a.* 未被利用的，未开发的
5. release [ri'li:s] *vt.* 发表，释放
6. behavior [bi'heivjə] *n.* 行为，举止，表现，性质，状态
7. acronym ['ækrənim] *n.* 词头，只取首字母的缩略词

8. environment	[in'vaiərənmənt]	*n.*	环境，围绕，周围状况
9. audiovisual	['ɔːdjəu'viʒuə]	*n.*	视听设备
10. merely	['miəli]	*ad.*	仅仅，只不过
11. synthetic	[sin'θetik]	*a.*	合成的，人工制造的
12. modify	['mɔdifai]	*vt.*	修改
13. encoder	[in'kəudə]	*n.*	编码器
14. decoder	[diː'kəudə]	*n.*	译码器
15. proprietary	[prə'praiətəri]	*vt.*	先占有，先取
16. unmanageable	[ʌn'mænidʒəbl]	*a.*	难管理的

Phrases and Expressions

1. bear an resemblance to	与……有相似之处
2. aborted project	流产了的计划
3. mobile phone	移动电话
4. go unexplored	不被利用的
5. courtesy of	多亏(因为)有了……
6. a bewildering number of	一系列令人困惑的

Notes

1. But this time, …this month.
   可是这一回，有了 MPEG-4 这项本月才发布的革命性的通讯标准，这一大好时机就不会白白溜走了。
2. the Geneva-based International Organization for Standardization (ISO)
   总部设在日内瓦的国际标准化组织。
3. Recorded images and sounds…to suit the transmission rate and quality.
   录制好的图像及声音和计算机生成的同时并存；一种新的声音语言以极低的数据速率保证产生和光盘一样好的音质，而且多媒体的内容甚至可以根据传输速率和品质进行自我调节。
4. Authors of content…could set it spinning.
   内容的作者能给用户改动画面的主动权（如删除，增加，或移动对象，或者改变对象的行为），例如，只要（鼠标）在小方框上点击一下，它就会旋转起来。
5. It supplies tools with…of proprietary formats.
   它为国际互联网提供了建造统一的(高质量的)视听编码和解码的工具，这就预先防止了发生专用制式无法控制的混乱。

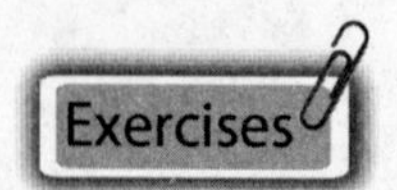

Decide whether the following statements are true[T] or false[F] according to the text:

1. The multimedia content could even adjust itself to suit the transmission rate and quality. [ ]

2. Possibly the greatest of the advances made by MPEG-4 is that viewers and listeners need longer be passive. [ ]

3. MPEG-4 allows the user to interact with objects within the scene. [ ]

4. Perhaps the most immediate need for MPFEG-4 is defensive. [ ]

Multimedia in Our Time(II)

Of all the new and useful features in MPEG-4, perhaps the most entertaining is its ability to map images onto computer-generated shapes. When the shapes are animated, the gap between synthetic and real can be bridged quite efficiently. In principle, any mesh (currently 2-D, with 3-D in next version of the standard) may have any image mapped onto it. A few parameters to deform the mesh can create the impression of moving video from a still picture-a waving flag, for instance. For more advanced effects, moving video image could also be mapped onto the mesh.

Pre-defined faces are particularly interesting meshes. These are compute models with a repertory of independent motions and a few common emotional states.

With MPEG-4's text-to-speech interface the animated face is an attractive tool for building anavatar-a digital, on-line stand-in for a human or synthesized presence.

The appearance of the face may be left to the decoder, or complete, custom facial models may be downloaded. The wireframe face model may have any surface, including even a snapshot of a person, though as the face is inherently 3-D, a special snapshot is required. Any feature on the model, such as lips, eyes, and so on, may be animated by special commands that make them move in sync with speech.

Part II Foundation

Lesson 6 Tolerances and Fits

Although standardized measurement is essential to modern industry, perhaps even more important are the design specifications that indicate the dimensions of a part. These dimensions control the size of a part, its features, and/or their location on the part or relative to other parts. Through this, parts are able to be interchanged and mated to each other to form complete assemblies. The purpose of this text is to introduce the basic terminology of tolerances and fits.

Limit and tolerance

Since it is impossible to machine a part to an exact size, a designer must specify an acceptable range of sizes that will still permit the part to fit and function as intended. The maximum and minimum sizes in part dimension that are acceptable are limits between which the actual part dimension must fall.

The difference between the maximum and minimum limits is tolerance, or the total amount by which a part dimension may vary. Tolerances on drawings are often indicated by specifying a limit, or by plus and minus notations (Fig.6-1).With plus and minus tolerancing, when the tolerance is both above and below the nominal (true theoretical) size, it is said to be bilateral (two sides). When the tolerance is indicated all on one side of nominal, it is said to be unilateral (one side).

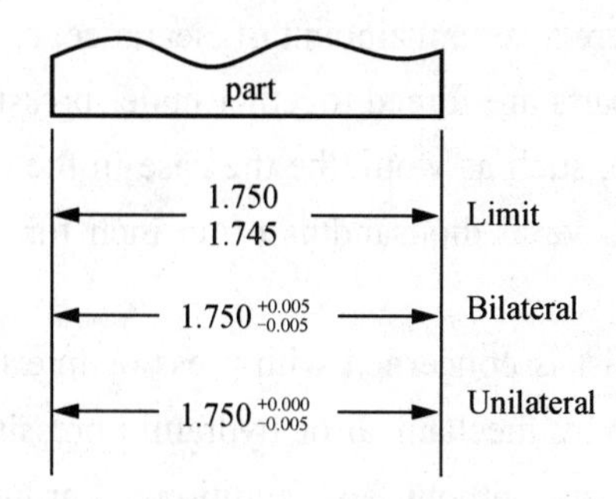

Fig.6-1 Tolerance notations

How tolerance affects mating parts

When two parts mate or are interchanged in an assembly, tolerance becomes vitally important. Consider the following example (Fig.6-2). The shaft must fit the bearing and be able to turn freely. The diameter of the shaft is specified as $1.000^{+0.001}_{-0.001}$. This means that the maximum limit of the shaft is 1.001 and the minimum is 0.999. The tolerance is then 0.002 and bilateral.

The maximum limit of the bearing bore is also 1.001 and the minimum limit is 0.999. The tolerance is once again 0.002. Will the shaft made by one machine shop fit the bearing made by another machine shop using the tolerances specified? If the shaft is turned to the maximum limit of 1.001 and the bearing is bored to its minimum limit of 0.999, both parts would be within acceptable tolerance, but would not fit to each other since the shaft is 0.002 larger than bearing. However, if the bearing bore was specified in limit form or unilateral tolerance of $1.002^{+0.002}_{-0.000}$, the parts would fit as intended. Even if the shaft was turned to the high limit of 1.001, it would still fit the bearing even though the bore was machined to the low limit of 1.002. Although a machinist is not usually concerned with establishing tolerance and limit specifications, you can easily see how fit problems can be created by overlapping tolerances discussed in this example.

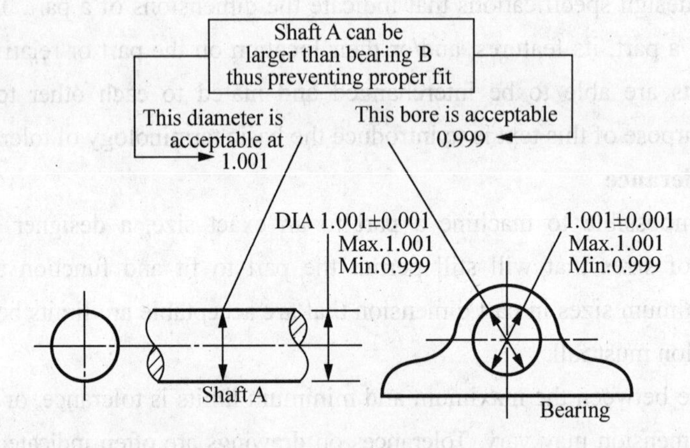

Fig.6-2 Tolerance overlap can prevent proper fit of mating parts

Fits

Fit refers to the amount or lack of clearance between two mating parts. Fits can range from free running or sliding, where a certain amount of clearance, exists between mating parts, to press or interference fits where parts are forced together under pressure. Clearance fits can range from a few millionths of an inch, such as would be the case in the component parts of a ball or miler beating, to a clearance of several thousandths of an inch for a very low speed drive or control lever application.

Many times a machinist is concerned with press or interference fits. In this case two parts are forced together usually by mechanical or hydraulic pressing. The frictional forces involved then hold the parts together without any additional hardware such as keys or setscrews. Tolerances for press fits can become very critical because parts can be easily damaged by attempting to press fit them if there is an excessive difference in their mating dimensions. In addition, press firing physically deforms the parts some extent.

This can result in damage, mechanical binding, or require a secondary resizing operation such as hand reaming or honing after the parts are pressed together.

New Words

1. standardize	[ˈstændədaiz]	*vt.*	使标准化，使规格化
2. specification	[ˌspesiˈfikeiʃən]	*n.*	规定，技术要求，规范
3. interchange	[ˌintəˈtʃeindʒ]	*vt.*	交换
4. mate	[meit]	*v.*	配合，配成对；
		n.	配对物
5. assembly	[əˈsembli]	*n.*	总成，组件
6. terminology	[ˌtəːmiˈnɔlədʒi]	*n.*	术语，专门名词
7. drawing	[ˈdrɔːiŋ]	*n.*	图
8. plus	[plʌs]	*a.*	正的，略大的；正量
9. minus	[ˈmainəs]	*a.*	负的，减去的
		n.	负量，负号
10. notation	[nəuˈteiʃən]	*n.*	符号，标志
11. nominal	[ˈnɔminəl]	*a.*	公称的，名义上的
12. theoretical	[ˌθiəˈretikəl]	*a.*	理论的
13. bilateral	[baiˈlætərəl]	*a.*	双向的
14. unilateral	[ˌjuːniˈlætərəl]	*a.*	单向的
15. vitally	[ˈvaitəli]	*ad.*	非常
16. machinist	[məʃiːnist]	*n.*	机械师，机械工人
17. overlap	[ˌəuvəˈlæp]	*v.*	重叠，相交，(部分)一致
18. interference	[ˌintəˈfiərəns]	*n.*	过盈，干涉，抵角
19. frictional	[ˈfrikʃənəl]	*a.*	摩擦的
20. hardware	[ˈhaːdwɛə]	*n.*	零件，附件，硬件
21. resizing	[riˈsaiziŋ]	*n.*	尺寸再生
22. honing	[ˈhəiniŋ]	*n.*	珩磨

Phrases and Expressions

1. (be) relative to	相对于，关于
2. attempt to (+inf.)	试图，企图
3. interference fit	过盈配合，压配合

Notes

1. The maximum and minimum sizes in part dimensions that are acceptable are limits between which the actual part dimension must fall.

零件尺寸可接受的极大值和极小值称为极限尺寸，零件的实际尺寸必须在这两个极限尺寸之间。

* 该句的基本句型是“主语+动词+表语”。

(1) 介词短语 in part dimensions 和定语从句 that are acceptable 均作定语修饰主语 The maximum and minimum sizes。

(2) 定语从句 between which the actual part dimension must fall 用于修饰主句中的表语 limits。在定语从句中 which 作介词 between 的宾语。

2. Fits can range from free running or sliding, where a certain amount of clearance exists between mating parts, to press or interference fits where parts are forced together under pressure.

配合范围可以从相配零件之间存在一定间隙量的间隙配合，变化至要用压力迫使零件装在一起的过盈配合。

* sliding 后面省略了名词 fits。

该句中有两个定语从句。第一个定语从句 where a certain amount of clearance exists between mating parts 用于修饰 free running or sliding(fits)，第二个定语从句 where parts are forced together under pressure 用来修饰 press or interference fits。

3. Tolerances for press fits can become very critical because parts can be easily damaged by attempting by press fit them if there is an excessive difference in there mating dimensions.

过盈配合时的公差非常关键，如果相配尺寸相差过大，零件很容易在进行加压配合的过程中被破坏。

* because 引导的为一原因状语从句，在从句中又嵌套一个由 if 引导的条件状语从句。句中 attempting to press fit them 中的 press fit 可视为一个复合动词，意为“加压配合”。本文中所有表示长度的数字，单位均为英寸。

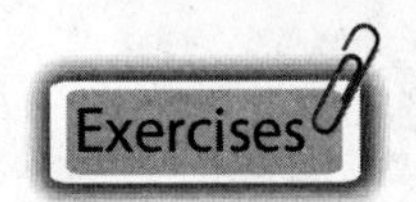

I. Answer the questions.

1. What is tolerance?
2. Why is tolerance important in manufacturing?
3. How do you indicate the tolerances on drawings?
4. What are fits?
5. Under which condition can a shaft fit a bearing and be able to run freely?

II. Decide whether the following statements are the true[T] or false[F] according to the text:

1. since it is impossible to machine a part to an exact size, a designer do not most specify an acceptable range of sizes that will still permit the part to fit and function as intended. [ ]

2. The shaft must fit the bearing and be unable to turn freely. [ ]

3. When the tolerance in indicated all on one side of nominal, it is said to be bilateral(Two

sides). [ ]

4. Many times a machinist is concerned with press or clearance fits. [ ]
5. Tolerances for press fits can not become very critical. [ ]

Dimension Measurement

A machinist is mainly concerned with the measurement of length; that is the distance along a line between two point (Fig.6-3). It is length that defines the size of most object. Width and depth are simply other names for length. A machinist measures length in the basic units of linear measure such as inches, millimeters, and in advanced metrology wavelengths of light. In addition, the machinist sometimes needs to measure the relationship of one surface to another, which is commonly called angularity(Fig. 6-4). Squareness, which is closely related to angularity, is the measure of deviation from true perpendicularity. A machinist will measure angularity in the basic units of angular measure, degrees, minutes and seconds of arc.

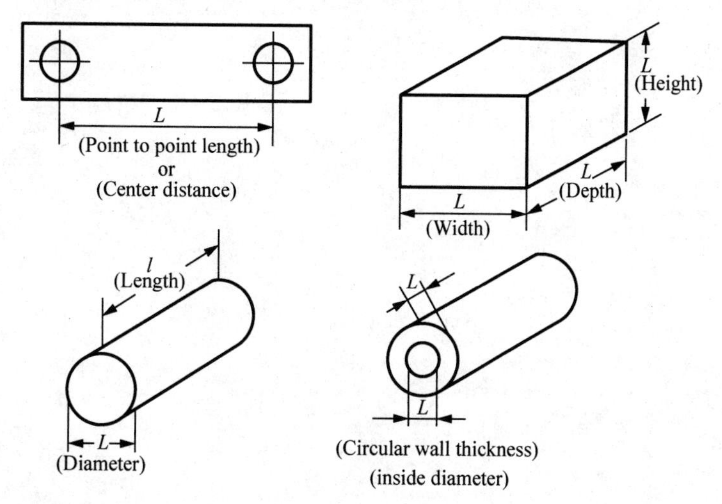

Fig. 6-3 The measurement of length may appear under several different angularity

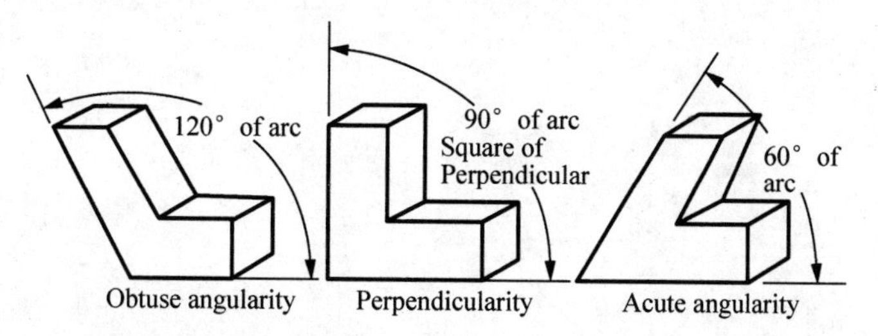

Fig. 6-4 Measurement of surface relationships or angularity

In addition to the measure of length and angularity, a machinist also needs to measure such things as surface finish, concentricity, straightness, and flatness. He or she also occasionally comes in contact measurements that involve circularity, sphericity, and alignment. However, many of these more specialized measurement techniques are in the realm of the inspector or laboratory metrologist and appear infrequently in general machine shop work.

Lesson 7 Couplings, Keys, Shafts and Springs

Couplings are used to connect two shafts. For example, a coupling is used to join the shaft of an electric motor to the line shaft of a machine or a hydraulic turbine to an electric generator or, for practical reasons, is used to sectionalize a long shaft, and so on. Couplings used for such typical applications are called permanent couplings because their connections would only be broken for repairs and or general maintenance. Those applications which require the shafts to periodically disengage are called clutches. Permanent couplings are classified into two groups rigid couplings and flexible couplings.

Keys are used to prevent relative motion between a shaft and machine elements such as gears, pulleys, sprockets, cams, levers, flywheels, impellers, and so on. There are numerous kinds of keys (some of which have been standardized) for various design requirements. The keys most frequently used are the square key, the tapered key, and the woodruff key.

A shaft is a rotating or stationary member, usually of circular cross section, having mounted upon it such element as gears, pulleys, flywheels, cranks, sprockets, and other power-transmission elements. Shafts may be subjected to bending, tension, compression, or torsional loads, acting singly or in combination with one another. When they are combined, one may expect to find both static and fatigue strength to be important design consideration, since a single shaft may be subjected to static stresses, completely reversed stresses, and repeated stresses, all acting at the same time. The word"shaft"covers numerous variations, such as axles and spindles. An axle is a shaft, either stationary or rotating, not subjected to a torsion load. A short rotating shaft is often called a spindle.

Mechanical springs are used in machines to exert force, to provide flexibility, and to store or to absorb energy. In general, springs may be classified as either wire springs or flat springs, although there are variations within these divisions. Wire springs include helical springs of round, square, or special-section wire and are made to resist tensile, compressive or torsional loads. Under flat springs are included the cantilever and elliptical types, the clocktypes power springs and the flat spring washers, usually called Belleville spring.

New Words

1. coupling [kʌpliŋ] *n.* 联轴器，连接
2. sectionalize ['sekʃənəlaiz] *vt.* 分段，分布
3. permanent ['pəːmənənt] *a.* 永久的，固定的，恒定的
4. disengage [ˌdisin'geidʒ] *vt.* 脱开，分离，解脱
5. clutch [klʌtʃ] *n.* 离合器
6. flexible ['fleksəbl] *a.* 易弯的

7. key	[kiː]	*n.*	键，钥匙
8. pulley	[ˈpuli]	*n.*	皮带轮
9. sprocket	[ˈsprɔkit]	*n.*	链轮
10. cam	[kæm]	*n.*	凸轮
11. flywheel	[ˈflaiwiːl]	*n.*	飞轮
12. impeller	[imˈpelə]	*n.*	叶轮，转子

Phrases and Expressions

1. tapered key	斜键
2. woodruff key	半圆键
3. power-transmission-element	传递动力的零件
4. fatigue strength	疲劳强度
5. cantilever-spring	半悬臂式(汽车)弹簧
6. elliptical type spring	双弓式板簧
7. Belleville springs	蝶形弹簧(贝氏弹簧)
8. hydraulic turbine	水力透平机
9. rigid coupling	刚性，联轴器

Notes

1. Couplings used for such typical applications are called permanent couplings because their connections would only be broken for repairs and/or general maintenance.
由于这类用途的联轴器其接合状态只是在修理或一般维修时才脱开，故称作固定联轴器。
* use for such typical applications 是过去分词短语作后置定语，修饰名词 couplings。permanent couplings 是主语 couplings 的补足语。
because their connections would only be broken for repairs and/or general maintenance 是原因状语。

2. Shafts may be subjected to bending, tension, compression, or torsional loads, acting singly or in combination with one another.
轴可以承受弯曲、拉伸、压缩或扭转载荷，作用的载荷既可以是单一的，也可以是复合的。
be subjected to… 经受、遭受、承受。
* actins singly or in combination with one another 为现在分词短语作补充说明，副词 singly 和介词短语 in combination with one another 均作状语，修饰现在分词 acting。其意为：以单一的形式起作用或以相互结合的形式起作用。

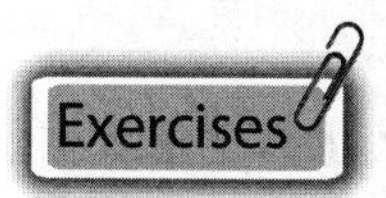

1. What are coupling used?
2. What is the function of the key?
3. Give the example of the keys most frequently used?
4. What is the function of mechanical spring?
5. Which several categories can springs be divided into?

Stress and Strain

When a load is applied to a material a balancing force is set up within the material, and this internally acting force is termed a stress. The types of stress normally considered are tensile, compressive and shear stresses. When a material is in a state of stress its dimensions will be changed. A tensile stress will cause an extension of the length of the material, while a compressive stress will shorten the length. Tensile and compressive stresses are termed direct stresses. The dimensional change caused by stress is termed strain.

In elastic behavior the strain developed in a material is subjected to a stress, is fully recovered immediately when the stress is removed. Some materials show elastic properties up to quite high levels of stress while others possess little, if any, elasticity. In 1678 Hooke enunciated his law, stating that the strain developed is directly proportional to the stress producing it. This law holds, at least within certain limits, for most materials.

(Fig.7-1) is a force-extension diagram for a metal stressed in tension. The first portion of the curve, OA, shows that the length of the specimen increases in direct proportion to the applied load, hence strain will be proportional to stress. Hooke's law does not hold beyond point A. Behavior within the region OA will be elastic. Beyond point A the extension of the material ceases to be wholly elastic and some permanent strain is developed. The elastic permanent strain is termed plastic strain. Point A is known as the elastic limit.

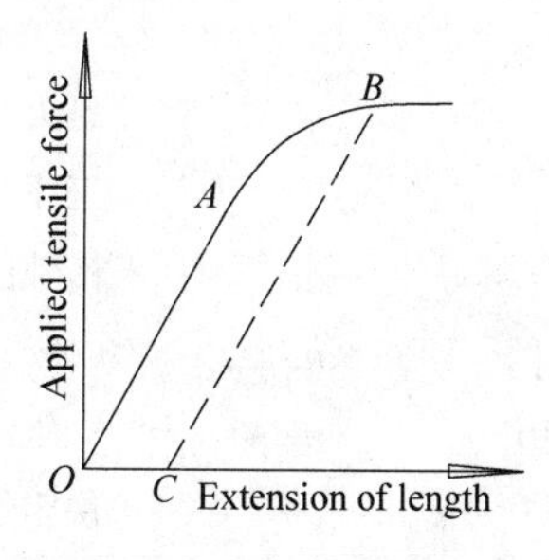

Fig. 7-1 Force-extension curve for a metal

Lesson 8 Annealing and Normalizing of Plain Carbon Steels

Process Annealing

Cold-worked low-carbon steels(in the form of strip, sheet, wire) are heated, in an insert atmosphere, to 550~600℃, i.e. to below the lower critical temperature, so that the process is also known as "sub-critical annealing". The subsequent cooling rate is not important, but contact of the steel with air should be avoided in order to prevent oxidation. Process annealing is cheaper than full annealing because the latter is carried out at a higher temperature, namely above the upper critical temperature.

Full annealing

Full annealing is the treatment given to produce the softest possible condition in hypoeutectoid steels; the resulting microstructure is completely refined, with accompanying high ductility. It involves heating the steel to about 30℃ above the upper critical temperature and then cooling slowly(e.g. in the furnace).

Full annealing is often used to produce softening and grain refinement in hot-worked hypoeutecoid steels and in steel castings. The soaking time depends on the section thickness(e.g. 20 minutes per cm thickness) and the treatment temperature varies with the carbon content as show:

Carbon	%	0.1	0.2	0.3	0.5	0.7	0.8
Temperature	℃	900	860	830	810	780	770

Normalizing

Normalizing is carried out on low and medium carbon steels(i.e. material containing less than about 0.6% carbon). The process is applied to achieve the best combination of mechanical properties when it is undesirable for the material to be in the softest possible condition(i.e. fully annealed). The treatment involves heating the steel to about 30℃ above its upper critical temperature ((i.e. the same temperature as for full annealing) but followed by cooling in still air. The more rapid cooling(as compared with full annealing) produces a finer pearlite and smaller ferrite grain size, resulting in a slightly harder and stronger material. However, the properties actually obtained in a normalized steel will vary with the section thickness; large normalized sections may show properties similar to those of a fully annealed steel of smaller section.

New words

1. anneal	[ə'ni:l]	*vt.*	退火
2. process annealing			工序间退火
3. inert	[i'nə:t]	*a.*	惰性的
4. contact	['kɔntækt]	*n./v.*	（使）接触
5. atmosphere	['ætməˌsfiə]	*n.*	大气（压），气氛，环境
6. critical	['kritikəl]	*a.*	决定性的，关键性的，危急的；批评的，批判的

7. undesirable ['ʌndi'zaiərəbl] *a.* 不合需要的
8. subsequent ['sʌbsikwənt] *a.* 随后的，后来的
9. microstructure ['maikrəu'strʌktʃə] *n.* 显微结构
10. refine [ri'fain] *v.* 细化，改善，精炼
11. ferrite ['ferait] *n.* 铁素体
12. pearlite ['pə:lait] *n.* 珠光体

Phrases and Expressions

1. subcritical annealing 亚临界退火
2. depend on 依靠
3. hype-eutectoid 亚共析(的)，亚共析体

Notes

Cold-worked low-carbon steels (in the form of strip, sheet, wire) are heated, in all inert atmosphere, to 550～600℃, i. e to below the lower critical temperature, so that the process is also known as "sub-critical annealing".
工序间退火是在惰性气氛中，把经过冷成形的低碳钢(带钢、钢板或线材)加热到550～600℃，也就是其下临界温度以下。所以，工序间退火又叫“在临界温度以下退火”。

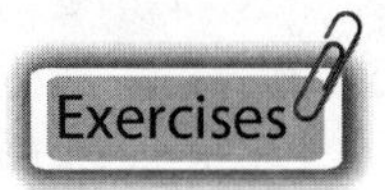

1. Why is process annealing also known as "sub-critical annealing"?
2. Why is process annealing cheaper than full annealing?
3. Describe the process of full annealing.
4. Describe the process of normalizing.

Reading Material

Hardening and Tempering of Plain Carbon Steels

Steels with less than 0.3% carbon cannot be effectively hardened, while the maximum hardness is obtained at about 0.8% carbon. Beyond about 0.8% carbon there is an increasing tendency to retain some austenite in the quenched structure, and this austenite offsets any possible increase due to a harder martensite, so that the net hardness remain more or less the same.

The quench hardening of hypo-eutectoid steels involves heating to 30℃ to 50℃ above the upper critical temperature, holding at this temperature (about 20 minutes per cm thickness), followed by quenching in water. Hyper-eutectoid steels, however, are not treated according to the above rules. If a hyper-eutectoid steel was quenched from above its Ac3 temperature, then the free cementite present would precipitate at the austenite grain boundaries and thus embrittle the steel. The first step in dealing with these steels is to ensure, by means of hot work (e.g. forging), that the free cementite is dispersed throughout the structure as small particles. The steel is then hardened by heating to about 30℃ above the lower critical temperature, holding and then quenching. This treatment results in a microstructure of spheroidal particles of cementite dispersed in a matrix of martensite.

Tempering: Hardened steels may be tempered by heating them within the temperature range 200~700℃. This treatment will remove internal stresses set up during quenching, remove some, or all, of the hardness, and increase the toughness of the material.

Lesson 9 Soldering and Brazing

There are a number of methods of joining metal articles together, depending on the type of metal and the strength of the joint which is required.

Soldering gives a satisfactory joint for light articles of steel, copper or brass, but the strength of soldered joint is rather less than a joint which is brazed, riveted or welded. These methods of joining metal are normally adopted for strong permanent joint. Soldering is the process of joining two metals by a third metal to be applied in the molten state. Solder consists of tin and lead, while bismuth and cadmium are often included to lower the melting point. One of the most important operations in soldering is that of cleaning surfaces to be joined, this may be done by some acid cleaner. Although the oxides are removed by the cleaning operation, a new oxide coating forms immediately after cleaning, thus preventing the solder to unite with the surface of the metal. Flux is used to remove and prevent oxidation of the metal surface to be soldered, allowing the solder to flow freely and unite with the metal. Zinc chloride is the best flux to use for soldering most ferrous and nonferrous metals, for soldering aluminum stearine or vaseline is to be used as fluxes.

The soldering copper is a piece of copper attached to a steel rod having a handle. Soldering coppers are made in different lengths, forms and weights. The quality of soldering depends to a great degree on the form and size of the soldering copper. Two parts may be perfectly soldered only when the surfaces to be joined have absorbed enough heat to keep solder melted for some time.

In some cases it may be necessary to connect metal surfaces by means of a hard spelter solder which fuses at high temperature. This kind of soldering is called brazing.

New Words

1. solder	[ˈsɔldə]	*n.*	焊料
2. spelter	[ˈspeltə]	*n.*	硬钎焊料，锌铜焊料
3. braze	[breiz]	*vt./n.*	铜焊，硬钎焊
4. brazing	[breiz]	*n.*	铜焊（接），硬钎焊
5. join	[dʒɔin]	*vt.*	连接，结合
6. joint	[dʒɔint]	*n.*	接缝，接合处
7. bismuth	[ˈbizməθ]	*n.*	铋
8. cadmium	[ˈkædmiəm]	*n.*	镉
9. flux	[flʌks]	*n.*	助熔剂，焊剂
10. stearine	[ˈstiːərin]	*n.*	甘油，硬脂
11. vaseline	[ˈvæziliːn]	*n.*	凡士林

Phrases and Expressions

1. acid cleaner 酸洗液
2. oxide coating 氧化膜
3. zinc chloride 氯化锌
4. soldering copper 纯铜铬铁
5. spelter solder 硬焊料

Notes

1. One of the most important operations on soldering is that of cleaning the surface to be joint, this may be done by some acid cleaner.
   钎焊的最重要工序之一是将需要焊接的接缝表面擦干净，这一工序可用某种酸洗液进行。
   * 句中的 that 用作代词，代表 operation。
   To be joined 是不定式的被动式作定语，修饰名词 the surface，译作"需要焊接的接缝表面"。
2. Two parts may be perfectly soldered only when the surfaces to be jointed have absorbed enough heat to keep solder melted for some time.
   只有在接缝表面吸收足够热量后，使焊料有一段时间保持熔融状态，这样才能将两部分焊牢。
   * to keep solder melted 是不定式 to keep 带有宾语 solder 以及宾语补语 melted，可译为：使焊料保持熔融状态。
3. Oxyacetylene welding is the heating of two pieces of metal with a flame which burns a mixture of oxygen and acetylene gas.
   氧-乙炔焊（气焊）是用氧气和乙炔混合燃烧后的火焰来加热两块金属。
   * which burns a mixture of oxygen and acetylene gas 为定语从句，修饰名词 a flame。

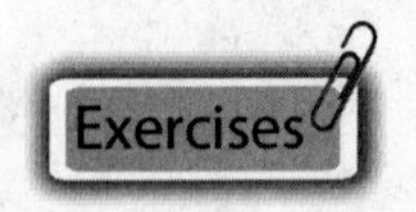

Decide whether the following statements are the true[T] or false[F] according to the text:

1. Welding produces joining of metals by heating them to suitable temperature, with or without application of pressure or by the application of pressure alone and with or without the use of filler metal. [ ]

2. Brazing produces joints stronger than those made by soldering. [ ]

3. Oxyacetylene welding is the heating of two pieces of metal with a flame which burns a mixture of hydrogen and acetylene gas. [ ]

4. Soldering is the process of joining two metals by a third metal to be applied on the solid state. [ ]

5. Soldering and brazing processes differ from welding in the sense that there is no direct melting of the base metals being jointed. [ ]

6. Perhaps, the most important commonly used of all the welding processes is the arc welding. [ ]

Adhesive bonding of metal parts is a rapidly growing field that influences the design of products of nearly all kinds. The advantages of adhesive are many. No holes (which weaken the part) are required, as with screws and rivets. No temperatures high enough to produce warping and residual stresses are involved, as with welding. When the joint is loaded, stresses are spread over a large area, with only minor stress concentration at the edges of contact. This often permits the use of thinner members, resulting in a weight saving. Adhesive bonding permits smooth, unbroken exterior surfaces for good appearance, easier finishing, and reduced fluid friction (in applications involving a flowing liquid or gas, as all airplae wing or helicopter rotor blade). Almost any solid materials, can be bonded with a suitable adhesive. When bonding dissimilar metals, the adhesive layer can provide effective insulation against galvanic currents. Flexibility of the adhesive material can be made to adapt differential thermal expansion of the bonded members. This flexibility also aids in absorbing impact loads. Furthermore, adhesive bonds can provide damping to reduce vibration and sound transmission.

On the negative side, adhesives are more temperature-sensitive than mechanical fasteners. Most adhesives currently in common use are limited to the -129℃ to 260℃range. Adhesives vary greatly in temperature response, and this must always be considered when selecting all adhesive for a specific application. Inspection, disassembly, and repair of adhesivesjoints may not be practical. Also, long-term durability for some adhesives is questionable.

Lesson 10 Sand Casting

The first stage in the production of sand castings must be the design and manufacture of a suitable pattern. Casting patterns are generally made from hard wood and the pattern has to be made larger than the finished casting size to allow for the shrinkage that takes place during solidification and cooling.

Sand moulds for the production of castings are made in a moulding box. The mould is made in two or more parts in order that the pattern may be removed. With a two-part mould the upper half of the moulding box is known as the cope and the lower half is termed the drag. The drag half of the mould box is placed on a flat firm board and the drag half of the pattern placed in position. Facing sand is sprinkled over the pattern and then the mould box is filled with moulding sand. The sand is rammed firmly around the pattern. When ramming of the sand is complete, excess sand is removed to leave a smooth surface flush with the edges of the moulding box. The completed drag is tumed over and the upper, or cope, portion of the moulding box positioned over it. The cope half of the pattern is placed in position, correct alignment being ensured by means of small dowel pins. A thin coating of dry parting sand is sprinkled into the mould at this stage. This is to prevent the cope and drag sticking together when the cope half is moulded. The cope is now filled with moulding sand and this is rammed firmly into shape in the same manner as in the making of the drag. After the ramming of sand in the cope is completed and excess sand has been removed from the top surface the two halves of the moulding box are carefully separated. The patterns are carefully removed from both cope and drag. The mould is reassembled by placing the cope upon the drag and it is then ready for use. Liquid metal is poured smoothly into the mould via the feeder.

When the metal that has been poured into a sand mould has fully solidified, the mould is broken and the casting is removed.

New Words

1. casting ['ka:stiŋ] *n.* 铸件，铸造
2. mould [məuld] *n.* 模型，铸型，压模
3. stage [steidʒ] *n.* 阶段，步骤
4. pattern ['pætən] *n.* 模型，试样，图案
5. shrinkage ['ʃriŋkidʒ] *n.* 收缩，缩水
6. solidification [salidifikeisən] *n.* 凝固，固化
7. cope [kəup] *n.* 上箱
8. drag [dræz] *n.* 下箱
   v. 拖，拉

9．sprinkle	[ˈspriŋkl]	*n./v.*	洒，喷
10．ram	[ræm]	*vt.*	锤击，夯紧；
		n.	伸杆，滑枕，夯
11．flush	[flʌʃ]	*a.*	齐平的；
		ad.	齐平地；
		vt.	使齐平
12．alignment	[əˈlainmənt]	*n.*	对准，准线
13．dowel	[ˈdauəl]	*n.*	定位销，销钉
14．pin	[pin]	*n.*	销，钉
15．feeder	[ˈfiːdə]	*n.*	冒口，送料器
16．reassemble	[ˈriːəˈsembl]	*vt.*	重新组合，重新装配
17．via	[ˈvaiə]	*prep.*	经过，经由

Phrases and Expressions

1．be poured into	浇入
2．allow for	考虑到，估计
3．facing sand	复面砂
4．moulding box	砂箱
5．parting sand	分型砂

Notes

1．Casting parterre ate generally made from hard wood and the pattern has to be made larger than the finished casting size to allow for the shrinkage that takes place during solidification and cooling.

铸造木模通常由硬质木材制造，考虑到铸件在凝固及冷却过程中的收缩，木模的尺寸必须比铸件大一些。

*（1）整个句子是由 and 前后的两个分句组成的并列句。

（2）to allow for…and cooling 是目的状语，修饰第二个分句，其中 that 引导的定语从句修饰 shrinkage。

2．After the ramming of sand in the cope. is completed and excess, sand has been removed, from the top surface the two halves of the moulding box are carefully separated.

上箱的砂子夯实以后，除去顶面多余的砂子，然后小心地分开上箱和下箱。

*（1）从 after the 到 from the top surface 是状语从句，修饰后面的主句。

（2）状语从句由两个并列分句组成。

3．When the metal that has been poured into a sand mould has fully solidified the mould is broken and the casting is removed.

当浇入砂型的铁水完全凝固之后，打破砂型取出铸件。

*（1）When the…fully solidified 是状语从句修饰主句。其中，that has…sand mould 是定语从句修饰：metal.

（2）后面的主句由 and 连接的两个并列分句组成。

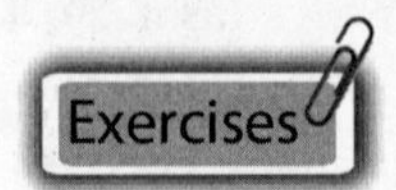

1. What is the first stage in the production of sand castings?
2. Why must casting patterns be made larger than the finished casting size?
3. Why is the mould made in two or more parts?
4. Describe the process in the production of a sand mould.

Forging

There are two kinds of forging process, Impact Forging and Press Forging. In the former, the load is applied by impact, and deformation takes place over very short time. Press forging, on the other hand, involves the gradual build up of pressure to cause the metal to yield. The time of application is relatively long. Over 90% of forging processes are hot.

Impact forging can be further subdivided into two main types.

(a) Smith forging

(b) Drop forging

Smith forging is undoubtedly the oldest type offorging, but it is now relatively uncommon. The impact force for deformation is applied manually by the blacksmith by means of a hammer. The piece of metal is heated in a forge and when at the proper temperature is placed on an anvil. While being hammered the metal is held with suitable tongs. The easiest metals to forge are the low and medium carbon steels and most smith forgings are made of these metals. The high carbon and alloy steels are more difficult to forge and require great care. Most non-ferrous metals can be successfully forged.

Drop forging is the modem equivalent of smith forging where the hmited force ofthe blacksmith has been replaced by the mechanical or steam hammer. The process can be carried out by open forging where the hammer is replaced by a tup and the metal is manipulated manually on an anvil. The quality of the products depends very much on the skill of the forger. Closed-die drop forging is widely used and the tup and anvil are replaced by dies. (Figure 10-1) illustrates the principle of an impact forge.

Press forging: Whereas impact forging umany involves a mechanical press, press forging, oil the other hand, requires hydraulic power. The largest forgings are invariably produced on large hydraulic presses. These have vertically moving rams which move down slowly under considerable pressure. The equipment required is therefore much bigger and (Figure 10-2) shows such a forge. A typical press forge would be capable of loads of the order of 6000 to 10, 000 tones. Forgings up to 100 tons weight can be handled easily in this forge and the highest-quality products are manufactured by this technique.

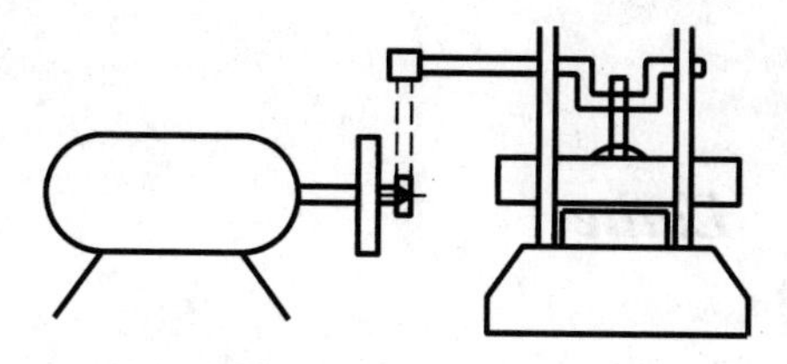

Fig. 10-1 Impact forge

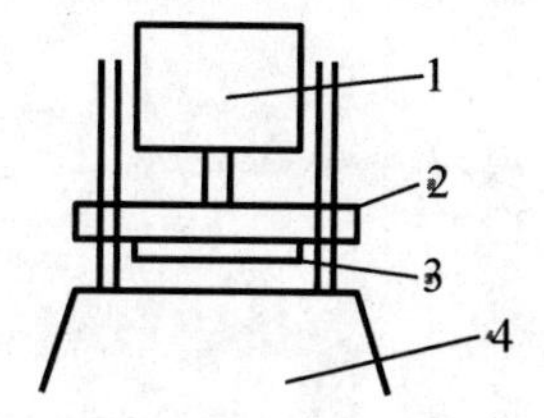

Fig. 10-2 press forge

1-Hydraulic cylinder 2-Crosshead

3-Tup 4-Anvil

Part III Speciality

Lesson 11 Lathe

Machine tools are machines for cutting metals. The most important of machine tools used in industry are lathes, drilling machines, and milling machines. Other kinds of metal working machines are not so widely used in machining metals as these three.

A lathe is a machine tool for cutting metal from the surface of a round work fastened between the two lathe centers and turning around its axis (Fig.11-1). In turning the work a cutter moves in the direction parallel to the axis of rotation of the work or at an angle to this axis, cutting off the metal from the surface of the work. This movement of the cutter is called the feed. The cutter is clamped in the tool post which is mounted on the carriage. The carriage is the mechanism feeding the cutter in the needed direction. The lathe hand may feed the cutter by hand or may make it be fed automatically by means of special gears.

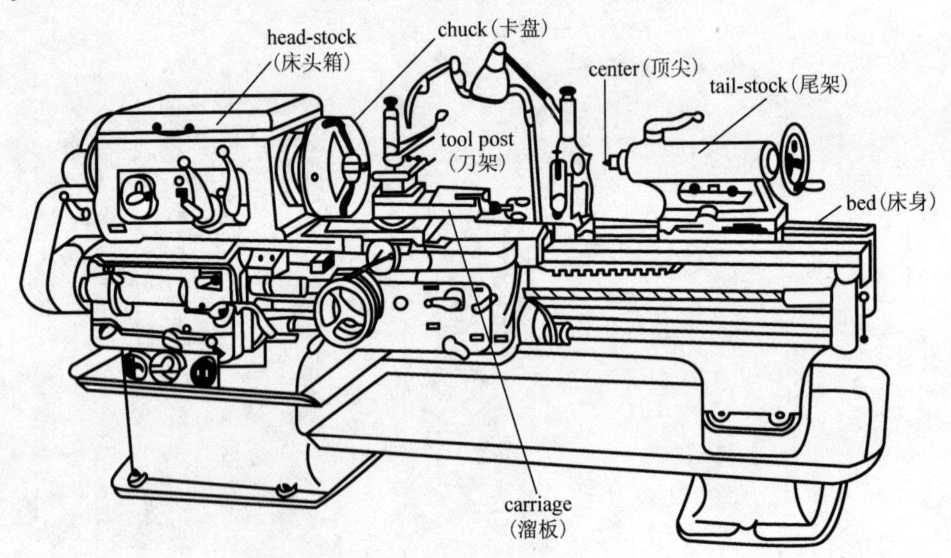

Fig.11-1 The Lathe

The largest part of the lathe is called the bed on which the head-stock and the tail-stock are fastened at opposite ends. On the upper part of the bed there are special ways upon which the carriage and tailstock slide.

The two lathe centers are mounted in two spindles one (the live center) is held in the head-stock spindle while the other (the dead center) in the tail-stock spindle.

The lathe chuck is used for chucking the work, that is for clamping it so that it will rotate without wobbling while turning. The chuck, usually mounted on the headstock spindle, may have different sizes and construction. If the work is perfectly round, it may be chucked in the, so-called three-jaw universal chuck all the jaws of which ale moved to the center by turning the screw. But if the work is not perfectly round, the four-jaw independent chuck should be used.

In turning different materials and works of different diameter, lathes must be run at different speeds. The gear-box contained in the headstock makes it possible to run the lathe at various speeds.

Before turning a work in the lathe, the lathe centers are to be aligned; that means that the axes of both centers must be on one line.

The alignment of the lathe centers may be tested by taking a cut and then measuring both ends of the cut with a micrometer.

Not all works should be fastened between the two centers of the lathe. A short work may be turned without using the dead center, by simply chucking it properly at the spindle in the head-stock.

New Words

1. lathe	[leið]	*n.*	车床
2. drill	[dril]	*n.*	钻头;
		vt.	钻（孔）
3. drilling	[ˈdriliŋ]	*n.*	钻削
4. mill	[mil]	*n.*	铣刀，铣床，铣
5. milling	[ˈmiliŋ]	*n.*	铣削
6. fasten	[ˈfɑːsən]	*vi.*	固定，紧固
7. turn	[təːn]	*vt.*	旋转，车削
8. feed	[fiːd]	*vt./n.*	进给，送给
9. cutter	[kʌtə]	*n.*	（切削）刀具
10. clamp	[ˈklæmp]	*vt.*	紧固，夹住
		n.	夹钳，夹板，压板
11. carriage	[ˈkæridʒ]	*n.*	溜板，拖板
12. bed	[bed]	*n.*	床，床身
13. head-stock	[ˈhedstɔk]	*n.*	头架，车床头，主轴箱，车头箱
14. tail-stock	[ˈteilstɔk]	*n.*	尾架，尾座

15. slide	[slaid]	*v.*	滑动
		n.	滑板，滑块
16. metalwork	['metlwə:k]	*n.*	金属加工（制造）
17. spindle	['spindl]	*n.*	心轴，主轴
18. chuck	[tʃʌk]	*n.*	卡盘，用（卡盘）夹紧
19. wobble	['wɔbl]	*vi.*	摇晃，摇摆
20. jaw	[dʒɔ:]	*n.*	卡爪，虎钳牙
21. align	[a'lain]	*vt.*	使成一直线；校正
22. axis	['æksis]	*n.*	轴线，轴心 axes（axis 的复数）
23. alignment	[ə'lainmənt]	*n.*	成直线，对准，同轴度
24. micrometer	[mai'krɔmitə]	*n.*	测微器，千分尺

Phrases and Expressions

1. cut off	切掉，切断，关掉
2. live center	主轴顶尖
3. dead center	尾架顶尖
4. three jaw universal chuck	三爪万能卡盘
5. four-jaw independent chuck	四爪卡盘
6. machine tool	机床，工具机
7. milling machine	铣床
8. tool post	刀座，刀架

1. Other kinds of metal working maching are not so widely used in machining metals as these three.

   其他类型的金属切削机床在金属切削加工方面不及这三种机床广泛。

   * not so…as…与……不一样

   as these three 为省略形式的比较状语从句。

   作原级形容词表示比较，通常有下述三种结构：

   （1）as+原级形容词+as：像……一样

   （2）not so+原级形容词+as：不如……那样

   （3）not as+原级形容词+as：不像……那样

   例如：Line AB is as long as line CD(is).

   Line AB is not so long as line CD.

   Line AB is not as long as line CD.

2. from the surface of a round work fastened between the two lathe centers and turning around its axis.
   车床是用来从圆形工件表面上切除金属的机床，工件安装在车床的两个顶尖之间，并绕顶尖轴线旋转。
   * fastened between the two lathe centers 和 turning around its axis 是两个并列的分词短语，fastened 含有被动的意义，turning 含有主动的意义，均作定语修饰名词 work。its 是指 round work。
3. In turning the work a cutter moves in the direction parallel to the axis of rotation of the work or at an angle to this axis, cutting off the metal from the surface of the work.
   车床车削工件时，车刀沿着工件的旋转轴线平行移动或者是与工件的旋转轴线交一斜角移动，将工件表面的金属切除。
   * 句中 parallel to the axis of rotation of work 做后置定语，修饰名词 direction；cutting, off the metal from the surface of the work 为分词短语作状语，表示伴随情况，这种状语往往放在句末，常用逗号与句子的其他成分隔开。
4. The lathe hand may feed the cutter by hand or may make it be fed automatically by means of special gears.
   车工可用手来实现手动进刀，也可借助于专门的齿轮组实现自动进刀。
   * 有些动词如 make, hear, see, watch 后的不定式作宾语补足语时，可不带不定式符号 to；be fed 是不定式的被动式作宾语 it 的补语；the lathe hand 为主语，带有两个并列的谓语 may feed 和 may make。
5. The gear box contained in the headstock makes it possible to run the lathe at various speeds.
   装入床头箱内的齿轮系统能使车床以不同的速度运转。
   * it 在句中作形式宾语，而真正的宾语是不定式短语 to run the lathe at various speeds，它通常放在宾语补足语（possible）的后面；contained in the headstock 作后置定语，修饰名词 the gear box。
6. Before turning a work in the lathe, the lathe centers are to be aligned; that means that the axes of both centers must be on one line.
   车床在车削工件前，它的顶尖要对准，即两全顶尖的轴线必须在一条直线上。
   * 句中有两个 that 前一个 that 是用作指示代词，它代表前面句子的内容，即代表 the lathe centers are to be aligned；后一个 that 用作连接词，无词义，引出宾语从句 that the axes of both centers must be on one line。to be aligned 是不定式的被动式在句中作表语。

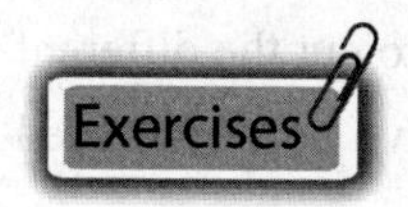

I. Decide whether the following statements are the true[T] or false[F] according to the text:
1. Lathe is a machine tool for holding and turning metal, plastic or other material against a

cutting tool to form a cylindrical product. [ ]

2. If the work is not perfectly round, it may be chucked in the so-called three-jaw universal chuck. [ ]

3. The lathe is one of the most important machines in a machine shop. [ ]

4. The head-stock which holds the other end of the work, moves along the bed, and can be damped in position at any point. [ ]

5. The most important of machine tools used on industry are lathes, drilling machines, and milling machines. [ ]

6. The smallest part of the lathe is called the bed on which the head-stock and the tail-stock are fastened at opposite ends. [ ]

II. Fill the blanks with the words and expressions given below.

Springs and pulleys	gears and pulleys	right	feeding	carrying	three-jaw
four-jaw left	short	measurement	alignment	long.	

1. The head-stock is mounted at the__________end of the lathe.
2. It contains the head-stock spindle, which is rotated by a combination of__________.
3. But if the work is not perfectly round, the__________independent chuck should be used.
4. The carriage is the mechanism__________cutter in the needed direction.
5. The__________of the lathe centers may be tested by taking a cut and then measuring both ends of the cut with a micrometer.
6. A__________work may be turned without using the dead center, by simply chucking it properly at the spindle of the head-stock.

III. Answer the following questions.

1. What is a machine tool?
2. Which machine tool is most widely used in metal working industry?
3. How many work center are there on a lather?
4. Where is the dead center mounted?
5. What is a chuck?

Cutting Tools

Metal cutting tools must possess a variety of different properties in order to cut the different metals under varying conditions of severity. To meet these demands, tools have been produced from a variety of materials.

The most important properties of cutting tools are hardness at high temperature, wear resistance, and impact strength.

As a tool cuts, high heat is developed as a result of compression and friction at the cutting edge of the tool. All metal cutting tools begin to lose hardness when heated to sufficiently high temperatures. As the tool softens due to heat, it wears and breaks down at the cutting edge or face. Various cutting tool materials begin to lose their hardness at different temperatures. Hence, the hardness of the tool and the degree to which it remains its hardness at high temperature are important in the selection of a cutting-tool material.

A cutting tool is wear-resistant if it resists abrasion at the cutting edge and along the tool face. Wear resistance improves as cutting tool hardness increases.

Cutting tools must also have high strength in order to be vibration and impact-resistant. Strength in cutting-tool material is not always proportional to hardness. Some of the hardest tool materials lack strength because they are too brittle.

The various materials from which most metal cutting tools are made can be classified under the following principal headings:

1. Carbon tool steel
2. High-speed steel
3. Cast alloys
4. Cemented carbides
5. Ceramics
6. Diamonds

Tool life or the number of pairs produced by a cutting-tool edge before regrinding is required, is a very important cost factor in manufacturing a part or product. Cutting tools must be reground at the first sign of dullness. If a tool is used beyond this point, it will break down rapidly.

In order to detect the time when a cutting tool should be changed, most modern machines are equipped with indicators that show the horsepower used during the machining operation. When a tool becomes dull, more horsepower is required for the operation, which will show on the indicator. When this occurs, the tool should be reconditioned immediately.

Lesson 12 Hydraulic Systems of Machine Tools

Hydraulic systems are now ever more widely used in machine tools as principal and feed movement drives, speed-changing devices, braking mechanisms, clamping devices, automatic control of machining cycle, etc. Hydraulic systems become the main type of drive in machine tools like grinders, shapers, copying millers, broaching machines, etc.

This extensive use of hydraulic systems is due to their capability of providing infinitely variable speed over a wide range, smooth reversal of moying machine members, automatic overload protection, easy lubrication, etc. Hydraulically controlled machine tools take less floor space, and their parts and units can be easily standardized. Among their shortcomings are leakage of hydraulic fluid through seals and gaps, ingress of air into fluid, effects of temperature and time on fluid properties etc.

Energy losses in hydraulic systems are made up of volumetric losses due to leakage of hydraulic fluid, hydraulic losses due to a drop in pressure, and mechanical losses due to friction of contact surfaces.

Total efficiency of the hydraulic system:

$$\eta = \eta_v \eta_h \eta_m$$

where $\eta_v \eta_h \eta_m$ is volumetric, hydraulic and mechanical efficiency, respectively.

Normal functioning of the hydraulic system largely depends on the type of working fluid employed. This fluid should be sufficiently viscous and uniform; it should possess good lubricity and protect mechanisms from corrosion; it should retain its properties with changes in temperature, pressure, speed and direction of movement. The working fluid should not become oxidized or evolve sediments, evaporate or inflame. These requirements are best met by mineral oils and their mixtures.

The principal property used in selecting and comparing oils is the viscosity index, which shows the change in the viscosity of an oil with its temperature. The higher the viscosity index, the hisber the quality of the oil and the higher its refinement. Oil viscosity index 90 is best suited for hydraulic systems.

Typically, the machine-tool hydraulic system includes: an oil tank; a pump to deliver oil into the system; control devices (valves, pressure relays, timers, etc.) to control pressure and volume of oil in the system; distributing devices to control the working cycle; operative cylinders for straight movement and hydraulic motors for rotating movement; piping to connect all the elements of the system.

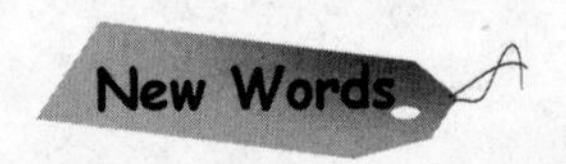

1. shaper [ˈʃeipə] *n.* 牛头刨床

2. extensive	[iks'tensiv]	*a.*	广泛的，广大的
3. standardized	['stændə,daizd]	*a.*	标准化的
4. leakage	['li:kidʒ]	*n.*	泄漏
5. seal	[si:l]	*n.*	密封垫
6. ingress	['ingres]	*n.*	进入
7. efficient	[i'fiʃənt]	*n.*	效率，功效
8. volumetric	[vɔlju'metrik]	*a.*	（测）容量的
9. viscous	['viskəs]	*a.*	黏性的
10. lubricity	[ju:'brisiti]	*n.*	润滑性能
11. evolve	['ivɔlv]	*vt.*	（使）逐渐形成
12. sediment	['sedimənt]	*n.*	沉淀（物）
13. retain	[ri'tein]	*vt.*	保持，保留
14. evaporate	[i'væpəreit]	*v.*	（使）蒸发
15. inflame	[in'fleim]	*v.*	（使）燃烧
16. viscosity	[vis'kɔsəti]	*n.*	黏性
17. valve	[vælv]	*n.*	阀
18. typically	['tipikəli]	*ad.*	典型地，具有代表性地
19. cylinder	['silində]	*n.*	液压缸
20. piping	['paipiŋ]	*n.*	管道

Phrases and Expressions

1. broaching machine	拉床
2. copying miller	仿形铣床
3. viscosity index	黏度指数
4. pressure relay	压力继电器

Notes

1. Hydraulic systems are, now ever more widely used in machine tools as principal and feed movement drives, speed-changing devices, braking mechanisms, clamping devices, automatic control of machining cycle, etc.
   现在，液压系统在机床中得到了更广泛的应用。主要用于主运动和进给运动的驱动，控制变速机构、刹车机构和夹紧机构及工作循环的自动控制等。
2. Energy losses, in hydraulic systems are made up of volumetric losses due to leakage of hydraulic fluid, hydraulic losses due to a drop in pressure, and mechanical losses due to friction of contact surfaces.
   液压系统的能量损耗包括：由于液体泄漏造成的流量损耗，由于压力下降造成的压力损耗及由于接触表面的摩擦造成的机械损耗。

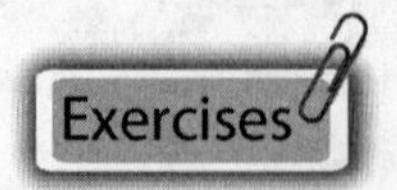

1. Why are hydraulic systems extensively used in machine tools?
2. What are the shortcomings of hydraulic systems?
3. What properties should working fluid have?
4. What is the principal property used in selecting and comparing oils?
5. What does the machine tool hydraulic systems include?

Pressure and Flow Control

Hydraulic energy is produced as long as the prime mover (usually an electric motor) drives the pump, and hydraulic pressure develops by resistance to pump flow. Hence, the hydraulic system suffers damage if the pump flow is not stopped or off-loaded (re-circulated) back to tank during non-action periods of the circuit. Non-action periods arise from stalling all actuator, or by reaching the end of the stroke or the circuit sequence, or during the time-delay periods of the circuit sequence.

In order to avoid hydraulic system damage, power wastage, and overheating of the hydraulic fluid, circuit designers use a variety of cleverly designed systems to control maximum system pressure and pump flow during non-action periods.

Pressure control valves are used in hydraulic systems to control actuator force (force= pressure×area), and to determine and (pre) select pressure levels at which certain machine operations must occur. Pressure controls are in the main used to perform the following system functions.

1. To limit maximum system pressure in a hydraulic circuit or sub-circuit, and thus provide overload protection.

2. To provide re-direction of pump flow to tank, while system pressure must be maintained (system unloading).

3. To provide re-direction of pump flow to tank while system pressure is not maintained (system off-loading).

4. To offer resistance to fluid flow at selectable pressure levels (counterbalance force).

5. To provide an alternative flow path for the fluid at selected pressure levels (pressure sequencing).

6. To reduce (or step down) pressure levels form the main circuit to a lower pressure in a sub-circuit.

Pressure control valves are often difficult to identify, mainly because of the many descriptive names applied to them. The function of the valve in the circuit usually becomes the basis for its name. The valves used to accomplish the abovementioned system functions are therefore given the following names, respectively:

1. Relief valves.
2. Unloading relief valve.
3. Offloading valve.
4. Counter balance valve and brake valve.
5. Pressure-sequence valves.
6. Pressure-reducing valves.

Flow-control valves are used in hydraulic systems to control the rate of flow from one part of the system to another. Flow-control devices accomplish one or more of the following control functions:

- limit the maximum speed of linear actuators and hydraulic motors (flowrate/piston area=piston speed).
- it the maximum power available to subcircuits by controlling the flow to them (power= flowrate ×pressure).
- proportionally divide or regulate the pump flow to various branches of the circuit.

A partly closed orifice or flow control valve in a hydraulic pressure line causes resistance to pump flow. This resistance raises the pressure upstream of the orifice to the level of the relief valve setting and any excess pump flow must pass via the relief valve to tank (Fig. 12-1).

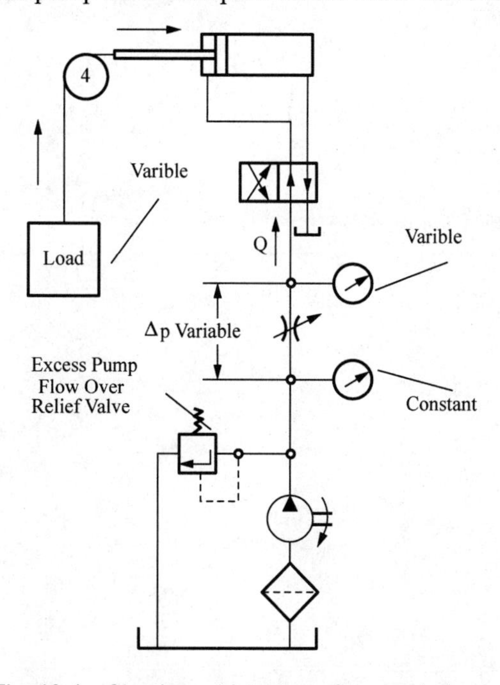

Fig. 12-1 Simple restrictor type flow control valve

In order to understand the function and operation of flow-control devices one must comprehend the various factors that determine the flowrate (Q) across an orifice or restrictor. These factors are.

- cross-sectional area of the orifice (mm2);
- shape of the orifice (round, square, triangular);
- length of the restriction;
- pressure differential across the orifice (△P);
- viscosity of the fluid(cst, depending on the temperature).

Thus, the law that govers the flowrate across a given orifice can by approximation be defined as $Q2 \propto \Delta P$. This implies that any variation in pressure up, or downstream of the orifice changes the pressure differential △P, and thus the flowrate through the orifice. The pressure upstream of the flow-control valve is normally kept constant by either the system relief valve or by the pressure controller on a variable displacement pump. Variations in the pressure differential(△P)are thus only caused by pressure fluctuations down stream, as a result of varying load forces on the actuator.

Lesson 13 Types of Control Devices

Several types of control devices are used in industry to satisfy the following control needs:

- Mechanical Control
- Pneumatic Control
- Electromechanical Control
- Electronic Control
- Computer Control
- Programmable Logic Control (PLC)

Mechanical control includes cams and governors. Although they have been used for the control of very complex machines, to be cost effectively, today they are used for simple and fixed-cycle task control. Some automated machines, such as screw machines, still use cam-based control. Mechanical control is difficult to manufacture and is subject to wear.

Pneumatic control is still very popular for certain applications. It uses compressed air, valves, and switches to construct simple control logic, but is relatively slow. Because standard components are used to construct the logic, it is easier to build than a mechanical control. Pneumatic control parts are subject to wear.

As does a mechanical control, an electromechanical control uses switches, relays, timers, counters, and so on, to construct logic. Because electric current is used, it is faster and more flexible. The controllers using electromechanical control are called relay devices.

Electric control is similar to electromechanical control, except that the moving mechanical components in an electromechanical control device are replaced by electronic switches, which works faster and is more reliable.

Computer control is the most versatile control system. The logic of the control is programmed into the computer memory using software. It not only can be for machine and manufacturing system control, but also for data communication. Very complex control strategies with extensive computations can be programmed. The first is the interface with the outside world. Internally, the computer uses a low voltage (5 to 12 volts) and a low current (several milliamps). Machine requires much higher voltages (24, 110, or 220 voltages) and currents (measured in amps). The interface not only has to convert the voltage difference, but also must filter out the electric noise usually found in the shop. The interface thus must be custom-built for each application.

New Words

1. pneumatic [nju(:)'mætik] *a.* 气动的，空气的
2. governor ['gʌvənə] *n.* 操纵杆，控制器
3. relay ['ri:lei] *n.* 继电器

4. timer	[ˈtaimə]	*n.*	定时器，计时员
5. counter	[ˈkauntə]	*n.*	计数器
6. construct	[kənˈstrʌkt]	*vt.*	修建，建立；构成，组成
7. computation	[ˌkɔmpju(ː)ˈteiʃ(ə)n]	*n.*	计算；估计；计算法；测定
8. milliamps(mA)	[miliˈmp]	*n.*	毫安
9. convert	[kənˈvəːt]	*vt./vi.*	(使)转变，(使)转化
10. interface	[ˈintə(ː)ˌfeis]	*n.*	[计]接口
11. voltage	[ˈvəultidʒ]	*n.*	电压，伏特数
12. memory	[ˈteməri]	*n.*	存储；存储器；记忆装置
13. strategy	[ˈstrætidʒi]	*n.*	战略，策略

Phrases and Expressions

1. pneumatic control	气动控制
2. electromechanical	机电的
3. electronic governor	电子调速器
4. screw machine	车丝机，攻螺纹机床
5. filter out	过滤
6. custom-built	客户定制

Notes

1. Although they have been used for the control of very complex machines, to be cost effective, today they are used for simple and fixed-cycle task control.
   尽管它们曾被用在对复杂机器进行控制的场合下，现在它们还应用于控制简单而固定循环的场合。
   * They 代替“cams and governors”.
2. Because standard components are used to construct the logic, it is easier to build than a mechanical control.
   由于可用标准件构成各种逻辑，因此气动控制的加工制造比机械控制更容易。
   * It is easier to do sth. … than … 更容易做……事情。
3. As does a mechanical control, an electromechanical control uses switches, relays, timers, counters, and so on, to construct logic.
   正像机械控制那样，机电控制使用开关、延时器、计数器和计时器等其他元器件构成各种逻辑指令。
   * “as does a mechanical control”由 as 引导的比较状语从句。
4. Electric control is similar to electromechanical control, except that the moving mechanical components in an electromechanical-control device are replaced by electronic switches, which works faster and is more reliable.

电气控制类似于机电控制，所不同的是将机电控制中的可动零部件被动作速度更快、可靠性更高的电气开关所代替。

*“except that…+从句”是介词短语引导的从句，为前面主句的状语。

5. The interface thus must be custom-built for each application.

因此须根据应用场合的不同构造用户接口。

*“custom”原意为“习惯，惯例”，在此引申为“用户”。

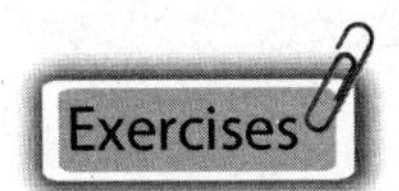

I. Answer the following questions briefly.

1. How many types of control can be divided into and give the details?
2. How does the computer control work?
3. What does an electromechanical control use to construct logic?

II. Translate the following sentences into Chinese.

1. Although they have been used for the control of very complex machines, to be cost effective, today they are used for simple and fixed-cycle task control.

2. Electric control is similar to electromechanical control, except that the moving mechanical components in an electromechanical-control device are replaced by electronic switches, which works faster and is more reliable.

3. The interface thus must be custom-built for each application.

PLC

In order to use the advantages of all those controllers and eliminate the difficulties, the programmable logic controllers were invented. A PLC was a replacement for relay devices. They are programmed using a ladder diagram, which is standard electric wiring diagram. As PLCs become more flexible, high-level as well as low-level languages are available to PLC programmers. PLCs have the flexibility of computers as well as a standard and easy interface with processes and other devices. They are widely accepted in industry for controlling from a single device to a complex manufacturing facility.

Programmable logic controllers (PLCs) were first introduced in 1968 as a substitute for hardwired relay panels. The original intent was to replace a mechanical switching device (relay modules). However, since 1968, the capabilities of the PLCs were to replace relay panels, modern PLCs have many more functions. Their use extends from simple process control to manufacturing system controls and monitoring.

They are used for high-speed digital processing, high-speed digital communication, high-level compute-language support, and, of course, for basic process control (Fig. 13-1).

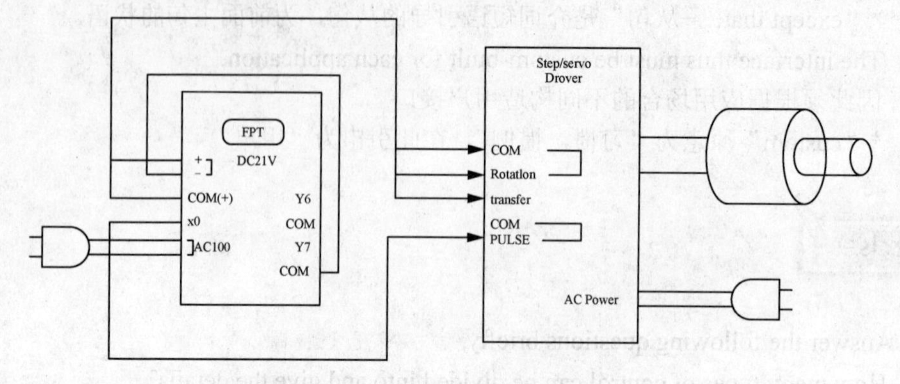

Fig. 13-1 Application of PLC(Control Step/Servo Motor)

PLCs vary in size and power. A large PLC can have up to 10000 I/O points and support all the functions discussed earlier. There are also expansion slots to accommodate PC and other communication devices. For many applications, a small PLC is sufficient. Fig. 13-2 shows a small PLC. It has 16 I/O points and a standard RS-232 serial communication port. The speed of PLC is constantly improving, even the low-end PLCs perform at high speed. One to two microsec/kbyte of memory speed is very common.

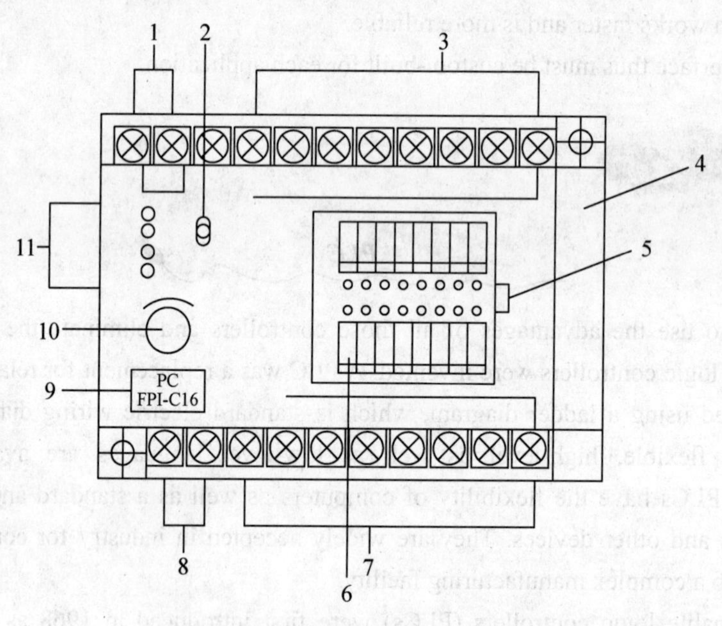

Fig. 13-2 PLC(FPI C16 Control Panel)

1—AC/DC Power Input 2—Mode Select 3—output 4—I/O Expansion Slots
5—I/O Status LED 6—Label 7—Input 8—DC Power Output 9—Programmer Interface
10—Adjustable Input 11—PLC Status LED

Lesson 14 Numerical Control Programme

Part Programming

A part programmer is a very crucial person in any NC manufacturing system. On obtaining the component drawing, he decides the sequence of operations, the speeds and feeds for the various operations and determines the magnitude of various motions desired. Therefore, it is important that he should be familiar with the various operations and machine tools to be used. He should be able to carry out calculations based on geometry and trigonometry.

Data Required for Programming

To prepare the manuscript for manual part prt6ogramming, the programmer needs to collect some data pertaining to the work to be carried out. This data would be as follows:

(1) Machine tools specifications.

(2) Specification of all tools.

(3) Specification of work material.

(4) Speed feed tables.

EIA/ISO Code

For coding on the tape, EIA or ISO codes are followed. NC machines are generally equipped to handle both types of information. Nowadays mostly ISO codes are used.

In a program this entire information is called block. There are 3 types of formats for representing the block in punched tape.

(1) Fixed sequential format.

(2) Word address format.

(3) Tab sequential format.

The following are the letter addresses used in programming:

N: operation sequence number address.

G: preparatory function address.

X, Y, Z, A, B, C...: dimension address.

S: spindle speed address.

F: feed rate address.

T: tool address.

M: miscellaneous function address.

Preparatory Function

This information is given by a word which is prefixed by the letter G followed by the numerical code for the operation for which the control unit is to instruct the machine tool. For example, G81 means that the instruction is to drill. The other parameters necessary for carrying out the operation would follow. The G...will not be able to operate the machine tool until all the relevant information, which follows is processed.

Absolute and incremental preparatory function

Preparatory function G90 and G91 are used for specifying that the data in the following block is in absolute mode(relative to a common datum) or incremental mode(relative to current position)respectively. G90 can be cancelled by G91 or vice versa.

Miscellaneous Function

For carrying out some operation, it may be desirable to start the spindle and have its rotation clockwise or anticlockwise. Words used for such instruction are termed as miscellaneous functions. Similarly, starting or stopping the coolant also fall under this category. These instructions are not pertaining to dimensions of the work but are required for carrying out the operation. The machine tools responds information is prefixed by the alphabet M followed by the numerical code for the function required. For example, M03 would mean spindle to rotate clockwise, while M04 anticlockwise.

New Words

1. crucial	[ˈkruːʃiəl]	*a.*	决定性的，紧要关头的
2. component	[kəmˈpəunənt]	*n.*	成分，组成部分，部件，元件
3. magnitude	[ˈmægnitjuːd]	*n.*	大小，积，量，长（度）；巨大；重要性
4. geometry	[dʒiˈɔmitri]	*n.*	[数]几何（学）
5. trigonometry	[trigəˈnɔmitri]	*n.*	三角法
6. convey	[kənˈvei]	*vt.*	运输；运送；表达，转达
7. sequential	[siˈkwinʃəl]	*a.*	按次序的，相继的，连续的
8. prefix	[ˈpriːfiks]	*n.*	[语]前缀
9. anticlockwise	[ˈæntiˌklɔkwaiz]	*a.*	逆时针的（地）

Phrases and Expressions

1. the sequence of operations	工序
2. are distinguished by	以……著称

Notes

1. Therefore, it is important that he should be familiar with the various operations and machine tools to be used.

   因此，他（编程员）应熟悉各种加工和所用机床，这一点很重要。

* It is+a. +that clause…，主语从句。

2. To prepare the manuscript for manual part programming, the programmer needs to collect some data pertaining to the work to be carried out.

   为了给零件手工编程准备好草稿，编程员需要收集与零件加工相关的资料。

   * to prepare…引导目的状语；carry out 意为执行，施行。

3. The information about an operation which would be necessary to be conveyed to the controller for the machine tool operation would consist of the following:

   必须传送给控制装置的与机床操作有关的信息如下：

   * about an operation 是 information 的定语，其后又有一个由 which 引导的定语从句。

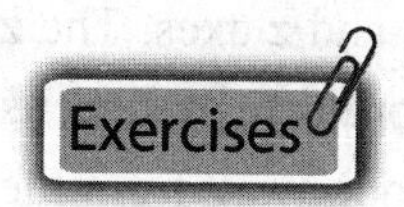

I. Translate the following expressions into Chinese.

1. part programmer
2. component drawing
3. geometry and trigonometry
4. preparatory function
5. miscellaneous function
6. incremental mode
7. clockwise direction and anticlockwise direction

II. There are a few preparatory and miscellaneous functions, translate and recite them.

G00 positioning
G01 linear interpolation
G02 clockwise circular interpolation (CW)
G03 anticlockwise circular interpolation (CCW)
G90 absolute data
M00 program stop
M02 end of program

III. Translate the following passage into Chinese.

A numerical control machine is a machine positioned automatically along a preprogrammed path by means of coded instructions. So, some has to determine what operations the machine is to perform and put that the information into a coded form that the NC control unit understands before the machine can do anything. Machine may be programmed manually or with the aid of a computer. Manually programming is called manual part programming, and programming done by a computer is called computer aided programming (CAP).

Coordinate System for NC Machines

In an NC system, each axis of motion is equipped with a separate driving source that replaces the hand wheel of the conventional machine. The driving source can be a DC motor, a stepping motor, or a hydraulic actuator. The source selected is determined mainly based off the precision requirements of the machine.

The relative movement between tools and workpieces is achieved by the motion of the machine tool slides. The three main axes of motion are referred to as the x, y, and z axes. The z axis is perpendicular to both the x and y axes in order to create a right-hand coordinate system, as shown in (Fig.14-1). A positive motion in the z direction moves the cutting tool away from the workpiece.

This is detailed as follows:

1. z AXIS

(1) On a workpiece-rotating machine, such as a lathe, the z axis is parallel to the spindle, and the positive motion moves the tool away from the workpiece (Fig. 14-1).

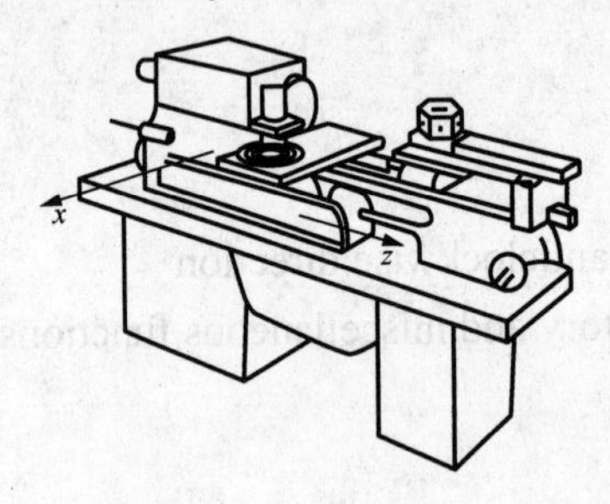

Fig. 14-1 Coordinate system for a lathe

(2) On a tool-rotating machine, such as a milling or boring machine, the z axis is perpendicular to the tool set, and the positive motion moves the tool away from the workpiece (Fig. 14-2 and Fig. 14-3).

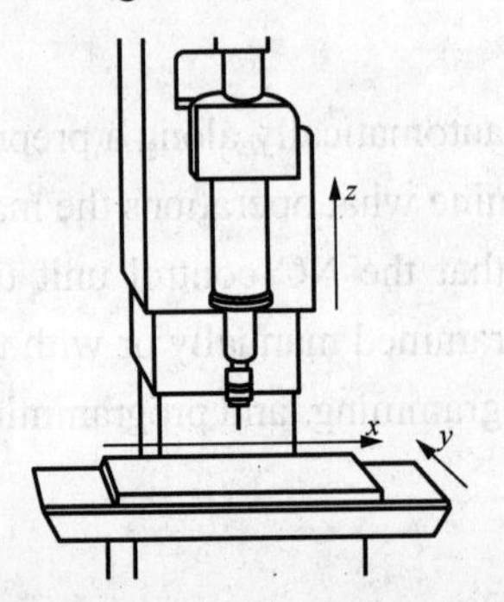

Fig. 14-2 Coordinate system for a drill

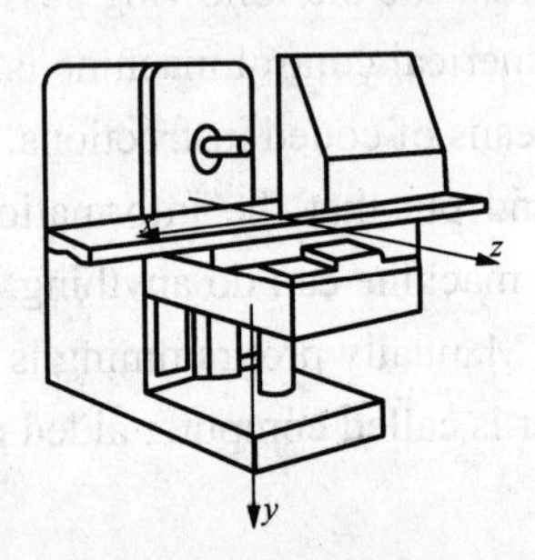

Fig. 14-3 Coordinate system for a mill

(3) On other machines, such as a press, a planing machine, or sheafing machine, the z axis is perpendicular to the tool set, and the positive motion increases the distance between the tool and the workpiece.

2. x AXIS

(1) On a lathe, the x axis is the direction of tool movement, and positive motion moves the tool away from the workpiece.

(2) On a horizontal milling machine, the x axis is parallel to the table.

(3) On a vertical milling machine, the positive x axis points to the right when the programmer is facing the machine.

3. y AXIS

The y axis is the axis left in a standard Cartesian Coordinate system.

Lesson 15 Jig Types

The term jig refers to any device used to ensure that holes are drilled, reamed, or tapped in the proper location.

Four common jig types will be covered below.

Box Jigs

A box jig is a special fabricated jig that assumes the basic shape of a box (Fig.15-1). The base of the box is normally used to locate and clamp the workpiece while supporting the sides of the jig. The sides of the box may also be used to aid in the clamping or locating of the workpiece while providing support for the bushing plate. The top of the box carries one or more bushings that are precisely positioned with respect to the location plane and points. This jig type is rigid and very accurate, making it a popular style for many applications. However, the fixed bushing plate slows the loading and unloading time invested in each production part. Chip removal from the interior of the box may also be difficult, periodically delaying the operation.

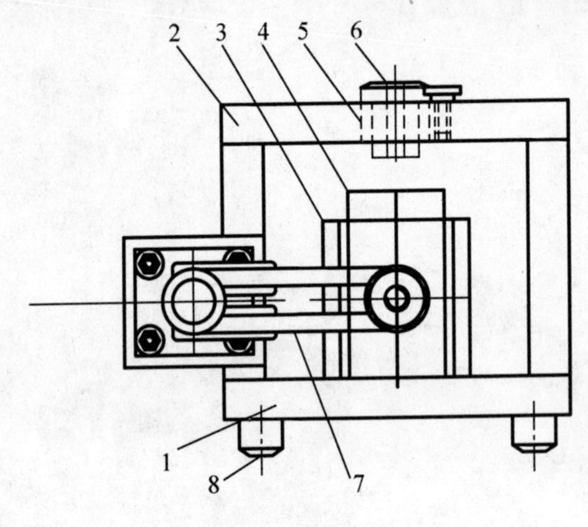

Fig.15-1 Box Jig

1—Base plate 2—Bushing plate 3—Vee block locator 4—Workpiece 5—Liner bushing 6—Fixed renewable bushing 7—Toggle clamp 8—Jig feet

Tumble Jigs

When a given workpiece requires the drilling of holes on more than one face, a tumble jig may be considered. A tumble jig is a variation of the box jig in which drill bushing are found in one or more sides of the jig. In low-volume applications, the workpiece is positioned inside the tumble jig and clamped. Then, by flipping the jig from one side to another, each drill bushing incorporated in the jig is exposed to the drill spindle. The major advantages of the tumble jig are: (1)reduced hole-to-hole spacing errors due to one location and clamping, (2)one jig takes the place of many, and (3) operation times are reduced with less handling.

Indexing Jigs

Indexing jigs, with either horizontal or vertical mounts, are commercially available standards designed to accommodate the drilling of circular hole patterns (Fig. 15-2). The workpiece is located and clamped under a single bushing. The position of the bushing is adjustable for height and location over the workpiece. This adjustment permits using a single jig for a wide variety of similar parts. Holes may be located from the first hole drilled by using the indexing head. Head may be equipped with special indexing plates that allow for special or odd angle indexing.

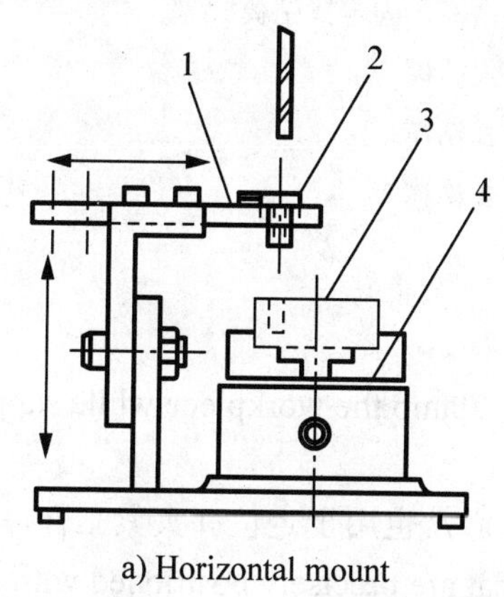

a) Horizontal mount

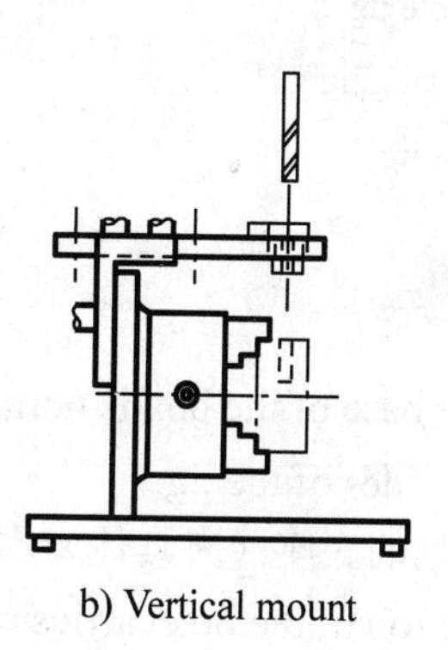
b) Vertical mount

Fig. 15-2 Indexing Jigs

1—Bushing tray 2—Bushing 3—Workpiece 4—Indexing head

Plate Jigs

The plate jig is distinguished by its main structural member, which is a plate. All other jig details are attached to this plate. The open construction of this jig type facilitates the loading and unloading of irregularly shaped workpieces.

New Words

1. jig	[dʒig]	*n.*	夹具，钻模
2. variation	[ˌvɛəri'eiʃən]	*n.*	变化，变动
3. indexing	['indeksiŋ]	*n.*	分度法，指标
4. fabricate	['fæbrikeit]	*vt.*	制作，装配，组合
5. locating	[ləu'keitiŋ]	*n.*	定位（法）
6. assume	[ə'sjuːm]	*vt.*	呈（某形式），假定，承担，接受
7. bushing	['buʃiŋ]	*n.*	钻套，衬套
8. interior	[in'tiəriə]	*n./a.*	内部（的）

9．tumble ['tʌmbl] *n.* 翻滚

10．flip [flip] *vt.* 使翻转，掷

11．incorporate [in'kɔːpəreit] *vt.* 结合，使混合

12．accommodate [ə'kɔmədeit] *v.* （使）适应

Phrases and Expressions

1．invest in 投资

2．be exposed to 招致，与……相接触

3．box jig 箱式钻模，固定式钻模

4．tumble jig 翻转式钻模

5．indexing jig 回转式钻模

6．plate jig 盖板式钻模

Notes

1．The base of the box is normally used to locate and clamp the workpiece while supporting the sides of the jig.

夹具的底座（夹具体）用于支承夹具的侧壁，通常也用于定位并夹紧工件。

2．The top of the box carries one or more bushings that are precisely positioned with respect to the location plane and points.

夹具的顶面装有一个或几个相对定位面（或点）精确定位的钻套。

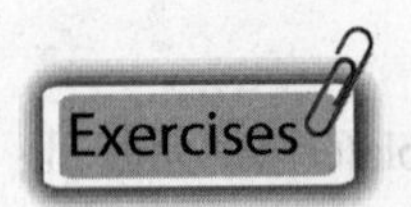

1. List two main hole-making processes.
2. Give definition of the term jig.
3. List four types of jig.
4. State the advantages and disadvantages of box jig.
5. What are the major advantages of the tumble jig?

Bushing Types and Applications

Headless Press Fit Bushing: The headless press fit bushing is specified in many low production jigs. The bushing is pressed into the bushing plate until it is flush with the top of the plate. The lack of a head minimizes clearance problems and allows two or more bushing to be placed on close centers.

Head Press Fit Bushings: The headpress fit bushing is similar to the headless type with the exception of the head or shoulder found on its top end. This bushing type is selected when high axial cutting forces are anticipated. The head prevents the bushing from being pushed through the bushing plate.

Fixed Renewable Bushings: A fixed renewable bushing is selected when the production life of the jig exceeds the normal wear life of one bushing. This bushing style is used with a press fit bushing liner and lock screw. The bushing slips into the liner and is held in place with a lock screw. When the bushing wears out, it can easily be replaces on the production floor.

Slip Renewable Bushings: Slip renewable bushing are also used with press fit-type liners. This bushing type is selected when more than one operation is to be completed on one hole using a single jig. In such a case, the hole is first drilled using one bushing, then that bushing is removed and replaced by a larger bushing sized to accommodate a reamer. In this manner, a hole can be drilled and reamed in the same jig. Both drill and reamer bushing will have identical outside diameters allowing them to fit perfectly into the liner.

Bushing Linear: Bushing liners, both headless and head types, are permanently pressed into the jig's bushing plate to protect it from wear when either fixed or slip renewable bushing are used. Headless liners are used when minimal axial loading is anticipated. Head liners are used when excessive axial cutting pressures are anticipated. The bushing plate is typically counterbored to allow a flush mounting of the liner's head.

Lesson 16 HTM125600 Turning and Milling Center

HTM125600 turning and milling center adopts disposition of twin-turret, simultaneous five-axis control linkages, and it possesses the load capacity of heavy-duty lathe. The machine is mainly used to machine high accuracy, multifarious process and complex shape gyro-rotor parts. Such as motor rotor, turbine rotor, roller and crankshaft, with high accuracy, multi-process and complex shape. The machine can be used to machine workpiece in small and medium batch and various varieties, saving tooling disposition, shortening preparing cycle of production. Key parts are all imported from world famous enterprise to ensure the accuracy and reliability of the machine and increase productivity.

Features of Machine Structure

- Bed of the machine is found by high-strength cast iron with integral tank structure, there is a bevel rack(m=8)with high intensity imported from Italian LICAT behind the bed for driving the column;
- Headstock adopts thermostatic lubricating oil, oil cooling cycle device is disposed on the outer front bearing;
- Main motor is larger power DC motor;
- Tailstock is consists of upper and lower parts and is provided with indicators that can separately display pushing force of weight of workpiece to be machined;
- The column is a side-hanging type structure and driving-driven driving system is provided for feed of Z-axis to eliminate reversal clearance;
- A working feeding machanism is provided at each side of the column. The feeding box and the right of a ram structure. X1 and X2 axis adopt double-driving to greatly increase the smoothness of motion and the machine is equipped with tool changing manipulator and tool magazine and BLUM measuring tool device;
- Control box suspends from under of the machine and it can be driven along Z-axis;
- With SIEMENS 840D numerical control system.

Table 16-1 Major Specification

Item	Unit	Remark
Max. turning length	mm	6000
Max turning diameter	mm	Φ1250
Max weight of workpiece between centers	kg	30000
Range of spindle speed	r/min	1-200
Output power of main motor	kW	75(直流 500-2000rpm)
Dia. of face plate	mm	Φ1250(手动四爪)
Max. torque of face plate	kN.m	35

续表

Item	Unit	Remark
Max. torque of C-axis	N.m	1200
Max. cutting force of single-tool	k.N	55
Travel of X1/X2 - axis	mm	1330/790
Travel of Y1-axis	mm	-300-+540(考虑换刀)
Travel of Y2-axis	mm	±190
Travel of Z-axis	mm	8130
Travel of B-axis		-90°-+180°
Travel of A-axis		0°-+90°
Speed of×1/Y1-axis rapid moving and feeding rate	mm/min	0-15000/0-12000
Speed of X2/Y2-axis rapid moving and feeding rate	mm/min	0-15000/0-12000
Speed of Z-axis rapid moving and feeding rate	mm/min	0-15000
Max. speed of B-axis	r/min	30
Max. speed of C-axis	r/min	20
Dia. / travel of failstock sleeve	mm	Φ300/200
Rapid speed of tailstock moving	mm/min	3500
Moving speed of tailstock sleeve	mm/min	660
Support range of steady rest(Optional)	mm	Φ150-Φ500
Power of boring and milling spindle	kW	52
Speed of boring and milling spindle step1/step2(max)	r/min	180/3150
Spindle torque of boring and milling stepl/step2(max)	N.m	2400/157
Weight of the machine	Kg	80000
Overall dimensions of the machine (L×H ×W)	mm	17020×7252×4707

New words

1. turning ['tə:niŋ] *n.* 车削
2. milling ['miliŋ] *n.* 磨，制粉，轧齿边 [机]铣（削），铣削法；铣出的齿边
3. disposition [dispə'ziʃən] *n.* 气质，天性，性格；安排，布置；支配；处理权
4. linkage ['liŋkidʒ] *n.* 连接；结合；联系；联动装置
5. capacity [kə'pæsiti] *n.* 容量，容积；才能，能力
6. multifarious [ˌmʌlti'fɛəriəs] *a.* 许多的，多方面的；各式各样的

7. turbine	[ˈtəːbin]	*n.*	涡轮机
8. rotor	[ˈrəutə]	*n.*	轮子，旋转器[物]旋度
9. roller	[ˈrəulə]	*n.*	滚压机；滚杠，滚柱；定型卷夹
10. crankshaft	[ˈkræŋkʃɑːft]	*n.*	机轴；曲轴，曲柄轴
11. productivity	[ˌprɔdʌkˈtiviti]	*n.*	生产率，生产力
12. eliminate	[iˈlimineit]	*vt.*	消除，排除；切断，分离
13. reversal	[riˈvəːsəl]	*n.*	反向，反转，倒转；运气不好
14. clearance	[ˈkliərəns]	*n.*	（公差中的）公隙，裕度，间隙，距离，容积
15. manipulator	[məˈnipjuleitə]	*n.*	操作者，操纵者，操纵器
16. specification	[ˌspesifiˈkeiʃən]	*n.*	说明书，详细的计划书[pl.]规范，规格，技术说明
17. torque	[tɔːk]	*n.*	扭转力，转矩，项圈

Phrases and Expressions

1. lubricating oil	润滑油
2. twin-turret	双塔刀架
3. is consists of	由……组成

Notes

1. HTM125600 turning and milling center adopts disposition of twin-turret, simultaneous five-axis control linkages, and it possesses the load capacity of heavy-duty lathe.
   HTM125600 车削和铣削加工中心采用双塔刀架，同时控制 5 轴联动，并拥有重型车床负载能力。
2. The machine is mainly used to machine high accuracy, multifarious process and complex shape gyro-rotor parts.
   该机主要用于加工精度高，工艺多和形状复杂的旋转零件。
3. The column is a side-hanging type structure and driving-driven driving system is provided for feed of Z-axis to eliminate reversal clearance.
   该立柱是一个侧面悬挂式结构和伺服驱动系统为 Z 轴进给，以消除反向间隙。

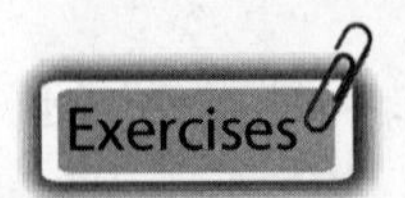

1. What does HTM125600 turning and milling center adopt?
2. Where are the key parts of HTM125600 turning and milling center imported?
3. Please say the features of machine structure.

Maintenance and Fault Diagnosis of CNC machine

Components of FANUC System are packed in detachable modules. There are 4 modules, namely: the computers with the interface, the drivers, the switching power supply and the transformer. The transformer takes a newly developed R-type structure of small size, high efficiency and noiseless. The switching power supply is specially designed for interference-free operation. The computer is packed on a two-layer printed-circuit-board to ensure high reliability; an individual driver-board is equipped for every axis and all the drivers are interchangeable. This flexible architecture provides great convenience in field maintenance, which turns out to be just the substitution of spare parts. The manufacturer provides spare parts as well as prompt services for the recovery of inactive component boards at reasonable prices.

The most common trouble that may occur in the system is the step-out of the stepper motor, and the following measures might be helpful in troubleshooting.

1. Check all the voltages from the power supply board for the correct values.

2. Switch to Manual Mode, drive the motor with pulsative step, and check the motor armature for regular motor by hand-touching. If the armature steps properly, feed step-out might be due to loosened fastening of the damper plate, which should be refitted and tightened, otherwise, (i.e. the armature does not step properly), the operation of the system must be subject to further inspection.

3. Remove the cover of the chassis. Interchange the signal input plugs in the sockets (XS-9 and XS-10) on the driver PCB's of the proper motor and the abnormal motor, then check again the two motors in Manual Mode as described in 2. If the abnormal motor now runs properly, troubles might be in the driver PCB; otherwise, they may be due to failures in the computer.

4. Check the voltage of the power input socket of the driver PCB (refer to Wiring Diagram), compare with the proper ones. When no voltage failures are found, check and compare the circuit components, mainly the power transistors, with an in-line measurement by a multimeter. Components with abnormal parameters might have been damaged.

5. In case when the voltages are correct, another way of trouble-shooting is interchanging the driver PCB's of the proper and the abnormal stepper motor.

6. Generally, small deviation in dimensions are due to mechanical hitches, while large deviation might be due to system circuitry troubles or loosened fastening of the motor damper.

7. When step-outs emerge at high-speed in dry run, the reduction gearbox should be examined.

8. When no failures are found in separate inspections all the functional modules, yet the

whole system works in unstable condition, the connecting cables should be carefully checked upon for soldering defects.

9. When errors such as confusing displays or keyboard defects occur in the mainframe board, cut off the main source to the Control Unit Chassis and examine the insertion the IC chips to ensure firm and sound connections.

We, the manufacturer, provide various post-sales services to solve problems in the applications. Please contact us. We are ready to support and ensure the effective running of this system.

Lesson 17 Computer Aided Manufacturing

Computer aided manufacturing(CAM) started with NC in 1949 at MIT. This project, sponsored by the U. S. Air Force, was the first application of computer technology to control the operation of a milling machine.

Standard NC machines greatly reduced the machining time required to produce a part or complete a production run of parts, but the overall operation was still time-consuming. Tape had to be prepared for the part, editing the program would result in making a new tape, and tapes had to be rewound each time a part was completed. With this in mind, the machine manufacturers added a computer to the existing NC machine, introducing the beginning of CNC.

The addition of the computer greatly increased the flexibility of the machine tool. The parts program was now run from the computer's memory instead of from a tape that had to be rewound. Any revisions or editing of the program could be done at the machine, and changes could be stored.

As the machine tool manufacturers continued to improve the efficiency of their machines, the computer capabilities were greatly increased to programmable microprocessors, and many time-saving devices were introduced to increase the machine's cutting time and reduce downtime. Some of these machine options are automatic tool changers, parts loaders and unloaders, chip conveyors, tool wear monitors, in-process gaging and robots-which brings us to today's machining centers.

CAM uses all the advanced technologies to automate the operations in manufacturing and handle the data that drives the process. The tools of CAM include computer technologies, CAE, and robotics. CAM uses all these technologies to join the process of design with automated production machine tools, material handling equipment, and control systems. Without computers, the most important tool in industry, the productivity of the United States would be in serious trouble. Computers help people to become more productive and to do things that would almost be impossible without them.

CAM ties together all the major functions of a factory. The manufacturing or production operations are joined together with the process planning, production scheduling, material handling, inventory control, product inspection, machinery control, and maintenance to form a total manufacturing system.

A CAM system generally contains three major divisions:

Manufacturing: The physical operation of controlling the machine tools, material handing equipment, inspection operations, etc. , in order to produce the parts required.

Engineering: The process which involves design and engineering activities to ensure that the parts are designed properly in order to function as required.

Management：The information such as scheduling, inventory control, labor, and manufacturing costs, and all the data required to control the entire plant.

CAM increases the productivity and versatility of machine tools. Before the introduction of NC and CAM, most machine tools were cutting metal only about 5 percent of the time. The automated systems available now cut metal about 70 percent of the time, and the goal is to come as close as possible to having them remove metal 100 percent of the available time.

New Words

1. revision [ri'viʒən] *n.* 修正，修改
2. microprocessor [maikrəu'prəusesə] *n.* 微处理器
3. option ['ɔpʃən] *n.* 选项
4. automate ['ɔ:təmeit] *vt.* 使自动化
5. schedule ['ʃedju:l] *vt.* 排定，安排
6. inventory ['invəntri] *n.* 详细目录，存货清单

Phrases and Expressions

1. automatic tool changers 自动换刀架
2. in-process gaging 在线检测
3. machine centers 加工中心
4. time-saving 省时的

Notes

1. This project, sponsored by the U. S. Air Force, was the first application of computer technology to control the operation of a milling machine.

   由美国空军倡导的这项技术，是计算机技术控制铣削加工的第一次应用。

   * sponsored by the U. S. Air Force 是插入语，做进一步说明。

2. Standard NC machines greatly reduced the machining time required to produce a part or complete a production run of parts, but the overall operation was still time-consuming.

   标准的数控机床极大地减少了加工单一零件和完成零件整个生产过程所需要的加工时，但整个加工仍然费时。

   * required...修饰 the machining time。

3. The parts program was now run from the computer's memory instead of from a tape that had to be rewound.

   零件加工程序运行于计算机存储器中，从而取代了须重绕的纸带。

4. As the machine tool manufacturers continued to improve the efficiency of their machines, the computer capabilities were greatly increased to programmable microprocessors, and many time-saving devices were introduced to increase the machine's cutting time and reduce downtime.
随着机床生产厂家不断地提高它们的机床效率，计算机上编程微处理器的能力也极大地增强了，采用了很多节省时间的装置，用于切削加工的时间增长了，停机时间减少了。
* downtime 意为停机时间。
5. Some of these machine options are automatic tool changers, parts loaders and unloaders, chip conveyors, tool weal monitors, in-process gaging and robots-which brings us to today's machining centers.
有些机床具备自动换刀、零件自动装卸、切屑自动传输、自动监控刀具磨损、在线检测和机器人等功能——这就产生了现在的加工中心。
* which 指代前面所提的各种功能。
6. The manufacturing or production operations are joined together with the process planning, production scheduling, material handling, inventory control, product inspection, machinery control, and maintenance to form a total manufacturing system.
将制造或生产运营和工艺设计、生产计划、材料处理、报表控制、产品检验、机器控制和维修联系在一起，形成一个完整的加工系统。
7. The automated systems available now cut metal about 70 percent of the time, and the goal is to come as close as possible to having them remove metal 100 percent of the available time.
现有的自动加工系统其加工时间占总时间的 70%。我们的目标是要使它们的切削时间尽可能接近总时间的全部。

I. Translate the following expressions into Chinese.
1. the first application of computer technology
2. overall operation
3. making a new tape
4. each time a part was completed
5. the flexibility of the machine tool
6. improve the efficiency
7. programmable microprocessors
8. automatic tool changer
9. tool wear monitor
10. computer aided engineering(CAE)

II. Choose the term which best matches the definition given in Column 2 from Column 1.

〈Column 1〉	〈Column 2〉
1. Standard NC machines.	(a) three major divisions: manufacturing, engineering, managment.
2. Automatic tool changers	(b) can automatically change machine tools.
3. The computer greatly increased	(c) greatly reduced the machine time.
4. Punched tape	(d) increased the flexibility of the machine tool.
5. A CAM system generally contains	(e) have to be prepared for the part before any machine can be done.

III. Translate the following passage into Chinese.

CAD/CAM systems can be used to produce CNC data to machine a part. After preparing a tool list and setup plan for the required part, the CNC programmer starts by creating a database. Once this database has been created, the programmer can recall the part on the CRT screen. After the part displayed, the programmer describes the tools required from the information in the tool library, this library contains a description and either a name or a tool identification number for each and every tool available for use.

Useful Menu and Parameters For CAM

1. UG's Main Menu and Function (Table 17-1)

Table 17-1 UG's Main Menu and Function

Menu	Function
File	New, Open, Close, Save, Save Work Part Only, Save As, Save All, Save Bookmark, Options, Print, Plot, Send to Package File, Import, Export, Utilities, Properties, Recently Opened Parts, Exit.
Edit	Undo List, Redo, Cut, Copy, Copy Display, Paste, Paste Special, Delete, Selection, Object Display, Show and Hide, Transform, Properties, Curve, Feature.
View	Refresh, Operation, Perspective, Orient, Layout, Visualization, Camera, Information Window, Current Dialog Box, Show Resource Bar.
Insert	Sketch, Datum/Point, Curve, Curve from Curves, Curve from Bodies, Design Feature, Associative Copy, Combine Bodies, Trim, Offset/Scale, Detail Feature, Mesh Surface, Sweep, Facet Body, Direct Modeling.
Format	Layer Settings, Visible in View, Layer Category, Move to layer, Copy to layer, WCS, Reference Sets, Group, Group Features.

续表

Menu	Function
Tools	Expression, Spreadsheet, Material Properties, Update, Reuse Library, Customize, Drafting Standard, Iournal, User Defined Feature, Part Families, Define Deformable Part.
Assemblies	Context Control, Reports.
Information	Object, Point, Expression, PMI, Part, Assemblies, Other.
Analysis	Measure Distance, Measure Angle, Minimum Radius, Geometric Properties, Measure Bodies, Section Inertia, Examine Geometry, Strength Wizard, Simple Interference, Assembly Clearance, SpaceFinder, Units kg-mm.
Preferences	Object, User Interface, Plalettes, Selection, Visualization, Visualization Performance, 3D Input Devices, Work Plane, Modeling, Sketch, Assemblies, Annotation, PMI, Teamcenter Intergration, NX Gateway, IT.
Window	New Window, Cascade, Tile Horizontally, Tile Vertically, 1.model1.part, More.
Help	

2. Parts Feature

Features
Sketch
Extrude
Revolve
Sweeping
Sweep along Guide
Tube
Hole
Boss
Pocket
Pad
Emboss
Offset Emboss
Slot
Groove
Dart
User Defined Feature
Extract Geomertry
Instance Geomertry
Sheet from Curves
Bounded Plane
Thicken
Sheet to Solid Assistant

Feature Operations
Draft Body
Edge Blend
Face Blend
Soft Blend
Chamfer
Shell
Thread
Mirror Feature
Mirror Body
Sew
Patch Body
Wrap Geometry
Offset Face
Scale Body
Emboss Sheet
Split Body
Divide Face
Hole
Trim Body
Join Face
Instance Feature
Unite

Datum Plane.
Datum Axis
Datum CSYS
Block
Cylinder
Cone
Sphere
Spherical Corner
Text Below Icon
Subtract
Intersect
Assembly Cut
Promote Body
Text Below Icon
Reset Toolbar

Lesson 18 Computer Integrated Manufacturing System

Computer integrated manufacturing or CIM is the term used to describe the most modern approach to manufacturing. Although CIM encompasses many of the other advanced manufacturing technologies such as computer numerical control (CNC), CAD/CAM, robotics, and just-in-time defivery (JIT), it is more than a new technology or a new concept. Computer integrated manufacturing is actually an entirely new approach to manufacturing or a new way of doing business.

To understand CIM, it is necessary to begin with a comparison of modern and traditional manufacturing. Modern manufacturing encompassed all of the activities and processes necessary to convert raw materials into finishes products, deliver them to the market, and support them in the fields. These activities include the following:

(1) Identifying a need for a product.

(2) Designing a product to meet the needs.

(3) Obtaining the raw materials needed to produce the product.

(4) Applying appropriate processed to transform the raw materials into finished products.

(5) Transporting product to the market.

(6) Maintaining the product to ensure a proper performance in the field.

This broad, modern view of manufacturing can be compared with the more limited traditional view that focuses almost entirely on the conversion processed. The old approach separates such critical preconversion elements as market analysis research, development, and design for manufacturing, as well as such after-conversion elements as product delivery and product maintenance. In the other word, in the old approach to manufacturing, only those processes that take place on the shop floor are considered manufacturing. This traditional approach of separating the overall concept into numerous stand-alone specialized elements was not fundamentally changed witll the advent of automation. While the separate elements themselves became automated (i.e. computer aided drafting and design (CAD) in design and CNC in machining), they remained separate. Automation alone did not result in the integration of these islands of automation.

With CIM, not only are the various elements automated, but also the islands of automation are all linked together or integrate. Integration means that a system can provide complete and instantaneous sharing of information. In modern manufacturing, integration is accomplished by computers. With this background, CIM can now be defined as the total integration of all manufacturing elements through the use of computers.

Progress is being made toward the eventual full realization of CIM in manufacturing. When this is accomplished, fully integrated manufacturing firms will realize a number of benefits from CIM:

(1) Product quality increases.

(2) Lead times are reduced.

(3) Direct labor costs are reduced.

(4) Product development times are reduced.

(5) Inventories are reduced.

(6) Overall productivity increases.

(7) Design quality increased.

New Words

1. encompass	[in'kʌmpəs]	*v.*	包含或包括某事物
2. delivery	[di'livəri]	*n.*	递送. 交付
3. performance	[pə'fɔːməns]	*n*	履行，执行
4. conversion	[kən'vəːʃən]	*n.*	变换，转化
5. advent	['ædvənt]	*n.*	出现，到来
6. background	['bækgraund]	*n.*	背景，后台
7. instant	['instənt]	*a.*	立即的，直接的
8. maintenance	['meintinəns]	*n.*	维护，保持

Phrases and Expressions

1. computer integrated manufacturing system(CIMS)	计算机集成制造系统
2. lead time=delivery time	交货时间，交货期，生产周期
3. be defined as…	被定义为……

Notes

1. It is more than a new technology or a new concept.

   与其说它(CIM)是一个新的方法，还不如说是一个新的概念。

   * 句型…more than…or…意为“与其……不如……”。

2. Modern manufacturing encompassed all of the activities and processes necessary to convert raw materials into finished products, deriver them to the market, and support them in the fields.

   现代制造包括了把原材料转换成成品、把产品投向市场和进行售后服务所必需的一切活动和过程。

   * necessary to do…是形容词短语，作 the activities and processes 的后置定语，意为“必需……的”。

3. This traditional approach of separating the overall concept into numerous stand-alone specialized elements was not fundamentally changed with the advent of automation.
这种传统的将整个概念分割成许多独立的专用单元的方式并没有随着自动化的出现而发生根本性的变化。
* 分词短语 separating the overall concept into numerous stand-alone specialized elements 这里作介词 of 的宾语。

4. Progress is being made toward the eventual full realization of CIM in manufacturing.
制造业在最终完全实现 CIM 的方向正在取得进展。
* full realization of…意为完全实现。

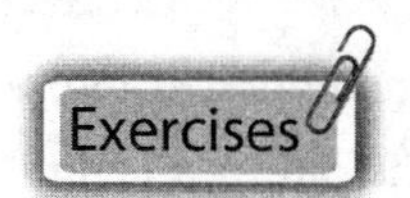

I. Decide whether the following statements are the true[T] or false[F] according to the text:

1. CIMS is a new type of enterprise. [ ]

2. Transporting product to the market is not encompassed in modern manufacturing. [ ]

3. Traditional manufacturing encompasses all of the activities and processes necessary to convert raw materials into finished products. [ ]

4. While such separate elements as CAD or CAM themselves became automated, integration of these islands of automation will fully realize. [ ]

5. In modern manufacturing, integration is accomplished by computers. [ ]

II. Answer the following questions.

1. What does CIMS means?

2. What's the difference between modern and traditional manufacturing?

3. What can we benefit from CIMS?

III. Fill the following blanks with appropriate words.

_____ or CIM is the term used to describe the most modern approach to manufacturing. Although CIM encompasses many of the other advanced manufacturing technologies such as computer numerical control _____, CAD/CAM, robotics, and just-in-time delivery _____, it is more than a new technology or a new _____. Computer integrated manufacturing is actually an entirely new approach to manufacturing or a new way of _____.

To understand CIM, it is necessary to begin with a comparison of modern and traditional manufacturing. Modern manufacturing encompassed all of the activities and processes necessary to convert raw materials into _____, deriver them to the market, and support them in the fields. These activities include the following.

This broad, modern view of manufacturing can be compared with the more limited _____ view that focuses almost entirely on the conversion processed.

In the other word, in the old approach to manufacturing, only those processes that take place on the _____ floor are considered manufacturing. This traditional approach of _____ the overall concept into numerous stand-alone specialized elements was not fundamentally changed with the advent of automation. While the separate elements themselves became _____, they remained separate. Automation alone did not _____ in the integration of these islands of automation.

Flexible Manufacturing Systems

The individual manufacturing system that were introduced here can be incorporated into a single large-scale system in which the production of part is controlled with the aid of a central computer. The advantage of such a production system is its high flexibility in terms of the small effort and short time required to manufacture a new product, and therefore it is denoted as a flexible manufacturing system (FMS).

Existing FMS in the United States are typically made up of machining centers working in concert with the types of machines, all under the control of a central computer. The work pieces are on pallets which move throughout the system, transferred by towlines(or drag chains)located beneath the floor or by some other mechanism. These FMS limit handling by the operators and can be more readily reprogrammed to handle new requirements.

Future FMS will contain many manufacturing cells, each cell consisting of a robot serving several CNC machine tools or other stand-alone systems such as an inspection machine, a welder, an EDM machine, etc. The manufacturing cells will be located along a central transfer system, such as a conveyor, on which a variety of different work pieces and parts are moving. The production of each part will require processing through a different combination of manufacturing cells. In many cases more than one cell can perform a given processing step. When a specific work piece approaches the required cell on the conveyor, the corresponding robot will pick it up and lead it onto a CNC machine in the cell. After processing in the cell, the robot will return the semi-finished or finished part to the conveyor. A semi-finished part will move on the conveyor until it approaches a subsequent cell where its processing can be continued. The corresponding robot will pick it up and load it onto a machine tool. This sequence will be repeated along the conveyor, until, at the route, there will be only finished parts moving, then they could be routed to an automatic inspection station and subsequently unloaded from the FMS. The coordination among the manufacturing cells and the control of the part's flow on the conveyor will be accomplished under the supervision of the central computer.

The advantages of FMS include the following:

(1) Increased productivity.

(2) Shorter preparation time for new products.

(3) Reduction of inventory of parts in the plant.

(4) Saving of labor cost.

(5) Improved product quality.

(6) Attracting skilled people to manufacturing (since factory work is regarded as boring and dirty).

(7) Improved operator's safety.

Additional economic savings may be from such things as the operator's personal tools, gloves, etc. Other savings are in locker rooms, showers, and cafeteria facilities-all representing valuable plant space, which will not require enlarging if company growth is achieved with flexible automation systems.

Lesson 19 Introduction to Electromechanical Products and Negotiation

Place: Shanghai Industrial Fair, Exhibition hall of NC Machines

Characters: Mr Zhou, Sales representative of a NC Machine Manufacturer

Mr. Xu, Deputy-headmaster in charge of teaching in a institute

Mr. Jiang, Dean of Electromechanical Department

Mr. Shi, Dean of the Scientific Research Section

Zhou: How do you do? Welcome to see our products. What kind of equipment are you most interested in?

Jiang: I am interested in your MC (Machining Center) Machine, Model SV-1000. Would you show me a manual of Model SV-1000?

Zhou: OK.What's your name?

Jiang: My name is Jiang Xhong Li. Here is my card. This is Mr. Xu, our deputy-headmaster and this is Mr. Shi, dean of our scientific resarch section.

Zhou: And here is my card. Thank you for coming Mr Jiang are you also interested in MC?

Jiang: Yes, ours is a comprehensive key institute integrated with electromechanical, trade and foreign languages. We not only have the specialties such as electromechanical integration and technological foreign languages but also NC simulation center and CAD/CAM laboratory. With the support of Shanghai Municipal Educational Commission and Finacial Bureau, we'll make more investment in equipment.

Zhou: Oh, Isee. I think you will mainly use the NC machine you are going to buy for teaching, won't you?

Jiang: Yes. Besides teaching and training, we'll also use it for scientific research and production. Therefore, we are very strict in choosing NC machines, which should meet the following requirments:

(1) Advanced technology.

(2) Multi-functionality.

(3) Higher precision which can meet the needs of teaching, scientific research and production.

Zhou: No problem. Established in 1943, our company has a long history and abundant experience in manufacturing machine tools. We are highly praised by our customers because of high quality of our products and our excellent after-sales services. Our products are widely sold in the world. From the sample products, you can see that our products are superior in function and precision index to those similar products. There are 16 tools in the storage, which will make them change automatically. The working table can move forward and backward in a wide scale, which is completely fit for the processing of conventional mold. It has a high performance and is quite suitable for your institute and middle-sized enterprises.

Shi: Besides guaranteeing the structural functions, and the technical precision listed in the sample, can you add a fourth axis to make the four axes(X, Y, Z, and B) move simultaneously?

Jiang: There should be RS-232 communication set on your MC, which can support the CAD/CAM communication and finish the complicated surface by DNC(Direct Numerical Contro1).

Xu: In addition. would you please provide the attachments suitable for this model, such as shanks, cutters, and trolleys?

Zhou: OK, No problem.

Xu: Would you give us your quotation?

Zhu: How many NC machines do you want to order?

Shi: One.

Zhou: Let me think it over. Five hundred and sixty thousand RMB.

Xu: Your quotation is on the high side.

Zhou: Considering the quality. I think our quotation is quite reasonable.

Jiang: Mr. Zhou, you know, colleges don't have a lot of funds and this time we have the rare chance to get the appropriation from the Municipal Educational Commission and Financial Bureau to renovate our NC training center. We have much equipment to buy and we are hard up for money. Please give us the most favorable price as your support for the educational cause.

Zhou: I have met three master-hands in negotiation today(1aughter). By the way, how would you make the payment?

Xu: I'll pay by installment.

Zhou: What about paying 30%upon signing the contract, and then paying the rest after delivery of the goods?

Xu: According to our practice, we'll pay 60%after delivery, and pay the additional 10% after three months' trial use.

Jiang: What about your after-sales services?

Zhou: We will ensure you "three warranties" (for repair replacement or compensation of faulty products) during one-year period of guarantee. Then we'll ensure you follow-up services. OK, just now Mr. Jiang said that you also want to buy NC equipment?

Jiang: Yes, we want to buy WFC(Wire Flame Cutter), and EDM(Electric Discharge Machine)

Zhou: We can be your agent.

Xu: Mr. Zhou, let's decide 5 hundred thousand for this NC machine. We'll discuss other equipment after we have done this one.

Zhou: I am afraid we can't. I don't think you'll let us sell the goods at a loss. I think we should decide it at 5 hundred and thirty thousand. This is our lowest quotation, and no further concession. Actually, we won't make a profit. We will just use it as an advertisement.

Xu: including freight?

Zhou: Um, OK.

Shi: When will you make the delivery?

Zhou: In about two months.

Xu: If you promise to deliver the goods 15 days ahead of time, We can accept your quotation.

Zhou: Please wait for a while, I'll talk it over with our manufacturing manager. Mr. Xu, I just talked it over with Yang, our general manager. He agrees to your requirement of delivery, 15 days ahead of time.

Jiang: Mr Zhou, during assembling the machine, can we go to your factory to learn from your technicians on how to test and adjust different kinds of precision index on the spot?

Zhou: Yes, you are welcome. You are experts in this line. We welcome you to supervise us. Please be assured that we'll use the advanced computer-laser feedback system to test and adjust the machine and make sure that every precision index will meet the requirements.

Shi: You can drop us a line.

Zhou: OK. Next, shall we sign a contract and a memorandum for the NC machine?

Xu: OK. Looking forward to mutual cooperation.

New Words

1. exhibition [ˌeksi'biʃən] *n.* 展览，展览会
2. hall [hɔːl] *n.* 门厅
3. representative [ˌrepri'zentətiv] *n.* 代表，代理人
4. institute ['institjuːt] *vt.* 建立，制定；开始，着手 *n.* 协会，学会；学院，研究院
5. equipment [i'kwipmənt] *n.* 设备；装备；配备；（工作必需的）知识，技能
6. manual ['mænjuəl] *a.* 用手的，手工的 *n.* 手册，指南
7. deputy ['depjuti] *n.* 副手，代理人，代表；议员，下院议员
8. comprehensive [ˌkɔmpri'hensiv] *a.* 广泛的，综合的

9. simulation	[ˌsimjuˈleiʃən]	*n.*	模仿；模拟
10. investment	[inˈvestmənt]	*n.*	投资
11. municipal	[mju(:)ˈnisipəl]	*a.*	市的，市政的
12. commission	[kəˈmiʃən]	*n.*	授权，委托；委员会
13. technology	[tekˈnɔlədʒi]	*n.*	科技（总称）；工艺；应用科学；工业技术
14. establish	[iˈstæbliʃ]	*vt.*	建立，成立；安置
15. quality	[ˈkwɔliti]	*n.*	质，质量；品质，特征，特性
16. superior	[sjuːˈpiəriə]	*a.*	（级别、地位）较高的；（品质、程度）优良的，较好的
17. index	[ˈindeks]	*n.*	索引；标志，象征；量度
		vt.	给……编索引，指示出
18. performance	[pəˈfɔːməns]	*n.*	演出，表演；性能，工作情况
19. enterprise	[ˈentəpraiz]	*n.*	事业，计划；企[事]业单位，公司
20. guarantee	[ˌgærənˈtiː]	*vt.*	保证；担保
		n.	保证，保障；保证书；保用期
21. precision	[priˈsiʒən]	*n.*	精确度，准确（性）
22. simultaneous	[ˌsiməlˈteinjəs]	*a.*	同时发生的；同时存在的
23. communication	[kəˌmjuːniˈkeiʃn]	*n.*	交流，交际，通讯
24. quotation	[kwəuˈteiʃən]	*n.*	引用，引述；引文，引语，语录；时价，报价，行情
25. appropriation	[əˌprəupriˈeiʃən]	*n.*	据为己有，占有，挪用（只指定用途的一笔），拨款
26. renovate	[ˈrenəuveit]	*vt.*	翻新；修复；整修
27. installment	[inˈstɔːlmənt]	*n.*	部分；分期付款
28. sign	[sain]	*n.*	标记，符号
29. contract	[ˈkɔntrækt]	*vt.*	缔结；订契约
		n.	契约，合同
30. warranty	[ˈwɔrənti]	*n.*	保证书；[律]（商品等的）保单
31. negotiation	[niˌgəuʃiˈeiʃən]	*n.*	协商，谈判
32. profit	[ˈprɔfit]	*n.*	利润，收益，赢利；益处，得益
33. concession	[kənˈseʃən]	*n.*	承认，允许；妥协，让步；特许权
34. technician	[tekˈniʃ(ə)n]	*n.*	技术人员，专家；技巧好的人
35. memorandum	[ˌmeməˈrændəm]	*n.*	（备忘的）记录；非正式商业书信，便函
36. mutual	[ˈmjuːtjuəl]	*a.*	相互的，彼此的；共同的，共有的
37. cooperation	[kəuˌɔpəˈreiʃən]	*n.*	合作

Phrases and Expressions

1. Industrial Fair　工业博览会
2. deputy-headmaster　副校长
3. Electromechanical Department　机电系
4. Financial Bureau　财政局

Notes

1. Yes, ours is a comprehensive key institute integrated with electromechanical, trade and foreign languages.
   是的，我院是一所集机电、商务、外语于一体的综合性重点高等技术学院。
   * integrated with electromechanical, trade and foreign languages 是 institute 的后置定语。
2. We not only have the specialties such as electromechanical integration and technological foreign languages but also NC simulation center and CAD/CAM laboratory.
   我院设有机电一体化和工业技术外语等专业，学院有数控实训中心，CAD/CAM 实验室。
   * not only… but also… 不但……而且……
   He not only studies hard but also works well.
   他不仅学习努力，而且认真工作。
3. From the sample products, you can see that our products are superior in function and precision index to those similar products. There are 16 tools in the storage, which will make them change automatically.
   从展品上，您可以看到其功能和技术精度指标优于其他同类产品。
   * superior 优势的，胜过……的（to; in）；超越……的（to）
   be superior in numbers 数量上占优势
   be superior to hardships 不屈服于艰难困苦
4. The working table can move forward and backward in a wide scale, which is completely fit for the processing of conventional mold.
   工作台范围较大，完全可以胜任常规的模具加工。

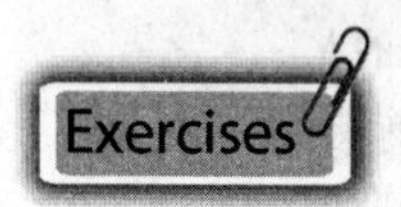

Please translate the following phrases into Chinese.

1. Exhibition hall of NC Machines
2. deputy-headmaster
3. in charge of

4. Finacial Bureau
5. machine tool
6. sign the contract
7. agree to
8. look forward to

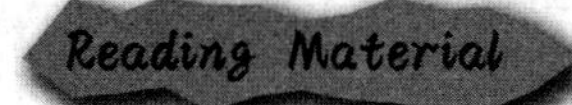

Operation Panel of the CNC System

The following panels are available.

7.2″Monochrome LCD/MDI Panel (Fig. 19-1)

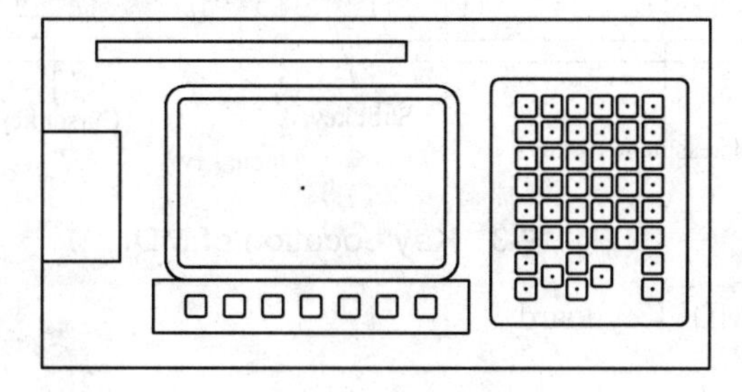

Fig. 19-1 7.2″Monochrome LCD/MDI Panel

14″color CTR/MDI Panel (Fig. 19-2)

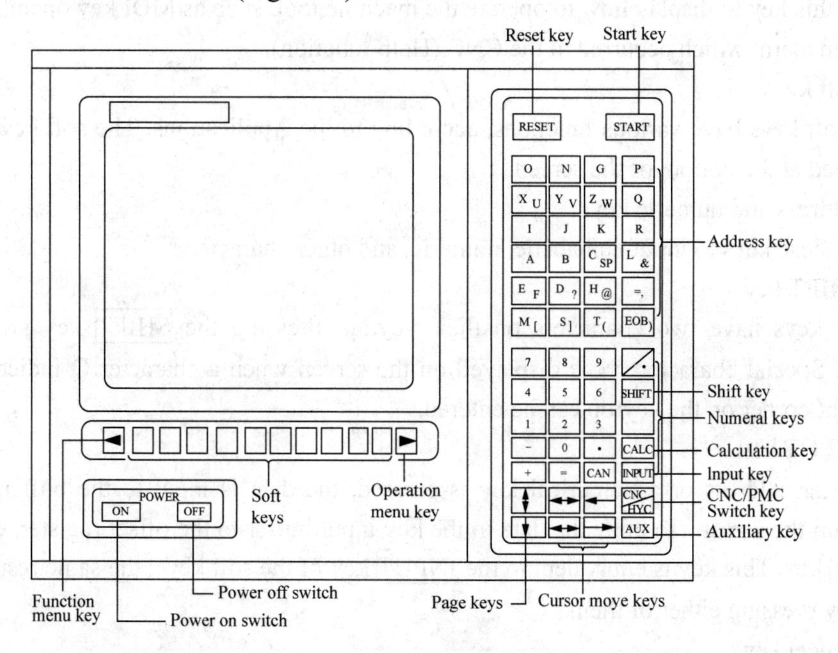

Fig. 19-2 14″color CRT/MDI Panel

Key Location of MDI (Fig. 19-3)

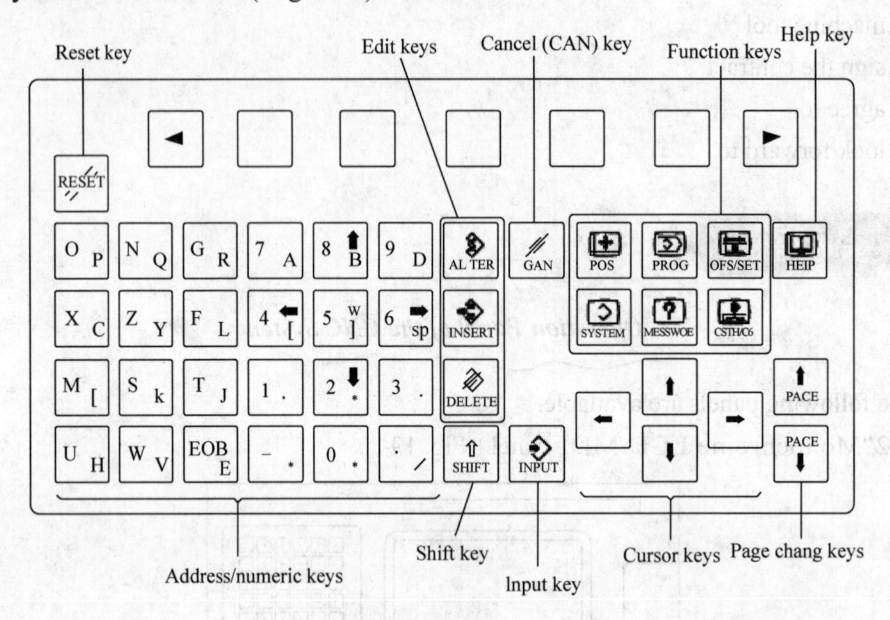

Fig. 19-3 Key Location of MDI

Explanation of the MDI Keyboard

1. RESET Key

Press this key to reset the CNC, to cancel an alarm, etc.

2. HELP Key

Press this key to display how to operate the machine tool, such as MDI key operation, or the details of an alarm which occurred in the CNC (Help function).

3. Soft keys

The soft keys have various functions, according to the Applications. The soft key functions are displayed at the bottom of the screen.

4. Address and numeric keys

Press these keys to input alphabetic, numeric, and other characters.

5. SHIFT key

Some keys have two characters on their keytop. Pressing the SHIFT key switches the characters. Special character ^N is displayed on the screen when a character Q indicated at the bottom right corner on the keytop can be entered.

6. INPUT key

When an address or a numerical key is pressed, the data is input to the buffer, and it is displayed on the screen. To copy the data in the key input buffer to the offset register, etc. , press the INPUT key. This key is equivalent to the INPUT key of the soft keys; the same results can be obtained by pressing either of them.

7. Cancel key

Press this key to delete the last character or symbol input to the key input buffer. When the key input buffer displays

>N001×1000Z

and the cancel CAN key is pressed, Z is canceled and

>N00l×1000__ is displayed.

8. Program edit keys

Press these keys when editing the program.

ALTER: Alteration

INSERT: Insertion

DELETE: Deletion

9. Function keys

Press these keys to switch display screens for each function.

Press this key to display the **position** screen

Press this key to display the **program** screen

Press this key to display the **offset/setting** screen

Press this key to display the **system** screen

Press this key to display the **message** screen

Press this key to display the **custom** screen (conversational macro screen) or graphics screen.

10. Cursor move keys

There are four different cursor move keys.

→: This key is used to move the cursor to the right or in the forward direction. The cursor is moved in short units in the forward direction.

←: This key is used to move the cursor to the left or in the reverse direction. The cursor is moved in short units in the reverse direction.

↓: This key is used to move the cursor in a download or forward direction. The cursor is moved in large units in the forward direction.

↑: This key is used to move the cursor in a upload or reverse direction. The cursor is moved in large units in the reverse direction.

11. Page change keys

redo↓: This key is used to changeover the page on the screen in the forward direction.

↑redo: This key is used to changeover the page on the screen in the reverse direction.

Lesson 20 Adjustment and Training of Installation of CNC Machines

A large quantity of NC equipment (such as Machining Center, Wire Flame Cutter, Electric Discharge Machine) are delivered to NC simulation center in a institute. Some NC equipment is fixed up and debugged by some technicians from the manufacturer. They are fixing and installing the NC and are training the users how to operate and maintain these new machines.

Place: Simulation Center in institute

Character: Engineers from the manufacture; Mr. Zhou; Mr. Li; Mr. Zhang; Mr. Shi and Miss You, technicians of the institute

Jiang: Hello, Mr. Zhou, Mr. Zhang and Mr. Li.
We have prepared the crane and transporting tools for this installation. Let's discuss how to install these machines and how to train us.

Zhou: We are responsible for the installation and adjustment of the equipment. You can divide into several groups to do the following things:
1) Make an inventory according to the shipping list ot the equipment.
2) Help our engineers fix up these machines.
3) Inspect the precision in accordance with some indexes of ex-factory set.
What do you think about it, Mr. Jiang?

Jiang: OK, you are very considerate, I agree with what you said.

Zhou: Mr. Jiang to save time, let's install the three machines in groups?

Jiang: OK, Mr. Zhou and I will be responsible for making an inventory to Machining Center. Mr.Shi and Li for EDM, Miss You and Mr. Zhang for Flame Cutter.

(*MC testing ground*)

Jiang: Mr. Zhou, first let's recheck every index of the MC equipment in accordance with manufacturing precision shall we?

Zhou: Yes, let's begin. I think there may be some changes in the original precision because of the bumping in transport. So, we should readjust them.

Jiang: OK. Since every index of geometric precision has met our standards, I want to design a part to finish on the machine, is it OK?

Zhou: Special sample and tools are needed.

Jiang: I've prepared everything.

Zhou: Oh, it's very complicated. There are many difficult processes such as milling the surface and the bench, pocket, drilling holes, tapping, free surface and so on. I think that we'll undergo an examination today (*laugh*). It will test both the machine and the operator.

Jiang: That's not my aim. We are not familiar with the new equipment. I want to know the actual processing ability of this equipment in order to know what's what, when we undertake some processing in future.

Zhou: OK, let's start.

Jiang: Mr Zhou, you'd better prepare something on one side of the machine. I will send an NC program to you on the other side. What's Baud Rates of the machine?

Zhou: 4800.

Jiang: Ready. Start.

Zhou: OK. The machine is beginning to process the sample. The tool is changed smoothly in magazine, mill the surface milling the slots, drilling hole, tapping and so on. A11 the processes are OK.

Jiang: Let's measure the finished sample. Oh, the precision fits with the requirements. Would you mind making up some sizes in this sample?

Zhou: That's right. After adjusting the value of the make up, we'll finish and measure it again.

Jiang: Now, that's very good. Size and precision totally meet the standards. Thank you very much.

(*EDM testing ground*)

Li: Mr. Shi, first of all, let's test the flatness and straightness of the working table, then the verticality of the principal axis against the working table. The above targets are within the precision limits of the delivery stipulation.

Shi: Next, can you test the two kinds of processing (rough and finish processing)?

Li: OK.

Shi: How do you guarantee the precision of processing?

Li: First, I guarantee the precision of the electrodes themselves; second, I guarantee the verticality of electrodes against the working table when installed; Finally I select the proper processing parameters, for example, voltage current intensity, pulse breadth, clearance, frequency and so on. All these should be accumulated through long-term experience.

Shi: Thank you.

(*Flame Cutter testing grounnd*)

You: Mr. Zhang, what should we pay attention to when processing Flame Cutter?

Zhang: First, avoid folding when tying the molybdenum wire; second, make sure of its proper tightness when screwing it. You should not screw it too tight, or it will break.

You: How can we improve the precision of flame cutter processing?

Zhang: First, pay attention to the coordination between the tightness and the feeding speed of the molybdenum wire; second, pay attention to the verticality of the molybdenum wire(try to use the straighter of electrode to correct its verticality); select the proper processing parameters according to different materials. This depends on accumulated experience, of course there is an experimental data base available for reference.

You: Thank you.

New Words

1. quantity	[ˈkwɔntiti]	*n.*	数目，数量
2. simulation	[ˌsimjuˈleiʃən]	*n.*	模仿；模拟
3. maintain	[menˈtein]	*vt.*	保持；继续；保养，维护；坚持；主张
4. crane	[krein]	*n.*	起重机，吊车，升降架，升降设备
5. transport	[trænsˈpɔːt]	*vt.*	运送；流放
		n.	运输，运输工具，激动，狂喜，流放犯[化]运输
6. installation	[ˌinstəˈleiʃən]	*n.*	安装，设置；就职；装置，设备
7. bump	[bʌmp]	*vt./vi.*	撞倒；冲撞
		n.	碰撞，猛撞
8. pocket	[ˈpɔkit]	*n.*	袋，口袋
		vt.	把……装入袋内
		a.	袖珍的；小型的
9. undergo	[ˌʌndəˈgəu]	*vt.*	经历，承受；遭受
10. verticality	[ˌvɜːtiˈkæləti]	*n.*	垂直性，垂直状态
11. electrode	[iˈlektrəud]	*n.*	电极
12. molybdenum	[məˈlibdinəm]	*n.*	钼
13. accumulate	[əˈkjuːmjuleit]	*vt./vi.*	堆积；积累
14. magazine	[ˌmægəˈziːn]	*n.*	刀库；自动储存送料装置；杂志，期刊
15. stipulation	[ˌstipjuˈleiʃən]	*n.*	[u]规定；[c]条款，条件

Phrases and Expressions

1. be responsible for	负责
2. in accordance with	按照
3. agree with	同意
4. be familiar with	熟悉
5. molybdenum wire	钼丝

1. Would you mind making up some sizes in this sample?
   你不介意补充加工试件中某几个尺寸吧？
   * mind + doing 介意+doing
   * make up 补充，弥补
   Work fast, to make up for lost time.
   加紧工作，来弥补损失的时间。
   You have to make up the French examination.
   你必须补考法语。
   I certainly will try to make up for it.
   我一定会设法补救的。
2. Mr. Shi, first of all, let's test the flatness and straightness of the working table, then the verticality of the principal axis against the working table.
   史先生，首先，让我们测试机床工作台面的平面度和时的直线度，然后，测试主轴对工作台的垂直度。

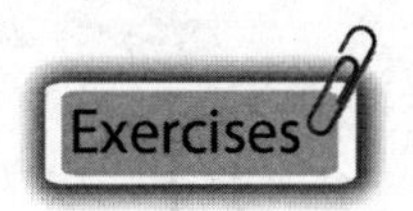

Please translate the following phrases into Chinese.

1. Wire Flame Cutter
2. Electric Discharge Machine
3. in accordance with
4. be familiar with
5. Baud Rates
6. make up
7. delivery stipulation
8. rough and finish processing

Installation

1. Unpacking

In unpacking, the shipping list must be first examined to ensure the proper configuration of the required system.

All the parts, attachments and spare parts of the shipped system have then to be checked item by item according to the shipping list for their types, quantities and external appearances to exclude confusions, mistake packing, shortages and damages.

The Control Unit Chassis must be subject to a further inspection for the correct types, good mechanical fastening and reliable electrical connections of all its component, such as PCB's switches and keys, transformers and so forth (refer to the Control Unit Assembly, and the Wiring Diagram) .

2. Mounting

Mount the Control Unit Chassis safely on the machine tool at a position convenient to operator. A cantilever bracket shown in (Fig.20-l) might be quite be helpful. In some systems, the driver circuitry with the power transformer are packed in a separate chassis, it should be fixed securely also.

Mount the stepper motors to the feed mechanism of machine tool.

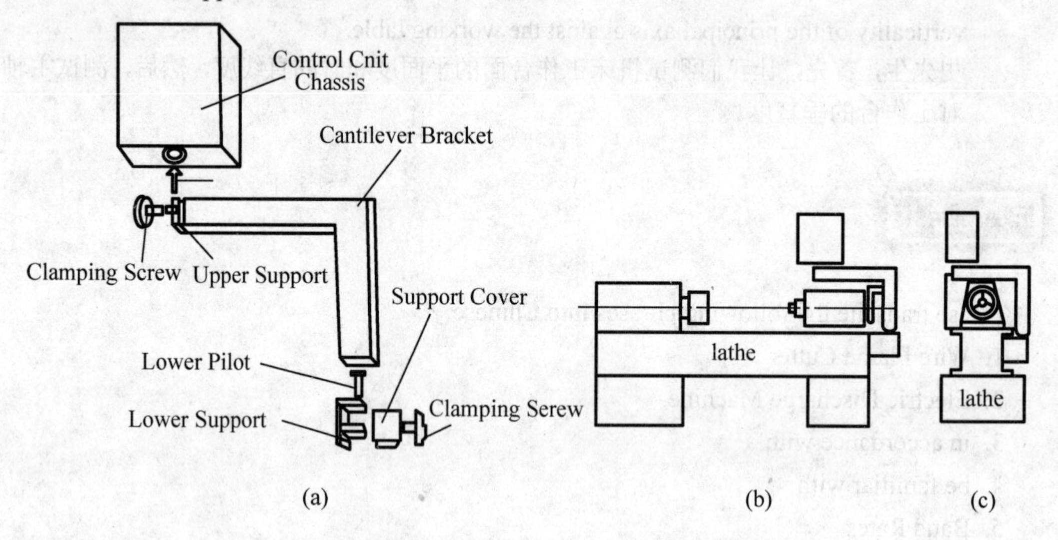

Fig. 20-1 Installation of Control Unit Chassis

(a) The Mounting Bracket (b) Installation-I (c) Installation-II

3. Powering-On

Connect the motor drives, the stepper motors and the main power supply to the Control Unit Chassis according to the Assembly and Wiring Diagram. Before the main source is turned on, the Load Button for the power amplifier must be set "OFF". Turn on the main source switch, and the Control Unit is now put in work. At this instant, the ventilator blowers must work properly, as the blowers prohibit the Control Unit work without the forced Ventilation. Then turn on the Load button as that the Control Unit, the Drivers, and the stepper motors can be tested by manual operations. When the manual operation inspection verifies the correct performances of all the component parts, a simple PMP ought to be prepared and be inputted to the system to check the various functions. If this functions check is confirmed, the system can now be the motor drives for combined debugging.

4. Points for Attention

(1) If the rotation direction of the motor is found to be opposite to the presumed one, it can be reversed by interchanging the pin-connections of the connectors at the ends of the cable joining the driver board and the stepper motor.

NOTE: Be sure to interchange both the two pairs of connections simultaneously, as a single interchange of either of the two pairs will cause damages to the power transistor.

(2) The IC chip in the system must be prevented from being touched by fingers and are strictly forbidden from being plugged or extracted when energized. When soldering is necessary in maintenance, all the power source to the system must be cut-off first, and all the plugging between the computer mainframe and the peripberals should be disconnected. To avoid damage when soldering in-circuit elements the power supply to the soldering iron must be cut off at the instant of soldering and the chip pins should be soldered with the residual heat of the iron.

(3) When the stepper motor is locked statically, there might be light high-frequency buzz, which is a normal phenomenon and needs no further care.

(4) When standing-by for a long period, the power amplifier must be switched off so as to minimize the power consumption and element depletion. For the same reason, longtime continuous fast feed over 4000 mm/min is also irrational as it might bring damages to the power transistor.

(5) Once the system main source is cuf off, the system must not be repowered within 10 seconds; similarly undue or frequent power on-off are prohibited as all these will cause defects in the computer and damages to the components.

(6) The characteristics of the VMOS high power transistors are strictly stipulated by the system, so all other types of transistors are prohibited for substitution.

(7) When connecting or disconnecting the plugs aid sockets, the main source must be cut off to secure safety for the system and the operator. Care should be taken to assure correct directions and steady insertion when mating them so as to avoid damages in the connectors.

(8) The framework of the control unit chassis is grounded, so the user must ensure the correct connection of the main source to guard the chassis from being energized, as an energized chassis frame will result in serious hazard.

Lesson 21 Method of Replacing Battery for CNC Machine Tool(I)

In a system using this CNC, batteries are used as follows:

Use	Component connected to battery
Memory backup in the CNC control unit	CNC control unit
Preservation of the current position indicated by the separate absolute pulse coder	Separate detector interface unit
Preservation of the current position indicated by the absolute pulse coder built into the motor	Servo amplifier

Used batteries must be discarded according to appropriate local ordinances or rules. When discarding batteries, insulate them by using tape and so forth to preservent the battery terminals from short-circuiting.

BATTERY FOR MEMORY BACKUP(3VDC)

Part programs, offset data, and system parameters are stored in CMOS memory in the control unit. The power to the CMOS memory is backed up by a lithium battery mounted on the front panel of the control unit. The above data is not lost even when the main battery goes dead. The backup battery is mounted on the control unit at shipping. This battery can maintain the contents of memory for about a year.

When the voltage of the battery becomes low, alarm message "BAT" blinks on the display and the battery alarm signal is output to the PMC. When this alarm is displayed, replace the battery as soon as possible. In general, the battery can be replace within one or two weeks, however, this depends on the system configuration.

If the voltage of the battery becomes any lower, memory can no longer be backed up. Turning on the power to the control unit in this state causes system alarm 935(ECC error) to occur because the contents of memory are lost. Clear the entire memory and reenter data after replacing the battery.

Therefore, FANUC recommends that the battery be replaced once a year regardless of whether alarms are generated.

The power to the control unit must be turned on when the battery is replaced. If the battery is disconnected when the power is turned off, the contents of memory are lost.

Observe the following precautions for lithium batteries:

WARNING

If an unspecified battery is used, it may explode.

Replace the battery only with the specified battery (A02B-0200-K102.)

In addition to the lithium battery built into the CNC control unit, commercial D-size alkaline batteries can be used by installing the battery case externally (Fig.21-1).

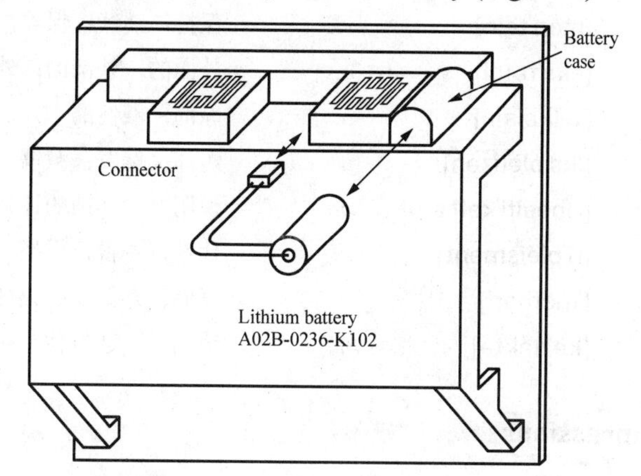

Fig. 21-1 Installing the battery

> **NOTE**
> A lithium battery is installed as standard at the factory.

(1) Prepare a new lithium battery (ordering drawing number:A02B-0200-K102).

(2) Turn on the power of the control unit once for about 30 seconds.

(3) Turn off the power of the control unit.

(4) Remove the old battery from the top of the CNC control unit.

First unplug the battery connector then take the battery out of its case. The battery case of a control unit without option slots is located at the top right end of the unit. That of a control unit with 2 slots is located in the central area of the top of the unit (between fans).

(5) Insert a new battery and reconnect the connector.

> **NOTE**
> Complete steps (3) to (5) within 10 minutes. Do not leave the control unit without a battery for any longer than the period shown, as this will result in the contents of memory being lost.

> **WARNING**
> Incorrect battery replacement may cause an explosion. Do not use a battery other than that specified (specification: A02B- 0020-K102).

New Words

1. battery ['bætəri] *n.* （蓄）电池（组）
2. component [kəm'pəunənt] *n.* 成分，组成部分，部件，元件
3. preservation [ˌprezə'veiʃən] *n.* 保存，保藏，储藏，保持

4. ordinance [ˈɔːdinəns] *n.* [正]条例，法令
5. lithium [ˈliθiəm] *n.* 锂
6. maintain [menˈtein] *vt.* 保持；继续；保养，维护
7. external [eksˈtəːnl] *a.* 外面的，外部的；外观的，表面的
8. alkaline [ˈælkəlain] *a.* 碱的，碱性的
9. explosion [iksˈpləuʒən] *n.* 爆炸；爆发；激增，扩大
10. specification [ˌspesifiˈkeiʃən] *n.* 说明书，详细的计划书
11. replacement [riˈpleismənt] *n.* 代替，替换，更换
12. memory [ˈmeməri] *n.* 存储；存储器；记忆装置
13. connector [kəˈnəktə] *n.* 连接器；连接体；接插件

Phrases and Expressions

1. backup battery 备用电池
2. discarding battery 丢弃的电池
3. servo amplifier 伺服放大器
4. the absolute pulse coder 绝对脉冲编码器
5. is mounted on 安装在

Notes

1. Preservation of the current position indicated by the absolute pulse coder built into the motor.
   在绝对脉冲编码器内显示当前位置的保存数值，绝对脉冲编码器内置到马达。
   * built into the motor 是 the absolute pulse coder 的后置定语。
2. Used batteries must be discarded according to appropriate local ordinances or rules.
   必须按照适当的地方条例或规则丢弃废旧电池。
   * according to appropriate local ordinances or rules 是本句的状语。
3. Part programs, offset data, and system parameters are stored in CMOS memory in the control unit.
   零件程序，刀具补偿和系统参数存储在控制单元的 CMOS 存储器中。
4. The power to the CMOS memory is backed up by a lithium battery mounted on the front panel of the control unit.
   到 CMOS 存储器电源的数据由安装在控制单元前面板上的锂电池进行备份。
5. Therefore, FANUC recommends that the battery be replaced once a year regardless of whether alarms are generated.
   因此，发那科建议不论是否产生报警，每年更换一次电池。
6. If the battery is disconnected when the power is turned off, the contents of memory are lost.

如果电池断开时，电源被关掉时，内存中的内容会丢失。

7. The battery case of a control unit without option slots is located at the top right end of the unit.

   无选择插槽一个控制单元电池盒位于机身顶部的右端。

8. That of a control unit with 2 slots is located in the central area of the top of the unit (between fans).

   1 个控制单元，2 个插槽，是位于该单位（在风扇）顶部的中心区域。

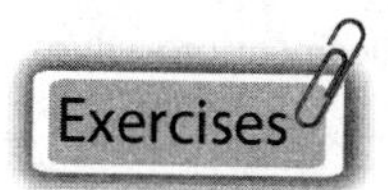

Answer the following question.

1. Where are batteries used in a system using this CNC?
2. By what is the power to the CMOS memory backed up?
3. How long can a lithium battery maintain the contents of memory?
4. When the battery is replaced, whether should the power to the control unit be turned on?
5. What happened when an unspecified battery is used?

Method of Replacing Battery(II)

Replacing the alkaline dry cells (size D)(Fig. 21-2)

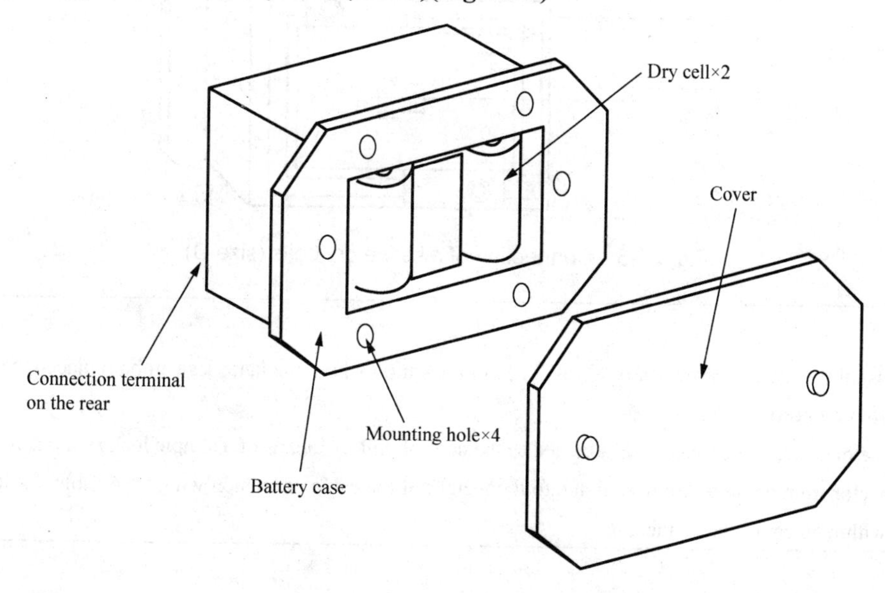

Fig. 21-2 Replacing the alkaline dry cells

(1) Prepare two new alkaline dry cells (size D).

(2) Turn on the power of the control unit once for about 30 seconds.

(3) Turn off the power of the control unit.

(4) Remove the battery case cover.

(5) Replace the batteries, paying careful attention to their orientation.

(6) Replace the battery case cover.

NOTE

When replacing the dry cells, use the same procedure as that for lithium battery replacement procedure, described above.

Connection of alkaline dry cells (size D)

Power from the external batteries is supplied through the connector to which the lithium battery is connected (Fig.21-3). The lithium battery, provided as standard, can be replaced with external batteries in the battery case (A02B-0236-C281) according to the battery replacement procedures described above.

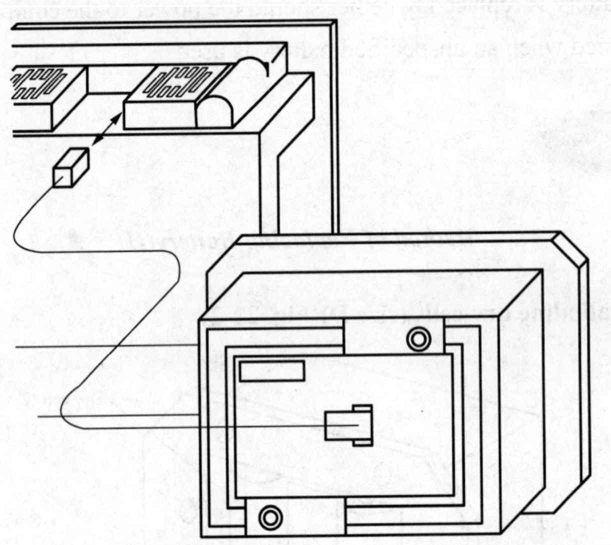

Fig. 21-3 Connection of alkaline dry cells (size D)

NOTE

1 Install the battery case (A02B-0236-C281) in a location where the batteries can be replaced even when the control unit power is on.

2 The battery cable connector is attached to the control unit by means of a simple lock system. To prevent the connector from being disconnected due to the weight of the cable or tension within the cable, fix the cable section within 50 cm of the connector.

Lesson 22 Automation Operation

Programmed operation of a CNC mchine tool is referred to as automatic operation.

There are the following types of automatic operation:

MEMORY OPERATION

Operation by executing a program registered in CNC memory.

MDI OPERATION

Operation by executing a program entered from the MDI panel.

DNC OPERATION

Operation while reading a program from an input/output device.

PROGRAM RESTART

Restarting a program for automatic operation from an intermediate point.

SCHEDULING FUNCTION

Scheduled operation by executing programs registered in an external input/output device.

SUBPROGRAM CALL FUNCTION

Function for calling and executing subprograms registered in an external input/output device during memory operation.

MANUAL HANDLE INTERRUPTION

Function for performing manual feed during movement executed by automation operation.

MIRROR IMAGE

Function for enabling mirror-image movement along an axis during automation operation.

MANUAL INTERVENTION AND RETURN

Function restarting automation operation by returning the tool to the position where manual intervention was started during automation operation.

MEMORY CARD-BASED DNC OPERATION

Automation operation by a program written to a memory card.

We will give an example:the memory operation of automatic operation:

MEMORY OPERATION

Programs are registered in memory in advance. When one of these programs is selected and the cycle start switch on the machine operator's panel is pressed, automatic operation starts, and the cycle start LED goes on.

When the feed hold switch on the machine operator's panel is pressed during automatic operation, automatic operation is stopped temporarily. When the cycle start switch is pressed again, automatic operation is restarted.

When the RESET key on the MDI is presed, automatic operation terminates and the reset state is entered.

The following procedure is given as an example. For actual operation, refer to the manual supplied by the machine tool builder.

Procedure for Memory Operation

Procedure

1. Press the MEMORY mode selection switch.

2. Select a program from the registered programs. To do this, follow the steps below.

(1) Press PROG to display the program screen.

(2) Press address O .

(3) Enter program number using the numeric keys.

(4) Press the [O SRH] soft key.

3. For the two-path control, select the tool post to be operated with the tool post selection switch on the machine operator's panel.

4. Press the cycle start switch on the machine operator's panel. Automatic operation starts, and the cycle start LED goes on. When automatic operation terminates, the cycle start LED goes off.

5. To stop or cancel memory operation midway through, follow the steps below.

(1) Stopping memory operation

Press the feed hold switch on the machine operator's panel. The feed hold LED goes on and the cycle start start LED goes off. The machine responds as follows:

a) When the machine was moving, feed operation decelerates and stops.

b) When dwell was being performed, dwell is stopped.

c) When M, S, or T was being executed, the operation is stopped after M, S, or T is finished.

When the cycle start switch on the machine operator's panel is pressed while the feed hold LED is on, machine operation restarts.

(2) Terminating memory operation

Press the RESET key on the MDI panel.

Automatic operation is terminated and the reset state is entered. When a reset is applied during movement, movement decelerates then stops.

After memory operation is started, the following are executed:

a) A one-block command is read from the specified program.

b) The block command is decoded.

c) The command execution is started.

d) The command in the next block is read.

e) Buffering is executed. That is, the command is decoded to allow immediate execution.

f) Immeidately after the preceding block is executed, execution of the next block can be started. This is because buffering has been executed.

g) Hereafter, memory operation can be executed by repeating the steps d) to f).

New Words

1. register	['redʒistə]	*vt./vi.*	记录；登记；注册
2. temporarily	['tempərərili]	*ad.*	临时
3. terminate	['tə:mineit]	*vt./vi.*	结束；使结束，使停止，使终止；解除(契约等)
4. decelerate	[ˌdi:'seləreit]	*vt./vi.*	（使）减速；降低速度，减速；慢化；制动
5. dwell	[dwel]	*vi.*	居留；居住，单居（at, in）
6. decode	[ˌdi:'kəud]	*vt.*	译（码），解（码）
7. buffer	['bʌfə]	*n.*	起缓冲作用的人（或物）；（机）缓冲器，减振器 vt. 缓冲，减轻
8. precede	[pri'si:d]	*vt./vi.*	（时间，位置，次序）在……之先[前]，领先于，在……之上；比……重要；在……前加上；为……加上引言（by, with）
9. command	[kə'mɑ:nd]	*n.*	命令
		vt./vi.	指挥；控制
10. execution	[ˌeksi'kju:ʃən]	*n.*	实行，执行

1. Operation by executing a program registered in CNC memory.
   此操作是运行在 CNC 内在中的程序。
   * registered in CNC memory 是 program 的后置定语。
2. Scheduled operation by executing programs registered in an external input/output device.
   通过执行在外部输入/输出设备程序的预定操作。
3. Restarting a program for automatic operation from an intermediate point.
   自动运行是从当前点重新启动一个程序。
4. Function for calling and executing subprograms registered in an external input/output device during memory operation.
   在存储器操作中调用和执行内部/外部设备中的子程序功能。
   * registered in an external input/output device 是 subprograms 的后置定语。
5. When one of these programs is selected and the cycle start switch on the machine operator's panel is pressed, automatic operation starts, and the cycle start LED goes on.
   当选择这些程序中的一个，按下机床面板上的循环启动按钮，自动运行启动，并且循环启动灯亮。
6. For the two-path control, select the tool post to be operated with the tool post selection

switch on the machine operator's panel.

对于两个路径的控制，选择刀架要与刀架在机器上操作的面板选择开关运作。

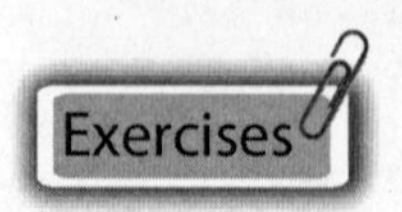

Please translate the following phrases into Chinese.

1. automatic operation
2. MDI
3. input/output device
4. manual feed
5. in advance
6. machine operator's panel
7. cycle start
8. refer to

Ultraprecision Machining

Beginning in the 1960s, increasing demands have been made for the precision manufacturing of components for computer, electronic, nuclear energy, and defense applications. Some examples include optical mirrors, computer memory disks, and drums for photocopying machines.Surface finish requirements are in the tens of nanometer (10^{-9}m or 0.001μm) range and form accuracies in the μm and sub-μm range.

Because the cutting tool for ultraprecision machining applications is almost exclusively a single-crystal diamond, the process is also called diamond turning. The diamond tool has a polished cutting-edge with a radius as small as a few nanometers. Wear of the diamond can be a significant problem, and recent advances include cryogenic diamond turning, in which the tooling system is cooled by liquid nitrogen to a temperature of about -120℃.

The workpiece materials for ultraprecision machining to the date include copper alloys, aluminum alloys, silver, electroless nickle, infrared materials, and plastics (acrylics). The depth of cut involved is in the nanometer range. In this range, hard and brittle materials produce continuous chips (the process is known as ductile-regime cutting)；deeper cutting produce discontinuous chips.

The machining tools for these applications are built with very high precision and high machine, spindle, and workholding-device stiffnesses. These ultraprecision machines, parts of which are made of structural materials with low thermal expansion and good dimensional stability, are located in a dust-free environment (i.e. clean rooms) where the temperature is controlled to within a fraction of one degree.

Vibrations from internal machine sources as well as from external sources, such as nearby machines on the same floor, are also avoided as much as possible. Laser metrology is used for feed and position control, and the machines are equipped with highly advanced computer control systems and with thermal and geometric error-compensating features.

Lesson 23 Test Operations(I)

The following functions are used to check before actual machining whether the machine operates as specified by the created program.

(1) Machine Lock and Auxiliary Function Lock

(2) Feedrate Override

(3) Rapid Traverse Override

(4) Dry Run

(5) Single Block

1. MACHINE LOCK AND AUXILIARY FUNCTION LOCK

To display the change in the position without moving the tool, use machine lock.

There are two types of machine lock: all-axis machine lock, which stops the movement along all axes, and specified-axis machine, which stops the movement along specified axes only. In addition, auxiliary function lock, which disables M, S, and T commands, is available for checking a program together with machine lock. (Fig. 23-1)

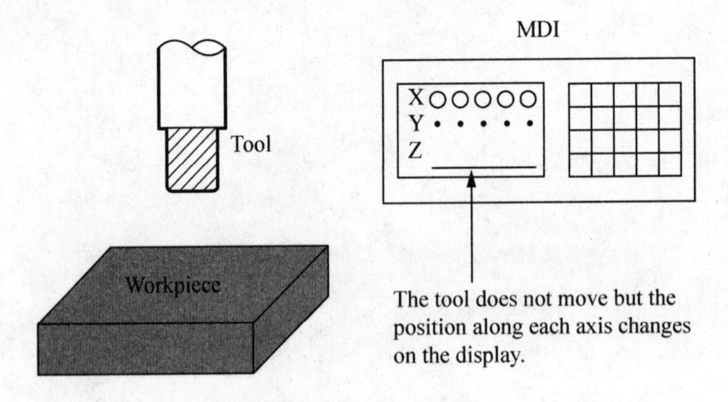

Fig. 23-1 Machine lock

Procedure for Machine Lock and Auxiliary Function Lock

Machine Lock

Press the machine lock switch on the operator's panel. The tool does not move but the position along each axis changes on the display as if the tool were moving.

Some machines have a machine lock switch for each axis. On such machines, press the machine lock switches for the axes along which the tool is to be stopped. Refer to the appropriate manual provided by the machine tool builder for machine lock.

Warning

The positional relationship between the workpiece coordinates and machine coordinates may differ before and after automatic operation using machine lock. In such a case, specify the workpiece coordinate setting command or by performing manual reference position return.

Auxiliary Function Lock

Press the auxiliary function lock switch on the operator's panel. M, S, T and B codes are disable and not executed. Refer to the appropriate manual provided by the machine tool builder for machine lock.

Restrictions

M, S, T, B command by only machine lock

M, S, T, B command are executed in the machine lock state.

Reference position return under Machine Lock

When a G27, G28, or G30 command is issued in the machine lock state, the command is accepted but the tool does not move to the reference position and the reference position return LED does not go on.

M codes not locked by auxiliary function lock

M00, M01, M02, M30, M98, and M99 commands are executed even in the auxiliary function lock state. M codes for calling a subprogram(parameters No. 6071 to 6079) and those for calling a custom macro(parameter No. 6080 to 6089) are also executed.

2. FEEDRATE OVERRIDE

A programmed feedrate can be reduced or increased by a percentage(%) selected by the override dial. This feature is used to check a program. For example, when a feedrate of 100 mm/min is specified in the program, setting the override dial to 50% moves the tool at 50 mm/min. (Fig. 23-2)

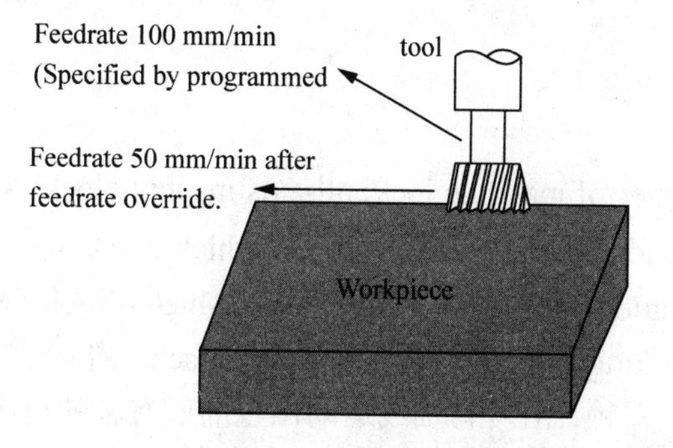

Fig. 23-2 Feedrate override

Procedure for Feedrate Override

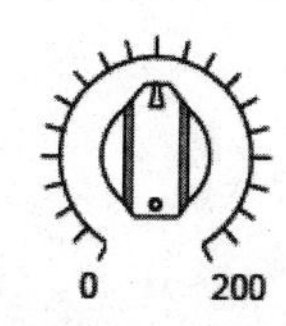 JOG FEEDRATE OVERRIDE	Set the feedrate override dial to the desired percentage(%) on the machine operator's panel, before or during automatic operation. On some machines, the same dial is used for the feedrate override dial and jog feedrate dial. Refer to the appropriate manual provided by the machine tool builder for feedrate override.
Resitrictions	

Override Range	The override that can be specified ranges from 0 to 254%. For individual machines the range depends on the specifications of the machine tool builder.
Override during thread	During threading, the specified override is ignored; the override is always assumed to be 100%.

New Words

1. execute ['eksikju:t] *vt.* 执行，实现；使生效
2. intermediate [,intə'mi:djət] *a.* 中间的；中级的
3. feedrate [fi:d reit] *n.* 进给速率
4. perform [pə'fɔ:m] *vt./vi.* 执行；履行
5. available [ə'veiləbl] *a.* 可用的或可得到的

Phrases and Expressions

1. in a canned cycle 在一个封闭的周期内
2. rapid traverse 快速进给，快速行程
3. dry run 空运行
4. jog feedrate override 点动进给倍率

Notes

1. There are two types of machine lock: all-axis machine lock, which stops the movement along all axes, and specified-axis machine, which stops the movement along specified axes only. In addition, auxiliary function lock, which disables M, S, and T commands, is available for checking a program together with machine lock.

   有两种类型的机器锁：沿所有轴线运动停止的所有轴的机床锁定，沿着指定的轴停止运动的指定轴机床锁。此外，能够使M，S，和T指令丧失功能的辅助功能锁可用于检查程序和机床锁。

   *（1）which stops the movement along all axes 作 all-axis machine lock 的后置定语；which stops the movement along specified axes only 作 specified-axis machine 的后置定语。

   *（2）is available for 可得到的

   例如：be available for use 可加以利用

   These tickets are available for one month.

   这些票有效期一个月。

He is not available for the job.
他不适宜做这个工作。
This book is not available here.
这里没有这本书。

2. Refer to the appropriate manual provided by the machine tool builder for machine lock.
请参考由机床锁生产厂家提供的合适的手册。
* provided by the machine tool builder for machine lock 作 manual 的后置定语。
3. Press the cycle start button to execute the next block.
按循环起动键以执行下一程序段。
* to execute the next block 作目的状语。
例如：Never once did I doubt that I would be able to execute my plan.
我从未怀疑过我能执行自己的计划。
4. If G28 to G30 are issued, the single block function is effective at the intermediate point.
如果 G28 到 G30 被使用，单段功能在中间点有效。
例如：This country is now at an intermediate stage of development.
这个国家目前正处于发展的中间阶段。

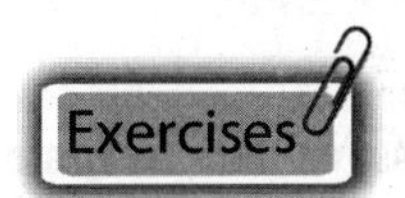

1. Which functions are used to check before actual machining?
2. Which two types of machine lock?
3. How many instructions about the reference position?

3. RAPID TRAVERSE OVERRIDE

An override of four steps (F0, 25%, 50%, and 100%) can be applied to the rapid traverse rate. F0 is set by a parameter (No.1421). (Fig. 23-3)

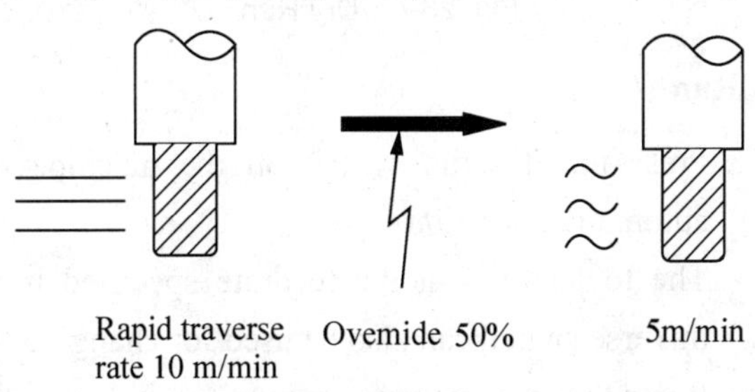

Fig. 23-3 Rapid traverse override

Rapid Traverse Override

Procedure

25 50

LOW 100

Rapid traverse overtime

Select one of the four feedrates with the rapid traverse override switch during rapid traverse. Refer to the appropriate manual provided by the machine tool builder for rapid traverse override.

Explanation

The following types of rapid traverse are available. Rapid traverse override can be applied for each of them.

1) Rapid traverse by G00
2) Rapid traverse during a canned cycle
3) Rapid traverse in G27, G28, G29, G30, G53
4) Mannual rapid traverse

Rapid traverse of manual reference position return

4. DRY RUN

The tool is moved at the feedrate specified by a parameter regardless of the feedrate specified in the program. This function is used for checking the movement of the tool under the state that the workpiece is removed from the table. (Fig. 23-4)

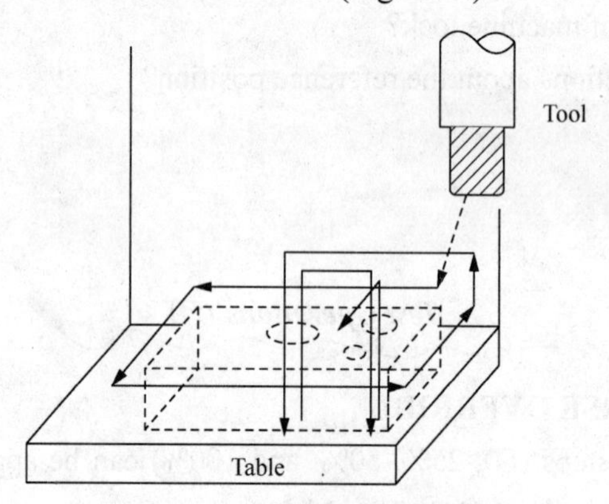

Fig. 23-4 Dry Run

Procedure for Dry Run

Procedure

Press the dry run switch on the machine operator's panel during automatic operation.

The tool moves at the feedrate specified in a parameter. The rapid traverse switch can also be used for changing the feedrate.

Refer to the appropriate manual provided by the machine tool builder for dry run .

Explanation

Dry Run Feed Rate

The dry run feedrate changes as shown in the table below according to the rapid traverse switch and parameters.

Rapid traverse button	Program command	
	Rapid traverse	Feed
ON	Dry run speed×JV, or rapid traverse rate*1)	Dry run feedrate×Max.×JV*2)
OFF		Dry run feedrate×JV*2)

Max.cutting feedrate… Setting by parameter No.1422

Rapid traverse feedrate… Setting by parameter No.1420

Dry run feedrate… Setting by parameter No.1410

JV: Jog feedrate override

(1) Dry run feedrate x JV when parameter RDR (bit 6 of No. 1401) is 1. Rapid traverse rate when parameter RDR is 0.

JV: Jog feedrate override

(2) Clamped to the maximum cutting feedrate

JVmax: Maximum value of jog feedrate override

5. SINGLE BLOCK

Pressing the single block switch starts the single block mode. When the cycle start button is pressed in the single block mode, the tool stops after a single block in the program is executed. Check the program in the single block mode by executing the program by block. (Fig. 23-5(a))

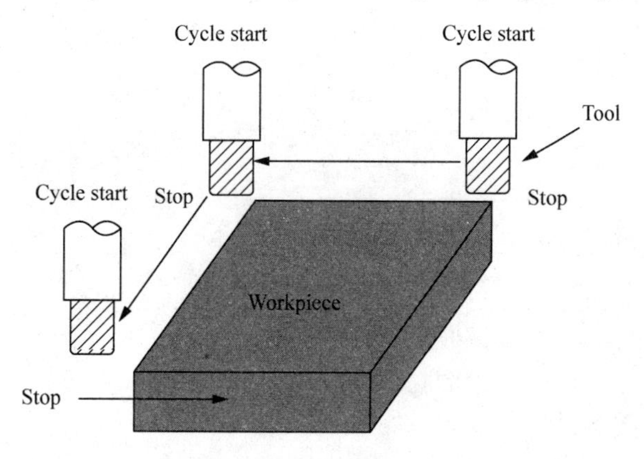

Fig. 23-5(a) Single block

Procedure for Single Block

1. Press the single block switch on the machine operator's panel. The execution of the program is stopped after the current block is executed.

2. Press the cycle start button to execute the next block. The tool stops after the block is

executed.

Refer to the appropriate manual provided by the machine tool builder for single block execution.

Explanation

Reference position return and single block

If G28 to G30 are issued, the single block function is effective at the intermediate point.

Single block during a canned cycle

In a canned cycle, the single block stop points are the end of 12 , and 6 shown blow. When the single block stop is made after the point 1 or 2 , the feed hold LED lights. (Fig. 23-5(b))

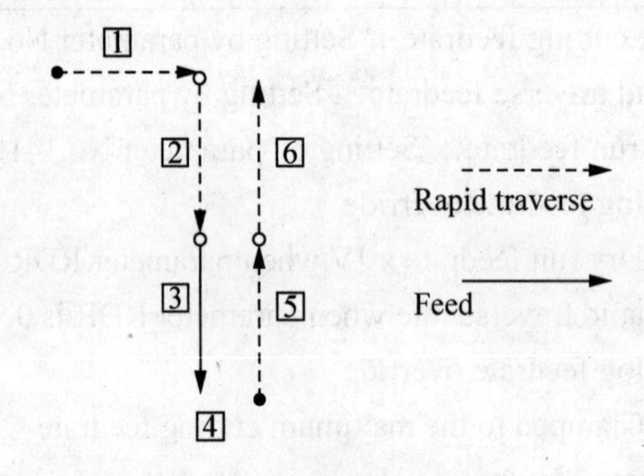

Fig. 23-5 (b) Single block during canned cycle

Single block stop is not performed in a block containing M98P; M99; or G65.

However, single block stop is even performed in a block with M98P; M99 command, if the block contains an address other than O, N, P, L.

Lesson 24 Agency Agreement

This agreement is made and entered into this first day of May, 2009 by and between Huaxia National Chemical Import and Export Corporation, SINOCHEM, a corporation duly organized and existing under the laws of the People's Republic of China, with its principal place of business at (...Address...) (hereafter called the Seller/principle) and Galaxy Import and Export Corporation, a corporation duly organized and existing under the laws of the United States of America, with its priciple place of business at (...Address...) (hereafter called Agent). Hereby it is mutually agreen as follows:

Article 1 Appointment

During the effective period of the agreement, Seller/principle hereby appoints the Agent as its exclusive agent to solicit orders/indents for the products stipulated in Article 3 and the agent accepts and assumes such appointment.

Article 2 The Agent's Duty

The agent shall strictly conform with any and all instructions given by the seller to the Agent (from time to time) and shall not to make any representation, promise, contract, agreement or do any act binding the seller. The seller shall not be held responsible for any and all acts or failures to act by the Agent in excess of or contrary to such instructions.

Article 3 Commodity/Products

The product under the agreement shall be dyestuffs produced by the Agent with the trademark "Diamond" (hereafter called the Product).

Article 4 Territory

The territory covered under this Agreement shall be expressly confined to the United States of America (hereafter called the Territory).

Article 5 Exclusive Right

In consideration of the exclusive right herein granted, the seller (principal) shall not, directly or indirectly, sell the Product in the Territory through other channels than the Agent; the Agent shall not sell, distribute or promote the sale of any product competitive with or similar to the Product in this territory and shall not solicit accept any order for the purpose of selling the Product outside the Territory.

Article 6 Minimum Transaction

During the first 12 month of the agreement, the Agent shall conclude transactions worth US $100, 000, US $140, 000 for the second 12 months and US $200, 000 for the third 12 months. In the event that the aggregate payment received by the Seller from the customers or others obtained by the Agent is less than the above stipulated amount in the respective period of the duration of this agreement, the Seller shall have the right to terminate this Agreement by giving thirty (30) days' written notice to the Agent.

Article 7 Selling Price

The Seller shall from time to time furnish the Agent with the minimum prices and the terms and conditions of sales at which the Products are to be sold respectively.

Article 8 Orders

In soliciting orders, the Agent shall adequately inform customers of the general terms and conditions of the Seller's Sales confirmation. The Agent shall immediately dispatch any orders received to the Seller for its acceptance or rejection.

Article 9 Expenses

All expenses and disbursement in connection with the sales of the Product shall be for the Agent's account.

Article 10 Commission

The Seller shall pay the Agent commission in US dollars at the rate of 3% for the first 12 months, 4% for the second 12 months and 5% for the third 12 months of the net invoiced selling price of the Product on all orders directly obtained by the Agent and accepted by the Seller. Such commission shall be payable every six(6) months on the condition that the Seller receives the full amount of payments due to the Seller. Payment of commission shall be made by way of bank transfer.

Article 11 Market Report

The Agent shall report monthly to the seller about its inventory, market conditions and other activities.

Article 12 Promotion

The Seller shall furnish the Agent, free of charge, with a sufficient amount of promotional materials, such as literature, catalogues, leaflets and whatnot.

The seller and the Agent shall together work out a promotion plan and schedule. The Agent shall diligently carry out the promotion plan and make necessary reports on the feedback impact of the promotional activity.

Article 13 Duration

This Agreement shall enter into force on the signing of both parties. At least three months before the expiration of the term, both the Seller and the Agent shall consult each other about renewal of this Agreement. If the renewal of this Agreement is ageed upon by both parties, this Agreement shall be renewed for another three years, with amendment, if agreed upon by both parties.

Article 14 Force Majeure

Neither party shall be held reponsible for failure or delay to perform all or any part of their duties due to an act of God, government orders or restrictions or any other events which could not be predicted at the time of the conclusion of this Agreement and could not be controlled, avoided or overcome by the parties of this Agreement. However, the party effected by such events of force Majeure shall inform the other party of their occurrence in written form as soon as possible.

Article 15 Trade Terms and Government Law

The trade terms under this Agreement shall be governed and interpreted under provisions of INCONTERM 2000 and this Agreement shall be governed as to all maters under the laws of the People's Republic of China.

Article 16 Arbitration

All disputes arising from the performance of this Agreement should be settled through friendly negotiations. Should not settlement be reached, the case shall then be submitted to the China Economic and Trade Arbitration Commission for arbitration, and the rules of this Commission shall be applied. The award of the arbitration shall be final and bending upon both parties. The arbitration shall be borne by the losing party unless otherwise awarded by the Commision.

IN WITNESS THEREOF: This Agreement shall come into effect immediately after it is signed by both parties in two original copies; each party holding one copy.

Huaxia National Chemical Import Galaxy Import and Export Corporation
and Exprot Corporation

Signed by_________in Beijing　　　　Signed by_________in Beijing

New Words

1. agency	['eidʒənsi]	*n.*	代理处，代理权
2. corporation	[ˌkɔːpə'reiʃ ən]	*n.*	公司，社团
3. duly	['djuːli]	*ad.*	正确地，适当地；按时地，准时地
4. hereafter	[hiər'ɑːftə]	*ad.*	今后，从此以后
5. hereby	['hiə'bai]	*ad.*	（用于公文件中的）以此方式；特此
6. exclusive	[iks'kluːsiv]	*a.*	专用的；独家的
7. solicit	[sə'lisit]	*vt./vi.*	恳求，请求，乞求
8. indent	[in'dent]	*vt.*	一式两份（或两份以上）地起草（文件、合同等）；制作（合同、契约等）的复本
		vt.	订货，（向……）正式申请
		n.	合同，国外定货单
9. stipulate	['stipjuleit]	*vt.*	（尤指在协议或建议中）规定，约定，讲明（条件等）
10. representation	[ˌreprizen'teiʃ ən]	*n.*	（总称）代表，代表制；表现，表示，代理
11. warranty	['wɔrənti]	*n.*	保证书，保单；授权

12. contract	['kɔntrækt]	*vt./vi.*	缔结；订契约
		n.	契约，合同
13. contrary	['kɔntrəri]	*a.*	相反的，相违的
14. commodity	[kə'mɔditi]	*n.*	商品，货物
15. dyestuff	['daistʌf]	*n.*	染料
16. territory	['teritəri]	*n.*	领域，范围
17. confine	[kən'fain]	*vt.*	限制；局限于
		n.	界限，范围
18. aggregate	['ægrigət]	*n.*	合计，聚集
		a.	合计的，聚集的
19. dispatch	[dis'pætʃ]	*vt.*	派遣，快速处理
20. schedule	['ʃedju:əl]	*n.*	时间表，日程安排表
21. disbursement	[dis'bɜ:smənt]	*n.*	支付款，支出额
22. inventory	['invəntəri]	*n.*	财产等的清单，详细目录，存货清单
		vt.	把……编入目录
23. leaflet	['li:flit]	*n.*	传单，散页印刷品
24. whatnot	['wɔtnɔt]	*n.*	难归类（或难描写）的物（或人）；诸如此类的东西
25. invoice	['invɔis]	*vt.*	开……的发票
26. arbitration	[ˌɑ:bi'treiʃən]	*n.*	仲裁
27. transaction	[træn'zækʃən]	*n.*	（一笔）交易；（一项）事务
28. commission	[kə'miʃən]	*n.*	佣金，回扣
29. award	[ə'wɔ:d]	*vt.*	授予，奖给；判给

1. This agreement is made and entered into this first day of May, 2009 by and between Huaxia National Chemical Import and Export Corporation, SINOCHEM, a corporation duly organixed and existingg under the laws of the People's Republic of China, with its pricipal place of business at (…Address…) (hereafter called the Seller/pricipal) …

   本协议于 2009 年 5 月 1 日生效。当事人一方是华夏华工进出口公司，简称华夏化工。该公司是按中国有关法律组建及活动的，其主营业地位于……（公司地址）（以下简称卖方/委托人）……

   * 这句话中，enter into 表示进入……状态。例如：entered into combat readiness.（进入战争状态）。

2. During the effective period of the agreement, Seller/principle hereby appoints the Agent as its exclusive agent to solicit orders/indents for the products stipulated in Article 3 and

the agent accepts and assumes such appointment.

本协议的有效期内，卖方/委托人指定代理者为本协议第三条项下商品的独家代理。代理商同意并接受上述委托。

* 合同中的语言很严谨，译成中文时应注意译文要符合中文语言的逻辑关系。例如：the agent accepts and assumes such appointment. 直译成中文是：代理商接受并承担上述委托。但是，如果译成“代理商同意并接受上述委托”，则不仅评议通顺，也符合中文评议逻辑关系。

3. The Agent shall immediately dispatch any orders received to the Seller for its acceptance or rejection.

   代理商应立即将收到的定单转交卖方确定是否接受。

   *（1）received 是后置定语，修饰 orders.

   （2）for its acceptance or rejection.作状语

4. The Agent shall diligently carry out the promotion plan and make necessary reports on the feedback impact of the promotional activity.

   代理商应努力执行促销计划，并将促销活动的效果及反馈信息向卖方做必要的汇报。

5. Neither party shall be held reponsible for failure or delay to perform all or any part of their duties due to an act of God, government orders or restrictions or any other events which could not be predicted at the time of the conclusion of this Agreement and could not be controlled, avoided or overcome by the parties of this Agreement.

   协议任何一方对由自然灾害、政府采购的限制及其他双方在签约时无法预料、无法控制且不能避免和克服的事件而导致的不能或暂时不能改选全部或部分协议的义务不承担责任。

   * 这里 an act of God 是指不可抗力（如风暴、地震等）。

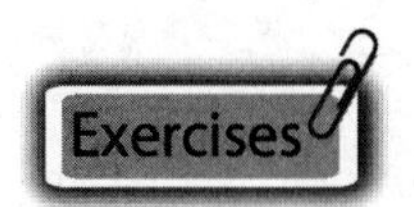

Turn the following into Chinese:

1. We’d like to renew our sole **agency agreement** for another two years.
2. Since the **agency agreement** was signed, your turnover has amounted to $50, 000.
3. The **agency agreement** has been drawn up for the period of one year.
4. Our **agency agreement** calls for a timely market report.
5. Since the **agency agreement** was signed, your turnover has amounted to $500.

Reading Material

Sales Contracts

No.: ______________________

Signed at: ______________

Date: ____________________

Seller: ____________________________________

Address: __________________________________

Tel: __________________ Fax: _______________

E-mail: _____________________________________

Buyer: _____________________________________

Address: __________________________________

Tel: ________________ Fax: _______________

E-mail: _____________________________

The undersigned Seller and Buyer have agreed to close the following transactions according to the terms and conditions set forth as below:

1. Name, Specifications and Quality of Commodity:
2. Quantity:
3. Unit Price and Terms of Delivery:

The terms FOB, CFR, or CIF shall be subject to the International Rules for theInterpretation of Trade Terms (INCOTERMS 2007) provided by International Chamber of Commerce (ICC) unless otherwise stipulated herein.

4. Total Amount:
5. More or Less:______%。
6. Time of Shipment:

Within _____ days after receipt of L/C allowing transhipment and partial shipment.

7. Terms of Payment:

By Confirmed, Irrevocable, Transferable and Divisible L/C to be available by sight draft to reach the Seller before______and to remain valid for negotiation in China until______after the Time of Shipment. The L/C must specify that transshipment and partial shipments are allowed.

The Buyer shall establish a Letter of Credit before the above-stipulated time, failing which, the Seller shall have the right to rescind this Contract upon the arrival of the notice at Buyer or to accept whole or part of this Contract non fulfilled by the Buyer, or to lodge a claim for the direct losses sustained, if any.

8. Packing:

9. Insurance：

Covering_____Risks for_____110% of Invoice Value to be effected by the__________

10. Quality/Quantity discrepancy：

In case of quality discrepancy, claim should be filed by the Buyer within 30 days after the arrival of the goods at port of destination, while for quantity discrepancy, claim should be filed by the Buyer within 15 days after the arrival of the goods at port of destination. It is understood that the Seller shall not be liable for any discrepancy of the goods shipped due to causes for which the Insurance Company, Shipping Company, other Transportation Organization /or Post Office are liable.

11. The Seller shall not be held responsible for failure or delay in delivery of the entire lot or a portion of the goods under this Sales Contract in consequence of any Force Majeure incidents which might occur. Force Majeure as referred to in this contract means unforeseeable, unavoidable and insurmountable objective conditions.

12. Arbitration：

Any dispute arising from or in connection with the Sales Contract shall be settled through friendly negotiation. In case no settlement can be reached, the dispute shall then be submitted to China International Economic and Trade Arbitration Commission (CIETAC), Shenzhe Commission for arbitration in accordance with its rules in effect at the time of applying for arbitration. The arbitral award is final and binding upon both parties.

13. Notices：

All notice shall be written in_____and served to both parties by fax/e-mail /courier according to the following addresses. If any changes of the addresses occur, one party shall inform the other party of the change of address within_____days after the change.

14. This Contract is executed in two counterparts each in Chinese and English, each of which shall be deemed equally authentic. This Contract is in_____copies effective since being signed/sealed by both parties.

Part IV Appendix

Appendix I The Characteristics of Scientific English

科技英语的特点

随着科学技术的发展和经济技术交流的增长，英语已被公认是国际上主要的科技语言。全世界越来越多的科学家、工程技术人员以及攻读某一专业的学生需要阅读日益增多的以英语撰写的科技文献资料、科技文章和教科书。这种表达科技概念、理论和叙述事实的英语，统称为科技英语。(English for Science and Technology，EST)。

虽然科技英语并非与日常会话和文字语言截然不同，但它确实有自身的特点和风格。了解这些特点，并在反复的阅读实践中不断地熟悉这些特点，有助于迅速提高阅读理解能力，这样才能充分发挥科技英语在科技工作中的作用。

本文拟就科技英语书面语的主要特点做扼要介绍。

一、科技英语的一般特点

科技文章与文艺小说、新闻报道等的文体风格迥然不同，它力求严谨周密，概念准确，逻辑性强，行文简练、重点突出、句式严整，具有严肃书面体风格。

下面摘录两段科普文章，以说明普通英语（A）与科技英语（B）的某些不同特点。

A

We made a hole in a cork and pushed into it a narrow glass tube. Then we pushed this into the neck of a bottle which we had filled with colored water. When we did this，some of the colored water went up into the tube. We marked the level of the colored water into the tube. Then we put the bottle into a pan of hot water.

Almost at once，the water level in the tube went down a little，but then it started to go up until the water poured out over the top.

B

After a hole was made in a cork, a narrow glass tube was inserted and the cork was inserted into the neck of a bottle filled with colored water. On doing this, some of the colored water rose in the tube. The level of the colored water in the tube was marked. Then the bottle was placed into a pan of hot water.

Almost immediately, the water level in the tube fell slightly, but then it started to rise until the water overflowed.

上面 A 和 B 谈及同一内容，用词方面的不同是显而易见的。

1. to push into = insert（嵌入）
2. which we had filled =filled（装有）
3. when we did this = on doing this（这样做时）
4. to go up =to rise（上升）
5. to put =to place（放）
6. at once = immediately（立刻）
7. a little = slightly（一点儿）
8. to pour out over the top = to overflow（溢出）

一般说来，科技文章文体的特点可以概括为：准确（precise）、精炼（concise）、清晰（clear）、严密（restricted）。那么，这些语言结构特点是如何体现出来的呢？下面分别加以简要介绍。

二、词汇特点

科技英语中除了使用普通英语词汇以外，还使用大量的适合各门学科的半技术词汇、适用于特定学科专业的专业词汇，以及大量的规范动词。

（一）半技术词汇

半技术词汇是指那些既适用于普通英语又适用于科技英语，而且在不同专业领域中出现时，又具有不同词义的词汇。因此，这类词汇是最难掌握的。例如，名词 cell，在普通英语中指“小房间”、“单人牢房”、“盒”和“槽”等；而在生物学中指“细胞”，在原子能领域中指“晶格”；在物理学中指“温差电偶”、“热电元件”，等等。这种一词多义现象，是由于各行各业都尽量借用普通词汇来表达各自不同的专业概念而造成的。

常见的这类词汇很多，例如：work, load, plant, reaction, flux, movement, revolution, solution, matter, mass, power, force, energy, efficiency, body, base, phase, centre, dog 等。

请注意下面例句中 power 的不同词义。

➢ I will do everything within my power to help you。

我愿意尽我的全力来帮助你。(能力)

➢ The transistor can go from an OFF condition to an ON condition with great speed and minimal power.

晶体管能以极高的速度和极小的功率由“关”的状态转换到“开”的状态。(功率)

➢ With the development of electrical engineering, power can be transmitted over a long distance.

随着电气工程的发展，电力能够输送到远距离之外。(电力)

➢ The power plant driving the machines is a 200 hp induction motor.

驱动机器的动力设备是一台二百马力的感应电动机。（动力）

半技术词汇是科技英语词汇的重要组成部分，也是最难掌握的一类词汇。由于半技术词汇可能适用于不同学科和专业，阅读中遇到这类词汇时，必须从科技著作涉及的具体专业内容来判断词义。

（二）专业词汇

专业词汇是高度技术性词汇，一般为单义词，其词义精确而且适用面窄，往往只适用于某一特定专业。例如：electron（电子），proton（质子），neutron（中子），bandwidth（频带宽度），flip-flop（触发器），polymerization（聚合作用），Oxygen（氧），Jupiter（木星），boring（镗削加工），lathe（车床），belt drive（带传动），flexible coupling（挠性联轴节），spur gear（直齿圆柱齿轮），involute gear teeth（渐开线齿形齿轮），mechanical brake（机械制动）等。

随着科学技术的发展，新词也不断涌现。据有关资料的统计，每年大约有 1500 个新词进入词库。如生态学（ecology）领域出现了新词 air pollution（空气污染），noise pollution（噪声污染），甚至还有 thermal pollution（热污染），visual pollution（视觉污染），cultural pollution（文化污染），以及 spiritual pollution（精神污染）等。

上面举出的专业词汇只是沧海一粟。专业词汇表面上看来令人眼花缭乱，实际上由于词义单一，记忆起来比半技术词汇容易很多。

（三）规范动词

日常英语习语中包括大量的短语动词，如 look over（检查、察看），throw out（扔出、逐出），find out（发现）等。这类短语动词中，有些具有词面意义，有些含有隐喻的意义，有的这两种意义兼而有之。在科技著作中，科技人员往往尽量使用规范动词来代替短语动词，以示态度严肃和表达的精炼、确切。例如：

➢ The valve has the effect of increasing the voltage.（用 increase 代替 make…greater）
➢ This work was formerly done manually，but it is now mechanized.（用 mechanized 代替 carried out by machines）

科技英语中使用的规范动词数量最大。下面再举一些例子：

discover—find out（发现）
achieve—carry out（完成，进行）
compensate—make up（补偿）
remove from—take out of（从……取出）
consume—eat up（消耗）
oscillate—swing to and from（摆动）
forecast—tell in advance（预测）
convey—carry along（输送）
establish—set up（确立、建立）

exceed—go beyond（超过）

retain—keep in（保持）

不过也有一些日常英语中使用的短语动词，没有适当的规范动词可以轻易地替换。这就是为什么科技英语中也偶尔使用短语动词的理由。例如：

➢ The boiler has to be shut down for inspection and repair. 该锅炉必须停火检修。

➢ The metal bar is cut down to the right size. 把这根金属棒切割到适当长度。

总之，为避免传达出模糊的易产生歧义的信息，科技英语崇尚词义明确的规范动词。

（四）简洁的修饰语和构词法

科技著作者力求文体简洁，能用一个词修饰的，绝不用短语和从句。下面列举的利用词缀法、合成法构成的新词较为普遍。

1. 形容词+名词

例如：internal diameter（内径），stainless steel（不锈钢），cast iron（铸铁），hot iron（铁水），ferrous steel（黑色金属），wet grinding（湿磨法）。

2. 名词+名词

例如：carbon dioxide（二氧化碳），spot weld（点焊缝），oil well（油井），wedge key（楔形键）。

有时也连续用两个或三个名词修饰一个名词。例如：

vacuum distillation unit（真空蒸馏装置）

值得注意的是，在名词作修饰语的结构中由多种不同的修饰关系，不如其他定语那么容易确定。这些关系可以概括见表 A-1 所示。

表 A-1

关　系	举　例
A of B:	lathe carrier = the carrier of a lathe（车床刀架）
A for B:	a water pipe = a pipe for water
A with B:	a surface plate = a plate with a (flat) surface
A which has B:	a cylinder lathe = a lathe which has a cylinder
A used for B:	elevator motor = motor used for an elevator（升降电动机）
A used for B-ing:	a punch hole = a hole used for punching
A contains B:	alloy steel = steel contains alloy（合金钢）
A made of (from) B:	a brass bearing = a bearing made of brass（黄铜轴承）
A shaped like B:	a horse shoe magnet = a magnet shaped like a horseshoe（马蹄形磁铁）
A operated by B:	power saw = a saw operated by power（电动锯）
A for doing B:	a gas meter = a meter for measuring gas（气量计）
A which dose B:	a gas company = a company which supplies gas（煤气公司）

3. 利用词缀法构成新词

（1）动词+后缀构成形容词，如：workable metal = metal which can be worked（可加工的金属），worked metal = metal which has been worked（已加工的金属），working fluid = fluid which dose the work（工作流体）等。

可见，利用词缀法构词简直可以代替一个短句，非常实用、精炼。下面是最重要的后缀：

① 以后缀-able（-ible，-uble）结尾的形容词大多数由相应的及物动词派生而来，在意思上一般是被动的，常译为"能……"、"可……"。例如：machinable steal 能加工的钢，controllable reaction 能控制的反应。

② 由动词加后缀-ive 和-ent、-ant 构成的形容词也属此类。如：effective range 有效范围（距离），absorbent carbon 活性炭。

③ 凡能用于被动意义的动词，都可以加后缀-ed 用作形容词，其意义表示被动。如：heated metal 已加热的金属，machined parts 已加工的零件。

④ 由动词加后缀-ing 用作形容词时，其意义表示主动。如：circulating water 循环水，rotating flied 旋转磁场，cutting edge 切削刃，lubricating system 润滑系统。

（2）其他重要的前缀和后缀：为了使文本精练，科技文章中使用很多来自希腊语、拉丁语或法语的词汇。如果我们熟悉这些词的前缀或后缀所代表的意义，在阅读中就能很容易地猜出并记住这些词的词义。下面略举其中最常见的几种：

① em-、en-把名词或形容词派生为动词。例如：enable 使能……，enlarge 扩大，embrittle 使变脆

② inter-(= between or among)表示在……之间，相互。例如：intersection 横断（切），交叉点

③ counter-(= against，opposition to)表示反，逆，对。例如：counterweight 配重，counterforce 反力

④ sub- (= beneath，less than)表示在……下，次（低）于。例如：subassembly 部（组）件装配，subway 地（下）道

⑤ in-表示在（向）内，进，入；非，无。例如：inlet（进）入口，inconstant 无规则的

⑥ out-表示在（向）外，远；超过。例如：outlet 出口，outweigh 比……重（要）

⑦ auto-表示自动（己，身）。例如：automation 自动化，autostop 自动停止器（装置）

⑧ multi-表示多。例如：multi-load 多负载

⑨ hydro-表示水，流体。例如：hydro-motor 液压马达

⑩ electr-表示电的。例如：electricity 电（学、气、力）

⑪ -ics(= subject)表示学科。例如：mathematics 数学，statistics 统计学

⑫ -free 表示无……的，没……的。例如：dust-free 无尘的

⑬ -proof 表示防（耐、不、反）……的。例如：water-proof 防水的，shock-proof 防振的

此外，具有否定意义的前缀有：de-、dis-、il-、im-、in-、ir-、non-、un-、mal-、mis-，

这些前缀均表示不……、无……、非……等意义。

具有动作意义和动作结果的后缀有：-tion、-sion、-al、-ance、-ence、-ag 等。动词后缀有：-en、-ise、-ate、-fy 等。

三、文体特点

科技英语的文体以说明文为主，也有一定数量的论说文和少量记叙文。

（一）说明文

说明文是用来说明事物的形状、性质、功用或者发展过程的。例如：用于介绍材料、产品、结构，描述实验过程、生产过程、工作原理、科研方法，或者介绍一本著作、一篇文章等。

说明文的特点是主要用一般现在时表达，以突出所说明的科技问题不受特定时间和地点的限制，是客观存在的事实。在说明文体中，最常用的方法有以下五种：

1. 叙述

说明文体最常用的方法就是叙述，它集中体现了科技文本简洁明快的特点。例如：

The main components of the lathe are the headstock and tailstock at opposite ends of a bed, and a tool-post between them which holds the cutting tool. The tool-post on a cross-slide which enables it to move sidewards across the saddle of carriage as well as along it，depending on the kind of job it is doing.

这段文字叙述了车床的主要部件名称、位置以及部分功用，主要用一般现在时和定语从句来表达；每个词都有恰如其分的作用和含义，多一个词则显累赘，少一个则使叙述内容不够精确。

2. 定义

为了对名词概念进行更本质的说明，定义性的语言结构也是不可缺少的。最常见的定义方法可用下面的公式来表达：

被定义名词 + is + 所属类别名词 + wh-word…。其中 wh-word 代表引出阐述部分定语从句的相应关系词。例如：

- An engineer is a person <u>who</u> designs machines，buildings or public works.
- An alloy is metallic substance <u>which</u> is composed of two or more elements.

另外，上述公式中类别名词也可以用动词-ing、for + 动词-ing 以及 with 引出的介词短语来界定类别名词。例如：

- A tangent is a straight line <u>touching</u> a curve at once point.
- A triangle is a plane figure <u>with</u> three sides.
- A thermostat is a device <u>for regulating</u> temperature.

从以上例句可以看出，下定义的句子常用的系动词是“is”。有时也使用“be”的其他形式或“can be defined as”结构，但这些形式出现的频率较低。

3. 分类

分类列举是说明事物的重要方法，能使读者的认识加以深化和条理化。例如：

➢ We can divide bearings into several types according to their position on the shaft.

我们可以根据轴承在轴上的位置将它分为几类。

说明事务分类的表达方法主要有以下几种（均以简单例句代表其句型）：

（1）There are two kinds (types、sorts、classes、varieties) of bearings.

（2）Bearings are of two types (etc.)

（3）We can divide bearings into two kinds (etc.) according to…

（4）We can classify bearings according to…

（5）Bearings can (may) be divided into…

（6）Bearings can (may) be classified as…

利用上述某一种表示方法将要说明的事物分类之后，科技著作者还常常用 first，second，…，to begin with，another point，…，finally 等进行罗列，逐一详细说明。

4. 举例

举例常作为例句出现，是说明文体中不可缺少的表达方法。例如：

➢ With certain metals，such as copper or iron，the change in resistance which attends on changes in temperature is relatively large—a fact which is utilized in the resistance thermometer，in which it is possible to measure temperature changes，as in the windings of an electric motor，for instance，by the change in resistance.

某些金属如钢或铁，其电阻随温度变化而变化的程度是相当大的—电阻温度计就是利用这一特点而研制的。例如，使用这种温度计能够根据电阻的变化来测定诸如电动机绕组的温度变化。

上面一个长句中使用了 such as，as 和 for instance 来引导具体例证。举例常用的连接型插入语还有：for example，as an example，namely，that is，in particular，as an application，including 等。

另外，举例还可以用来补充“定义”或“分类列举”。

5. 比较和比拟

对不易理解的科技内容作类比说明，是帮助人们认识事物的重要方法。例如：

➢ Like the human brain，a computer also has a memory.（比拟）

➢ Steel is far stronger than cast-iron.（比较）

科技工作者为了做更精确的说明时，也常用比较方法来补充“分类列举”的内容。例如：

➢ Engines used on ships include the diesel engine and the steam engine. A diesel engine is at least 50 percent more efficient than a steam engine.

6. 对比

为了说明问题的另一方面或表示相反意见时，科技著作者经常采用对比说明的方法，请看下面的例句：

➢ The centrifugal pump is compact and requires little maintenance. <u>But</u> it suffers from certain disadvantages.

上述第一句说明“离心泵”的优点，第二句以 But 开头引出问题的另一方面，指出“离心泵具有某些特点”。这类表示对比的常见句型有：but，instead，nevertheless，however，on the other hand，in contrast，in the contrary，conversely，in fact，yet。其中 in fact 也可以用来强调。

以上是说明文体中经常使用的六种方法。除此以外，科技文献资料或教科书中还经常用图表或公式进行说明。

（二）论说文

论说文也是科技书面英语中常见的文体。由于在内容安排上要求有必然的逻辑联系，因此其主要特点是逻辑严密，为了使逻辑性更强，内容层次更清楚，论证更有力，科技著作者主要使用以下五类词语。

（1）表示因果关系、依据或原因。

例如：thus，as a result，therefore，as a result (of)，hence，thereby，result in，so that，lead to，such…as to，consequently，because (of)，owing to，since，due to，as，depend on，in view of，(be) dependent on，for this reason，according to，the reason why…is (was) that…等。

（2）表示前提、条件的。

例如：if，suppose，even if，assume，only if，assuming，provided that，let，providing，when，unless，in case of，once，on（+动名词短语），on condition that，given（+名词）等。

下面两个例句用来说明不太常见的以 given 引出限制性条件的用法。

➢ <u>Given</u> plenty of labor，the job will be completed on schedule.
<u>假如</u>有充足的劳动力，这项工作将准时完成。

➢ <u>Given</u> sufficient turbulence in the combustion chamber，detonation is unlikely to occur.
<u>假定</u>在燃烧室中形成充分的湍流，就不可能产生爆炸。

需要指出的是，上面列出的词语均可以用于引出“真实条件句”（the open condition），即如果或假设首先发生某一现象或事件，则可能引起另一现象或事件的发生。当假定或设想某事发生但事实上它不可能发生或者根本没有发生过时，谓语动词要用虚拟语气的结构。这种结构在科技著作中偶有出现。不过，一般说来，科技著作者不喜欢做这样的假设（hypothesis）。

（3）表示对比、转折。对比、转折表达法是论说文的常用方法，比说明文用得更为普遍。下面再举出一些表示对比、转折的词语，以引起重视。

例如：whereas，while，regardless，otherwise，despite of，alternatively，in spite of，although，though 等。

（4）表示强调、肯定、结论和概括性的词语。

例如：above all，clearly，without any question，certainly，undoubtedly，obviously，actually，surely，really，of course，indeed，to be sure，in fact，especially，true，essentially，practically， in practice，naturally，in effect，briefly，in short，reviewing，in summary，conclusively，to sum up，in the end 等。

（5）表示附加说明的词语有。

例如：in addition，besides，alternatively，further，in other words，furthermore，in simple language，moreover，on the other hand，also 等。

以上列举的五类词语在科技著作中是经常见到的。事实上，从语言学角度看，这些词语起到“话语标志”（discourse markers）的作用，表示句和句之间以及比单一句更长的语言段落之间存在的意义上的关系。读者凭借这些“话语标志”可以更准确地理解科技著作的内容。

四、语法特点

科技著作在风格和结构上与文学作品截然不同，它不会采用诸如隐喻、含蓄、夸张、拟人、反话以及幽默等修辞手段。科技著作者崇尚通俗、清楚、简洁和准确的风格和语言结构。因此，科技英语在语法结构上具有以下特点。

（一）动词时态种类少

由于科技著作中以说明文和论说文为主，主要说明事物的一般特性、形状、功能、发生和发展的过程，或论说一般的因果关系等。这些科技知识是客观事实，不受时间和地点的限制，因此用一般现在时居多。例如：

➢ Action and reaction are opposite and equal.

➢ On average，women live longer than men.

有时是对实验过程的描述，无论谁做或在何时何地做，都会发生相同的情况，因此需要用一般现在时来叙述。例如：

➢ The temperature rises until it reaches 100℃，but after that it remains constant.

除经常大量地使用一般现在时之外，在科技著作中有时也使用其他少数几种动词时态。例如，用一般过去时和现在完成时对事物过去的状况进行记叙或对变化后的现状进行说明。

➢ We took a zinc plate which was negatively charged. When this plate was illuminated by ultraviolet light it quickly lost its negative-charge.（记述过去的实验）

有时也需要用过去完成时表示在某种行为之前发生的事情或过去存在的状态。

➢ Before our investigation many advances had been made in the technology.

另外，由于所记述的内容的需要，有时也使用进行时，一般将来时和过去将来时等。

（二）使用被动语态的句子多

据有关资料统计，在科技著作中大约有三分之一以上的句子其谓语动词使用被动语态。有些科技著作或文章绝大多数句子是被动句。究其原因，大致有下述四点：

（1）科技著作者力求客观地对待事物，而不强调行动的主体，因此通常不用“I”、“you”或“the operator”等作为句子主语。例如：

➢ Screws can be cut on a lathe.

（2）为使句意更加清楚。例如：

➢ People heat the specimen carefully.

上句中主语 people 是谓语动词 heat 的施动者，但是这个 people 究竟是谁呢？是作者？是读者？还是其他有关人员？还是任何人？要避免这些令人迷惑的问题，可以使用下面的被动句：

➢ The specimen is carefully heated.

（3）为把最重要的信息突出地置于句首，即主语位置，立刻吸引住读者的注意力。例如：

➢ The characteristics of steel can be altered in various ways.

（4）使句子更为简洁。例如：

➢ The driver started the engine.

➢ The engine was started.

显然，第二句被动句比第一句更加简洁。

试比较下面两段短文的特点。

➢ We can store electrical energy in two metal plates separated by an insulating medium. We call such a device a capacitor，or a condenser，and its ability to store electrical energy capacitance. We measure capacitance in farads.

我们能够把电能储存在由一绝缘介质隔开的两块金属板内。我们把这样的装置称为电容器，把其储存电能的能力称为电容。我们以法拉为单位测量电容。

➢ Electrical energy can be stored in two plates separated by an insulating medium. Such a device is called a capacitor，or a condenser，and its ability to store electrical energy is termed capacitance. It is measured in farads.

第二段文字各句使用了被动语态，各句主语分别为 Electrical energy，Such a device，its ability to store electrical energy 和 It，四个主语完全不同，避免了反复使用代词 We，主语包有较多信息，给读者以前后连贯、自然流畅、简洁客观的感觉。

（三）名词结构多

科技文体崇尚行文简洁、内容确切、信息量大，强调客观事实，而非某一行为动作。因此，在普通英语中通常使用动词之处，科技著作者习惯于使用名词结构。试比较下面两组例句：

➢ The filament is heated by applying a voltage.

➢ The filament is heated by the application of a voltage.

➢ Considerable lateral pressure is exerted by the concrete while it is being compacted.

➢ Considerable lateral pressure is exerted by the concrete during compaction.

上面每组例句的第二句是科技英语中经常使用的典型的名词结构。使用典型的名词结构、减少句子中的动词数量，可以使概念更加明确，有些也使原来的动词结构缩短。

在这类名词结构中，有相当数量的名词是由动词派生而来的含有动作意义的抽象名词。下面举几例以引起读者注意（见表 A-2）。

表 A-2

动词	抽象名词	动词	抽象名词
classify	classification	apply	application
combine	combination	develop	development
achieve	achievement	maintain	maintenance
replace	replacement	equip	equipment

（四）尽量用短语代替从句或分句

科技著作中复杂的长句往往带有各种从句。为了保持语言简洁明快，科技著作者经常使用以下表达方法避免从句过多的趋向。

（1）常用分词短语和分词独立结构作状语，以代替表示时间、原因、方式、目的、结果、条件等的状语从句。例如：

➢ The rivet contracts as it cools，drawing the plates together.（结果）

铆钉冷却时收缩，把钢板坚固在一起。

有时在分词前加上 thus、thereby 等副词表示强调。如上句可以写成：

The rivet contracts as it cools，thereby drawing the plates together.

thereby 意为“因此”、“从而”

Given enough time，he could do it better.（表示时间）

从上面例中可以看出，分词短语的逻辑主语必须与句子主语一致；如果不一致，则必须在分词前加上其逻辑主语（名词或代词），构成分词独立结构。请看下面的例句：

There are many kinds of steel，each having its special uses in industry.（表示伴随情况）

钢有多种，每种在工业上都有其特定用途。

从上面例句可以看出，分词短语所表达的具体状语意义有时是很含蓄的，需要细心推敲才能判断准确。

（2）用介词短语和其他短语代替从句。例如：

➢ Before entering the nozzle，the steam is at very high pressure.

在进入喷嘴之前，蒸汽处于高压状态。

上句中介词短语 Before entering the nozzle 在意义上相当于 Before it enters the nozzle.

这类结构的不同情况还可以列举一些：

Prior to entering = Before it enters

When / While / In As } While / passing through = it is passing } through…

After / leaving… / On } = After it leaves

On separation… = When it is (was, …) separated…

After separation…= After it is (was, …) separated…

During manufacture = While it is (was, …) manufactured…

Before separation = Before it is (was, …) separated…

When separated = When it is (was, …) separated…

While separated = While it is (was, …) separated…

Once separated = Once it is (was, …) separated…

If separated = If it is (was, …) separated…

注意上面后四个结构中 when，while，once，if 后接过去分词，而不是名词。另外，也可以接形容词。例如：when necessary 必要时，if possible 如果可能的话，once full 一旦装满，while still hot 仍然热时。

（3）用过去分词短语代替定语从句。例如：

➢ The steel (which is) obtained in this way is suitable for machine tools.

上面例句中省去括号中的 which be 之后，实际上缩减为过去分词短语作定语，使句子缩短。

（4）用名词作定语代替其他各种后置定语。用名词作定语的特点，在前面的词汇特点（四）中已将做了介绍，这里不再举例详述。

（5）大量使用缩略词。在科技文献资料中经常使用缩略词是科技英语的一大特点。一些较为常用的缩略词往往径直引用，而不注明全称。

英语中缩略词大体上可以分为两大类：一是将一个单词缩写为词首的一个或几个字母再加上词尾的几个字母，例如：把 engineering 缩写为“Eng”；二是把一个词组缩写为几个字母，每个字母（间或为两个以上字母）代表该词组中的一个单词（该字母为该单词的首字母），但冠词和介词全部予以省略。例如，把 light amplification by stimulated emission of radiation（受激辐射式光频放大器）缩写为“LASER”或“laser”（激光）。

应该注意，同一缩略词可能代表许多不同的词义，甚至代表同一专业的不同词义。现举例说明如下（见表 A-3 所示）。

表 A-3

AA	absolute altitude	绝对高度
AA	Arithmetic average	算术平均数
AA	Assembly area	装配区
AA	Architectural Association	建筑（业）协会
AA	Automobile Association	汽车制造业协会（英）
AA	Australian Army	澳大利亚陆军
AA	American Airlines	美国航空（运输）公司
AA	acetaldehyde	[化]乙醛
AA	acrylic acid	[化]烯丙酸
AA	amino-acid	[化]氨基酸

从上面的例词可以看出，在阅读科技文献遇到缩略词时，切不可想当然地理解词义，应从上下文的具体专业内容出发查阅专业词典或缩略词词典来确定词义。

Appendix II The Characteristics of English Practical Writing

英语应用文的特点

随着时代的进步，人们的交往越来越频繁，不论在国内还是在国外，应用文的使用越来越广泛，它的形式也越来越复杂。英语应用文的范围非常广泛，不可能一一列举说明，这里仅就机械工程类专业常用的应用文形式，如产品说明书、产品合格证书及商业合同的特点做一简要说明。

一、产品说明书

产品说明书是帮助用户认识产品，指导用户使用产品的书面材料，它对产品的结构、功能、特性、使用方法、保养、维修、注意事项等作出详细的解释说明，既介绍产品又传授知识和技能。

由于产品的种类、性质不同，其说明方法、内容也不同，产品说明书的式样也就多种多样，但在写法上有许多共同的地方。一般说来，产品说明书大多都由标题、正文、落款三部分组成。

标题由产品名称和文种组成，例如：Miniature Electronic Calculator Operation，既说明了产品是 Calculator，又说明了是产品的操作说明书。正文分项排列所要说明的内容，并逐一解释。落款注明生产厂家名称，根据需要还可注明经营者名称，请参阅下例：

Quarts Travel Alarm Clock
Of “Three Five” Brand
Instructions
Operating Manual For
Model Q 2858 Quarts Travel Alarm Clock

Start Clock

First open the battery compartment cover，according to the location shown in figure in battery support and put into a new 1.5V battery.

Correcting Clock Time

Turn the hand setting knob to clocklike at that time will be corrected in direction indicated by arrowhead on back.

Correcting Alarm

Turn the alarm hand setting knob in direction indicated by arrowhead on back and alarm hand will be made to turn any desire alarm time in advance .At the same time，push up the alarm stop knob to operating position. So when it goes to desire alarm time in advance，it will automatically give off an alarm sound enough for making you suddenly wake from sleep right now. You only push down alarm stop knob to stop working position，that the alarm sound will be stopped immediately.

Notice:

1. This product needs to use one piece of No. 5 Battery. It will not work if you reverse the polarity of the battery.

2. When you turn hand setting knob，according to the direction indicated by arrowhead on back. Don't turn back! In order to avoid the clock work abnormally.

3. When you will be waked up by the alarm sound, please push down the alarm stop knob on time with stopping sound. So you can not only prevent to trouble others，but also prolong the useful life of the battery.

二、产品合格证书

产品合格证主要表示产品在出厂前经过严格的技术检验，用以提高它在市场上的信誉，使用户愿意购买，有的还可以起到保单的作用。产品合格证书至少应该包括以下内容：产品名称、商标、型号、制造厂家名称、制造日期、检验员姓名、购买日期、出售者姓名及日期及保修时间等。请参阅下例：

Lotus Flower Brand

Model 610 Radio receiver

Qualification Card

Name of Product：Radio Receiver

Brand of Product：Lotus Flower

Model：Model 610

Manufactory：Peony Radio Factory

Date of Manufacture：May 1997

Serial No：863378

Inspector：Liu Jie

Purchaser's Name：Wang Jiang

Date of Purchase：April 8，1998

Dealer's Name：Spring Thunder Dep. Store

Dealer's Address：Wenhui Rd. 12，Xianyang City，Shanxi Province

Guarantee Period：One Year after the date of purchase

This product，manufactured of choice materials to precise standards，has undergone rigid quality control. It is fully guaranteed against defective materials or workmanship under normal use. In the guarantee period，adjustments for defects or replacement of parts will be performed free of charge upon your presentation of this qualification card.

Peony Radio Factory

Address：× × × Road，× × × City，× × × Province

Tel No：× × × × × × ×

三、商业合同

商业合同属于契约形式之一，一般是团体和团体之间、团体和个人之间、个人和个人之间就某一特殊问题经过协商取得一致意见后而拟定的一种书面凭证。合同对各方都有约束力，要求各方都履行所规定的义务，保证享受充分的权力。合同有许多类型，但格式基本相同。一份正式的商业合同通常包括标题、前言、正文、结尾、附件等五部分。

（一）标题

标题常以“合同”(AGREEMENT、CONTRACT)为题。为使合同标题的内容更加明确，让人一目了然，可注明合同的性质或交易货物的名称。例如：AGENCY AGREEMENT。

（二）前言

前言部分一般要并列分行写明立约团体的名称（或简称用“甲方 PART A、乙方 PART B”）和代表人签约日期、地点、依据及缘由。

（三）正文

正文即合同的主体，分条列出各项条款的具体内容，一般包括：

（1）定义条款

（2）基本条款（即主要条款，是合同的核心）

（3）一般条款（共性条款，法律性比较强）

① 合同的有效期

② 违约及索赔

③ 合同的转让

④ 不可抗力

⑤ 全部协议（指合同签订后，所有在此以前有过的意向书、备忘录、协议等）都不再有效，而以该合同为准。

⑥ 依据的法律或适用的法律

⑦ 仲裁及法院管辖

⑧ 通知（规定通知的送达方式及由合同目的而确定的通知送达人）

⑨ 文字（规定合同所用的文字）

（四）结尾及附件

结尾即合同双方的签名。在合同正文以下，以双方的简称分别签署双方代表团体的名称。名称分列于左右两侧，代表的姓名要亲笔签于合同上。有的合同还要注明签约日期及正、副本份数，双方分持的份数等。合同根据需要可以备有附件，附件是合同不可分割的组成部分。

合同一经签署就具有法律的约束力。因此，表达要求严密、具体、完整，语言必须规范，逻辑要严谨，不可有模棱两可、含糊其辞的语句，各条款间要前后呼应、互相衔接，协调一致。

请参阅本教材所选合同的实例。

四、英语应用文的主要语言特点

(一)组句注重形合，用词准确、行文简洁，虚词(介词、连接词等)使用频繁

例如：

1. There are plans for new product introductions in IBM to compete with foreign companies.
   IBM 公司计划拿出一些新产品与外国公司竞争。
2. The VI 3021 modern is a microcomputer-controlled device that uses two separate frequency channels for transmitted date and received date.
   VI 3021 调制解调器是由电脑控制的装置，它使用两个分离的频道发送和接收数据。
3. Fast answers through logical entry system.
   通过逻辑进数装置即能快速求出答案。
4. Twice the performance at half the cost!
   花一半的钱，却能得到双倍的性能，何乐而不为！
5. Orders with customers' materials or samples are welcome.
   欢迎来样来料加工。
6. If your order is large enough，we are prepared to reduce our prices by as much as 5 percent.
   如果定货量大，我们准备给你 5%的回扣。
7. Can you give me a rough idea of the quantity you wish to order from us，so that we may adjust our price accordingly?
   你能否告诉我你的定货量大约是多少？这样，我们就可以根据定货量来调整价格。
8. This TV set is capable of presetting tuning of up to 8 channels，VHF，UHF or inactive channels for instance for monitoring the playback of a video tape recorder.
   本电视机可预调八个频道，甚高频、特高频或用于调节录像带播放的空白频道。
9. We trust that you will make all necessary arrangements to deliver the goods in time.
   我们深信你方将做出一切必要的安排，以便货物及时发送。
10. We are looking forward with interest to your reply.
    我们盼望你方赐复。

(二)为了行文便利或表示强调，句子常使用倒装结构

1. There stands a large hydro-electric power station on the river.
   江边矗立着一座大型水电站。
2. Punched on the tapes are numbers of holes which mean binary's 1 for the computer.
   带上打着许多孔，这些孔对计算机来说意味着二进位的 1。

3. In this design are involved a number of complicated problems which should be solved first.
   这个设计涉及许多必须首先解决的复杂问题。
4. Only after a program is prepared in every detail，can the electronic computer understand the problem it to solve.
   只有在十分详尽地编制出程序之后，电子计算机才能读懂要解的题目。
5. Never has a machine been so efficient and accurate as the electronic computer.
   从来不曾有过像电子计算机那样效率高而又准确的机器。
6. Should the current be cut off，the coil would return to its original position.
   如果切断电源，线圈即恢复到原来的位置。
7. No sooner has the current started running in one direction than back it comes again.
   电流刚开始朝一个方向流动就立即返回。

（三）为行文简单，常常出现“省略”形式

1. The direction (in which) a force acts is changeable.
   力的作用方向是可以改变的。
2. The two forces，as shown in the figure below，are paralleled.
   如下图所示，该二力是平行的。
3. A machine can never produce more work than was supplied to it.
   一台机器所做的功绝不会多于供给它的功。
4. Roller and ball bearings are used whenever necessary.
   一旦需要，就使用滚动轴承。
5. It is required that remote control (should) be applied to this plant.
   要求将遥控应用到这一装置上。
6. Design and specifications (are) subject to change without notice.
   本机外形规格如有变更恕不另行通知。
7. In non-conductors (insulators) there are few，if any，free electrons.
   在绝缘体中几乎没有自由电子，即便有，也是微乎其微。
8. The length is used in feet，the mass in pounds，and the time in seconds.
   长度以英尺、质量以磅、时间以秒来表示。

Appendix III The Basic Knowledge of English-Chinese Translation

英汉科技翻译基础知识

不同民族使用不同的语言，为了相互间能够更好地交往、交流思想，就需要翻译。翻译是利用译文语言把另一种语言所表达的思想内容准确而且完整地重新表达出来的一种语言活动。

译文应忠实于原文，准确地、完整地表达原文的内容(包括原文的思想、精神和风格)。译者不得随意对原文的思想加以歪曲、删除，也不得有遗漏和篡改。译文语言必须符合规范、符合译文民族语言的习惯；要用民族的、科学的、大众的语言来表达原文的思想内容，以求通顺、畅达。这些就是翻译的一般原则。在翻译科技文章时，译文应力求逻辑正确、术语定名准确、语句简洁明确、数据无误。

因限于篇幅，本文仅以英译汉为线索，介绍翻译的基本技巧和方法。

一、词义选择

英语的词形变化相对说来比较简单，但是一词多义现象较为普遍。在科技英语中也是如此。正确地选择和确定词义是正确理解原文的基本环节。

选择词义通常可以从以下三方面着手：

(一) 根据词类确定词义

以 light 为例：

- Aluminum is a light metal. 铝是一种轻金属。(形容词)
- Turn on the light please. 请开灯。(名词)
- We lit on a reference book. 我们偶然找到一本参考书。(动词)
- He often travels light. 他经常轻装旅行。(副词)

(二) 根据上下文中词的搭配关系确定词义

由于学科和专业不同，同一个词在不同上下文中有不同的词义。请看下面各句中 solution 一词的译法：

The solution the mathematics teacher told you is correct.
数学老师告诉你的解答是正确的。

- The chemist found that there were impurities in the solution.
  那位化学家发现溶液中有杂质。

- Two solutions were offered in meeting as a way out of the difficulty.
  为克服这一困难在会上提出了两种解决办法。

（三）根据译文（汉语）语言搭配习惯选择词义

英语和汉语中虽然都有一词多义现象，但搭配习惯却有很大差异。当涉及专业内容时同样如此。因此，翻译时应注意选择符合译文语言习惯的搭配，不可一律照搬词典上提供的基本词义死译或直译。以 heavy（基本词义为“重的”）为例，请看下面各短语的译文：

heavy rain	大雨
heavy fighting	恶战
a heavy heart	沉重的心情
heavy traffic	拥挤的交通
heavy industry	重工业
heavy current	强电流
heavy cut	强方切削
heavy lines	（图表中的）粗（黑）线

科技文章具有较强的科学性、逻辑性，词与词之间，段与段之间总是相互依存的。因此必须结合上下文推敲词义，做到词不离句，然后按译文语言—汉语的搭配习惯确定译文。请看下面的例句：

- The university houses all of its students in hotels.
  该大学为所有学生提供宿舍。
- An aluminum bush houses the bearing.
  一个铝质轴套套在轴承上。

综上所述，选择词义时应注意分清词类，从上下文联系去理解词义，从原文叙述的专业内容去判断词义，以及切实注意语言的搭配习惯。

二、词义引申

英汉两种语言在表达方式上存在着很大差别。英译汉时，有时会遇到某些词，在词典上查不到适当的词义。如果生搬词典上某一词义逐词死译，会使译文生硬晦涩，含糊不清，不能确切表达原文的意思，甚至会造成误解，传达给读者错误的信息。这时，应根据上下文和逻辑关系以及汉语的搭配习惯，从该词的基本词义出发，引申词义，从而准确地表达出原文的思想内容和语言风格，这就是所谓“取意忘形”的意译法。

需要引申的可以是词、词组，也可以是整个句子。例如：

- To make steel　炼钢
- cylindrical motion　旋转运动
- The car makes 120 kilometers an hour. 该轿车时速达 120 km。
- The chief purpose of a drilling machine is to make holes. 钻床的主要用途是钻孔。
- There is no physical contact between work piece and tool. 工件与刀具不直接接触。

- The light in the workshop is poor．车间里光线不足。
- Iron comes between manganese and cobalt in atomic weight．铁的相对原子质量介于锰与钴之间。
- This kind of wood works easily．这种木材容易加工。
- Other things being equal，copper heats up faster than iron．其他条件相同时，铜比铁热得快。
- The only limit on the power of human brain is the limit of what we think is possible.

人类大脑的能力恰恰是由于我们认为它有局限而被禁锢了。

（该句没有逐词死译为：人类大脑能力的限度就是我们认为其可能的那个限度。）

三、词类转译

英语和汉语在词类方面有许多相似之处，例如都有名词、动词、形容词和介词等。但是，也有不少差别。英语中有冠词、分词、动词不定式、关系代词和关系副词，汉语则没有这些词类。因此，英译汉时除了可以不译出某些词类之外，有时也不一定机械地将英语某一词类译成汉语的某一词类，即把英语名词仍译为汉语名词，英语动词仍译为汉语动词，等等。这就是所谓的“词类转译”。

有些英语句子不经转译也可译成通顺的汉语，如 I am a student.（我是学生。）但这毕竟是极少数。可以说绝大多数英语句子需要通过词类转换的技巧才能译成通顺的汉语。一般说来，词类转译还会伴随着句子成分的转换，二者不可能截然分开。

（一）转译成汉语名词

1. 英语代词转译成汉语名词

- The switch completes the circuit when you close it.

译文 1：当你合上它时，电闸把电路接通了。

译文 2：当你合上电闸时，电闸把电路接通了。

译文 3：当你合上电闸时电路便接通了。

译文 1 没有把代词 it 译成所指代的名词，汉语不通顺，还可能造成误解。译文 2 把 jt 译为名词“电闸”，是明显的改进。译文 3 巧妙地运用了汉语的意合法，最为明确简练。

- Energy can neither be created nor destroyed，although <u>its</u> form can be changed.

  虽然能量的形式可以转换，但能量既不能创造也不能消灭。

译文把原句中的代词译成“能量的”，这种译法符合汉语习惯，文字也通顺。

2. 英语动词转译成汉语名词

某些英语动词很难直接用汉语动词来表达其概念，这时可转换成汉语名词。例如：

- The new boring-machine <u>behaves</u> well.

  新镗床运转良好。
- Gases <u>differ</u> from solids in that the former have greater compressibility than the latter.

  气体和固体的区别在于前者比后者有更大的可压缩性。

➢ The electronic computer is chiefly <u>characterized</u> by its accurate and rapid computation.
电子计算机的主要特点是运算准确而且迅速。

3. 英语形容词转译成汉语名词

➢ Ships ale designed to be <u>stable</u>, and should return to an upright position after heeling over.
船舶设计要具有稳定性，有倾斜之后应能回复到垂直位置。

➢ Ice is not as <u>dense</u> as water and it therefore floats.
冰的密度比水小，因而能浮在水面上。

（二）转译成汉语动词

汉语中使用动词的频率比较高，而且也比较灵活，有时一短句可能用几个动词，如：他请求领导派他到最艰苦的地方去工作。其中“请求”、“派”、“到”、“去”、“工作”都是动词。而英语语法要求一个英语句子中只能有一个谓语动词，其他动词都需要以非谓语的形式出现。因此，英语中含有动词意义的名词、形容词、介词短语以及副词有时转译为动词，更符合汉语的表达习惯。

1. 英语名词转换成汉语动词

➢ The <u>operation</u> of a machine needs some <u>knowledge</u> of its performance.
操作机器需要了解机器的一些性能。

➢ The pure scientist his attention to <u>explanation</u> of how and why events occur.
理论科学家把注意力集中在解释事物发展的过程和原因上。

➢ The <u>flow</u> of electrons is from the negative plate to the positive.
电子由负极流向正极。

2. 英语形容词转译成动词

➢ He is <u>certain</u> (that) the machine will operate well.
他确信这台机器会运转良好。

➢ The author is <u>grateful</u> to his colleagues for valuable suggestions.
作者感谢同事们提供了宝贵的建议。

从上面的两例可以看出，英语中表达知觉、情感、信念、情态等的形容词作表语时往往可以转译为汉语动词。常见的这类形容词还有：confident 相信，ignorant 不知道，sure 确信，ready 准备好，afraid 恐怕，fond 喜欢，careful 注意，doubtful 怀疑，等等。

另外英语中某些形容词与介词的固定搭配也往往转译成汉语动词。例如：

➢ A is <u>similar to</u> B in many ways.
A 在许多方面<u>类似于</u> B。

常见的这类搭配很多，例如：equal to 等于，helpful to 有助于，familiar to 熟悉，relative to 和……有关，depend upon 依据，suitable for 与……相适应，short of 缺少，next to 次于，等等。

3. 英语副词转为汉语动词

英语中作表语的副词以及作宾语补语的副词往往可以转译成汉语动词，请看下面的例句：

- The sun is <u>up</u>. 太阳<u>升</u>起来了。
- The experiment is <u>over</u>. 这项实验<u>结束</u>了。
- That engineer took the engine <u>apart</u>. 那位工程师把发动机<u>拆开</u>了。

4. 英语中介词转译成汉语动词

- Machine parts at irregular shape call be washed very clean <u>by</u> ultrasonics.
  <u>用</u>超声波能把形状不规则的机器零件洗得很干净。
- A force is needed to move an object <u>against</u> inertia.
  为使物体<u>克服</u>惯性而运动，就需要一个力。
- They spoke to us <u>about</u> their work plan.
  他们跟我们讲了<u>关于</u>他们的工作计划。

（三）转译成汉语形容词

1. 英语副词转译成汉语形容词

当英语形容词转译成汉语名词时，修饰该英语形容词的英语副词往往同时转译为汉语形容词。例如：

- At ordinary temperature mercury is <u>greatly</u> stable in air.
  常温下，水银在空气中具有<u>很高</u>的稳定性。

当英语动词转译为汉语名词时，作状语的英语副词往往可以同时转译成汉语形容词。例如：

- He supposes boys think <u>differently</u> from girls.
  他认为男孩子的思维方式和女孩子<u>不同</u>。

2. 英语名词转译成汉语形容词

- This experiments is a <u>success</u>.
  这个实验很<u>成功</u>。
- I sin a perfect <u>stranger</u> in electric arc welding.
  我对电弧焊完全<u>陌生</u>。

（四）转译成为汉语副词

1. 英语形容词转译为汉语副词

当英语名词转译为汉语动词时，修饰该英语名词的形容词往往可以伴随着转译成汉语的副词。请看下面的例句：

- They make a <u>careful</u> study of the properties of this new alloy.
  他们<u>仔细地</u>研究了这种新型合金的特性。

➢ Below 4℃, water is in continuous expansion instead of continuous contraction.

水在4℃以下时，是在不断地膨胀，而不是不断地收缩。

2. 英语中作状语的名词或名词性词组往往可以转译为汉语副词。例如：

➢ Theory should go hand by hand with practice.

理论应与实践密切地结合。

➢ The compression ill the cylinder of an engine must be checked from time to time.

发动机气缸中的压缩情况，需要不时地进行检查。

在英语科普文章中这类词组较为常见，例如还有：year by year（逐年）、step bv step（一步一步地）、all the time（不断地）、day and night（夜以继日地）、side by side（一起），等等。

总之，词类转译现象是多种多样的，决不仅限于上述几种。同一个英语句子，由于处理方法不同，可能有不同的转译现象。但是，其中最重要的转译是英语名词和介词转译成汉语动词，应特别注意练习。

四、句子成分的转换

由于英汉两种语言表达方式不同，语言结构形式差别很大，为了使译文符合汉语表达习惯，除了运用词类转译技巧之外，往往还伴随着句子成分的转换。例如，在某些特定的句型中，英语句子的状语、定语、表语又可能转译成汉语句子的谓语，等等。下面仅列举常见的几种情况，供举一反三、类比推敲。

（一）转换成为汉语主语

1. 在英语"there be…"句型中，往往将状语略去介词转换为汉语主语。例如：

➢ There are a variety of machine-tools in the workshop.

这个车间有各种各样的机床。

➢ There has been a decrease in our imports this year.

今年，我们的进口商品减少了。

注意：该句作状语的介词短语"in our imports"实际逻辑意义是说明主语"a degrease"的具体内容，因此转译成汉语译文的主语。在其他句型中有时也有类似情况。请看下面的例句：

➢ When water freezes, it becomes larger in volume.

水结冰时，其体积变大。

➢ The machine is lighter in weight and simpler in structure.

这台机器的重量更轻，结构更简单。

另外，在科技文体中使用"there be"句型时常常译成汉语无主语句。例如：

➢ There are a lot of scientific journals in the reading room.

阅览室里有许多科普读物。

➢ There are a number of methods of joining metal articles together, depending on the type of metal and the strength of the joint which is required.

把金属连接在一起有许多种方法，选用哪种方法要视金属的类型和所要求接缝的强度而定。

2．英语被动语态句子由 by 或 in 引导的状语，往往可以转换为汉语的主语，同时略去介词不译。例如：

➢ The Fahrenheit scale was widely used in English and USA.
英美广泛采用华氏温标。

➢ Large quantities of steam ale required by modem industry.
现代工业需要大量蒸汽。

3．英语动词的宾语有时可以转换为汉语主语。例如：

➢ Aluminum has a combining combining power of three.
铝的化合价是三。（试比较：铝有一个三的化合价）

➢ A car battery has a voltage of 12 volts.
汽车蓄电池的电压为 12V。

4．英语表语转换成汉语主语。例如：

➢ Two widely used alloys of copper are brass and bronze.
黄铜和青铜是两种广泛使用的铜合金。

➢ Of all the metals the best conductors are silver,gold and copper.
银、铜、金是金属中最好的导体。

5．英语中介词短语作定语时，有时可以转换为汉语主语，同时略去介词不译。例如：

➢ There are three states of matter：gas、liquid and solid.
物质有三种状态：气体、液体和固体。

（二）转换为汉语谓语

1. 英语主语转换为汉语谓语

有些英语句子的主语为含有动作意义的名词，并且后跟介词短语作定语。这种结构中介词（多为 of）宾语往往在逻辑意义上为主语名词所表达动作的宾语。因此可以把这种英语主语转换成汉语谓语。请看下面的例子：

➢ The expression of the relation between pressure、volume and temperature follows:
压力、体积和温度的关系可以表述如下。

➢ Compaction of the concrete is done by vibrating machines.
用振动机压实混凝土。

2. 定语转换为汉语谓语

➢ There is a large amount of energy wasted owing to the friction.
由于摩擦耗费了大量能量。

➢ The two machines have the same efficiency.
这两台机器效率相同。

3. 表语转译为汉语谓语

➢ This explanation is against the natural laws.
  这种解释违反自然规律。

➢ Vapor is always present in small amount in the air.
  空气中总是含有少量蒸汽。

（三）转换为汉语宾语

1．英语中有大量使用被动语态的句子常常并无由 by 引出的逻辑上的主语（即行为主体这时，句子主语往往可以转换为汉语宾语译成汉语无主语句。例如：

➢ Work is done when an object is lifted.
  举起一个物体时就做了功。

➢ Bearings must be lubricated regularly.
  必须定期润滑轴承。

2．若使用被动语态的英语句子有由 by 引导的逻辑主语（行为主体），则往往可以转译为汉语主谓宾主动式结构，英语中的主语仍转换成汉语宾语。例如：

➢ The steam engine was invented by Watt.
  瓦特发明了蒸汽机。

➢ The work is gripped firmly by the jaws of the chuck.
  卡盘爪牢牢地夹紧工件。

（四）英语主语转换为汉语定语

1．当英语句中及物动词（多为 have）的宾语转换为汉语主语时，则英语句中的主语同时可以转换为定语。例如：

➢ Pig has poor mechanical properties.
  生铁的力学性能很差。

➢ Aluminum has poorer conductivity than copper.
  铝的导电性比铜差。（试比较：铝有比铜差的导电性。）

2．当英语句子中作表语的形容词可以转译为汉语名词时，则英语主语往往可以转译为汉语定语。例如：

➢ Steel is much stronger than wood.
  钢的强度比木材高得多。

3．当英语句中作谓语的不及物动词转译为名词作汉语主语时，原英语句子的主语往往以转译为汉语定语。请看下面的例句：

➢ Steel weighs about eight times as much as water.
  钢的重量约为水的八倍。

（五）英语从句的转换

1. 英语定语从句转换为汉语状语从句

英语定语从句并非在逻辑意义上都起修饰限定作用，有些定语从句有明显的状语意义；因此，必须根据上下文的逻辑关系，转换为汉语的状语从句。例如：

- Electronic computers，which have many advantages，can not carry out creative work.
  电子计算机虽然有很多优点，但不能进行创造性的工作。

2. 英语主句转换成汉语从句

为了符合汉语表达习惯，有时必须把英语主句译为汉语从句。例如：

- One must study hard before one could succeed in mastering a foreign language.
  一个人必须勤学苦练才能掌握一门外语。

3. 英语并列句译为复合句

英语中用并列连词 and，but，so，for，yet，or 等连接的并列句，大多数连词词意本身已经表示出其状语意义；而由 and 连接的并列句中，有些根据前后句的逻辑意义判断并无并列关系，也应转译出其表达的状语意义。例如：

- We study English and they study Japanese.
  我们学英语，而他们学日语。
- Start the sound into the air, and it will make waves which you can't see.
  如果向空中发送声音，就会产生你看不见的波。

该并列句中，前句为祈使句表示条件，以 and 连接的陈述句表示由此产生的后果。因此该句译为汉语主从复合句。

五、省译与增译

由于英语与汉语表达方式的差异，英语原文与汉语译文绝不是一一对应的关系。有些词，如冠词、介词、关系代词、关系副词等，在英语中是不可缺少的，但在汉语表达时。如果逐词译出又是多余的。另一方面，把很多英语句子译成汉语时又需要增加一些英语原文没有的词。这种省词不译与增词加译的翻译方法，是达到准确、畅达地表达原文不可缺少的方法。

应该指出，增译不是无中生有，省译也不是恣意删减。增译的词应是英语中无其形但有其意的词，省译的词应是汉语表达时按汉语规范显得多余的词。增译与省译是否恰当，取决于译者对原文语言和译文语言掌握的熟练程度，也就是取决于对英语原文理解的深度和运用汉语表达的准确度。

下面介绍一些常见的情况。

(一) 增译

1. 英语中含有动作意义的名词的增译

翻译英语科技文献资料时，经常遇到一些含有动作意义的名词。这时，必须根据上下文的逻辑意义，补充相关的表示动作意义的名词，以使译文更加通顺流畅。如增译“作用”、

“现象”、“效应”、“方法”、“过程”、“设计”、“变化”、“装置”等等。请看下面的例句：

- Considerable lateral pressure is exerted by the concrete during compaction.
  在压实过程中，混凝土施加了相当大的侧压力。
- This carelessness will be his ruin.
  这种粗心大意的作风会把他毁了。

这类增译的名词还可以举出一些。例如：neutralization 中和作用、oxidation 氧化作用、modification 修改方案、cycling 周期变化、working 工作条件、distribution 分布曲线等等。

2. 增译概括性的词、解说性的词或使语气连贯的词

- A designer must have a good foundation in statics，kinematics，dynamics and strength of materials.
  一个设计人员必须在静力学、运动学、动力学和材料力学这四方面有很好的。
- Considerable simplification in solving the above can be achieve.
  在解决上述问题时，是能够达到相当大的简化的。

这类增译的名词可能根据上下文的逻辑意义有所不同。例如 according to him，可以译为“按照他的观点”、“按照他的理论”、“按照他的方法”，等等，这要视上下文而定。

3. 增译英语句中省略的词

在不影响理解的前提下，为了避免重复，英语惯用法允许省略英语中的某些词语。但是，汉译时，为了使译文清楚、通顺、有时需要增译这些英语句中省去的词语。例如：

- Gears must be propered lubricated. If (they are) not (properly lubricated),there is a large amount of energy wasted due to the friction.
  齿轮必须适当润滑。如果不是这样，就会有大量能量由于摩擦而耗掉。
- The charges of nucleus and (the charges of) are equal so that the atoms is electrically neutral.
  原子核的电荷与电子的电荷相等，所以原子不带电。

以上例句中括号内的部分一般是省略不写出的，但在汉译时要增译出来。

应该说明，译成汉语时，并非所有英语句中省略的词都一定要增译出来。

- This substance does not solve in water whether (it is) heated or not.
  该物质无论加热与否，都不溶于水。
- The records are not so good as (they are) compared with the standards.
  这些记录和标准化比起来还不够好。

以上两句汉语译文中并没有增译原句括号内省略的部分，而采用了汉语意合法，仍能表达清楚而且通顺。

（二）省译

省略英语中某些词不译，是经常采用的一种翻译方法。这是因为，英语依靠介词、连词等表示出前后词语或前后句之间的逻辑关系或词语关系；而汉语则多借助于意合法，即

从语序上就能够做到明确上下文的逻辑关系。可见，有些英语词语可以省略不译。在翻译实践中，能否省略不译完全取决于汉语表达的需要。

1. 省略冠词

英语中冠词出现频率极高，有很多冠词只是用作名词的标记。不表示任何意义，因此省略不译。不过，有时冠词是否存在使词组意义有很大差异，虽然无需译出冠词本身的意义，但必须译出整个词组意义上的差异。这一点需要特别注意。请看下面的例句：

➢ The stability of an object is greatest when its centre of gravity is at the lowest level.
物体的重心处于最低点时，其稳定性最大。

（译文中省略了两个 the 和一个 an。不定冠词 an 是泛指某一个，句首的定冠词 the 虽为特指，但是从上下文中已经清楚了指的是什么，也不必译出；第二个定冠词 the 处在形容词最高级前面，是英语惯用法的要求，也不必译出。）

➢ When matter changes to substance different from what it was，the change is a chemical change.
当物质变成和原来不同的物质时，这种变化叫化学变化。

（该句原文中的两个不定冠词均未译出，而定冠词译为“这种”。

➢ In the past，to fly to the moon was out of the question.
在过去，飞往月球是绝对不可能的。

➢ In these days，to fly to the moon is out of question。
现在，飞往月球是不成问题的。

注意：在上面两个例句中 out of the question 与 out of question 意义上差别甚大，不能忽视。这类用或不用冠词引起意义上的差别的例子还有：to go to school 上学、to go to the school 去那个学校、to take place 发生、to take the place 代替、the number of the instruments 仪表的数量、a number of the instruments 一些仪表，等等。

另外，专有名词前面的 the，表示独一无二的事物，如：moon、sun 前面的 the 和形容词最高级前面的 the,都不必译出。

2. 省略介词

英语中常常用介词表达词组之间的关系，而汉语则主要借助于词序和逻辑关系来表达。因此，表示时间、地点等的英语介词往往可以省略不译。例如：

➢ Cast-iron is inclined to fracture under excessive tension.
张力过大，铸铁容易断裂。（省略 under）

➢ We have found a method for solving this problem.
我们已经找到了解决这个问题的方法。（省略 for）

3. 省略连词

为符合汉语规范，有些英语连词往往省略不译，有时还可以加译“就”、“却”、“再”等，使上下文语意更加明确。请看下面的例句：

➢ Air has weight，though it is very light.

空气要轻也有重量。(省译)(试比较：尽管空气很轻，但它也有重量。)

➢ A gas becomes hotter if it is compressed.
  气体受压缩，温度就会升高。(省译 if)

➢ Liquids are like solids in that they have a definite volume.
  液体和固体一样，都有一定的体积。(省译从属连词 that；同时也省略了介词 in).

4. 省译代词

英语中代词比汉语用得多，有些代词在英语句型中是不可缺少的，但译成汉语时又显得累赘。因此，可以省略不译。例如：

➢ Different metals differ in their electrical conductivity.
  不同金属具有不同的导电性。(省译 their)

➢ We cannot see sound waves as they travel through air.
  声波在空气中传播时是看不见的。(省译成称代词 We)

➢ It is necessary that the bearings should be lubricated regularly.
  这些轴承有必要定期加油润滑。(省译代词：It，同时也省译面连词 that)

5. 省译动词

英语动词的使用场合比汉语少。有时动词在英语句子中使用只是出于语法结构或惯用法的需要，没有实际词意。为了使汉语译文更加通顺、规范，在汉译时往往省略这样的动词不译。

例如：

➢ Which machine is better?
  哪台机器更好些？(省译 is)

➢ Steels possess good hardness and high strength.
  钢的硬度大，强度高。(省译 possess)

(试比较：钢具有好的硬度和高的强度。)

六、被动语态的译法

一般说来，英语中使用被动语态比汉语多。究其原因，无非出于以下几种情况：不必说出施动者，不愿说出施动者，无从说出施动者或者出于上下文联系的考虑。在科技文章中，被动语态使用范围更广，这是因为科技著作者需要客观地叙述事理，而不是强调动作的主体。汉语中很少使用被动语态，而常使用无主语句。把英语被动句译成汉语时，一般可以采用下列处理方法。

(一) 译成汉语主动句

1. 译成汉语无主语句。例如：

➢ A force is needed to stop a moving body.
  要使运动着的物体停止下来，需要用力。

2. 译成“……的”、“将(把)……加以……”等。例如：

➢ Resistance is measured in Ohm.

电阻是以欧姆为单位来度量的。

➢ This problem will be discussed tomorrow.

这个问题明天将加以讨论。

3．增译“人们”、“我们”、“有人”或“大家”等主语。例如：

➢ It has been found that this machine is similar to the other one.

人们已经发现，这台机器与那台机器在结构上相似。

➢ An interesting question was asked at the meeting.

会上，有人问了一个有趣的问题。

4．用英语句中的介词引导的施动者作汉语句的主语。例如：

➢ The workshop will be mechanized by us.

我们将使这个车间机械化。

➢ Large quantities of steam are required by modern industry.

现代工业需要大量的蒸汽。

5．将英语句中的主语转译为汉语宾语。例如：

➢ Measures have been taken to diminished friction.

已经采取措施来减少摩擦。

➢ Adequate heat must be supplied to melt the metal.

必须提供足够的热量，好使金属熔化。

6．将英语句中的一个适当成分译成汉语中的主语。例如：

➢ Iron and steel are widely used in every industry.

所有工业都广泛使用钢铁。

➢ None of this three factors should be neglected.

这三个因素一个也不能忽视。

（二）译成汉语被动句

有些英语被动句有时也可以译成汉语被动句。这时，更能发挥汉语的优势，用规范的汉语忠实地表达出原文的内容。译成汉语被动句时，根据原文结构情况一般有以下两种处理方法：

1．在汉语句谓语动词前加一助动词“被”字。例如：

➢ The metal hardened when it was cooled in the air.

这种金属在空气中被冷却时，就硬化了。

不难看出，这种译法使译文沿用了原文的主语，而在谓语动词前加“被”字，译成与英语原文相应的被动句。

2．用“被”、“由”、“受”、“靠”、“给”、“遭”等汉语中表达被动概念的介词引导出施动者。例如：

➢ This water is heated by the uranium fuel and is pumped to a boiler.

这种水被铀燃料加热后，由水泵压送到锅炉。

➢ Besides voltage，resistance and capacitance，an alternating current is also influenced by inductance.

除了电压、电阻和电容以外，交流电还量电感的影响。

七、英语长句的译法

（一）顺译法

英语长句的叙述层次与汉语相近时，基本上可以按英语原文的顺序依次译出。例如：

1. In the course of designing a structure， you have to take into consideration what kind of load the above mentioned structure will be subjected to， where on the structure the said load will do what is expected and whether the load on the structure is put into position all of a sudden or applied by degrees.

（你在）设计一个构件时，必须考虑到：（上述）构件将承受什么样的载荷，该载荷将在构件的什么地方起作用，以及该载荷是突然施加的，还是逐渐施加的。

原文 consideration 后有三个并列的宾语从句，分别由 what、where 和 whether 引导，在第二个由 where 引导的宾语从句中又有宾语从句 what is expected，译文中没有直译为“所期望的”，而是引申译为“起作用”。其主要结构仍按原文顺序译出。

2. Mathematicians who try to use computer to copy the way the brain works have found that even using the latest electronic equipment they would have to build a computer which weighed over 10，000 kilos.

试图用计算机复制人脑活动方式的数学家们已经认识到，即使使用最先进的电子设备，也得制造一台重一万公斤的计算机才行。

原文主语 Mathematicians 后有由 who 引导的定语从句和由 which 引导的定语从句；另外，the brain works 也是定语从句，因惯用法没有关系词引导。全句主要结构仍按原文顺序译出。

（二）逆译法

有时英语长句的展开层次与汉语表达方式相反，这时就需要逆着原文的顺序译出。例如：

1. Aluminum remained unknown until the nineteenth century，because nowhere in the nature is it found free，owing to its always being combined with ocher，elements，most commonly with oxygen， for which it has a strong affinity.

铝总是跟其他元素结合在一起，最普遍的是跟氧结合在一起，这是因为铝跟氧有很强的亲合力；因为在自然界任何地方都找不到处于游离状态的铝，所以直到 19 世纪人们才知道铝。

英语表达习惯是先说出主要的，然后才说次要的。原文主句很简单，后面 because 引出原因状语从句；其中又有由 owing to 引导的短语说明如（游离）的原因；后面还有 for which 引导的定语从句，从实际逻辑意义上仍是进一步说明 most commonly with oxygen 原因。从上面的汉语译文可以看出，除了把 for which 引导的定语从句独立译出外，主要结构与原文顺序相反。

2. A student of mathematics must become familiar with all, the signs and symbols commonly used in mathematics and bear them in mind firmly, and be well versed in the definitions, formulas as well as the technical terms in the field of mathematics, in order that he may be able to build up the foundation of the mathematical subject and master it well for pursuing advanced study.

为了打好数学基础，掌握好数学，以便学习深造，一个学数学的人必须掌握和牢记数学中常用的符号，精通定义、公式以及术语。

该句英语原文很长，共66个词构成，其中 in order that 引导出目的状语从句，按汉语习惯提到译文句首。

（三）分译法

有时英语长句中各个主要概念在意义上并无密切联系，具有相对独立性；可以拆成独立的短句，再按照汉语习惯重新安排次序。为使语气连贯，有时需要增译适当的词语。例如：

l. Manufacturing processes may be classified as unit production with small quantities being rnade and mass production with large numbers of identical parts being produced.

制造过程可分如单件生产和大量生产。单件生产就是生产少量零件，大量生产就是大批量生产出相同零件。

英语原文中，由两个 with 引出的定语不好安排，因此采用“先译出后加以说明”的方法。

2. Radial bearings, which carry a load acting at right angles to the shaft axis, and thrust bearings, which take a load acting parallel to the direction of the shaft axis, are two main bearing used in modern machines.

承受的载荷方向与轴心线成直角的是径向轴承；承受的载荷方向与轴心线平行的是推力轴承。这是现代机器所采用的两种主要轴承。

该句英语原文的主语 Radial bearings 和 thrust bearing 后分别有一非限制性定语从句，从内容看是对其先行词下定义。为使译文通顺，需要把这两个定语从句的内容先行译出，然后再译出原文主干的内容分。

3. In the last 25 of the many thousands of years which separate the discovery of electrum from the discovery of the electrons, we have at last come to realize how much the properties of the former depend on the behavior of the latter.

把金银合金的发现和电子的发现看成毫不相干已有几千年了。在最近的25年中，我们才认识到，金银合金的性质在相当大的程度上取决于电子的性质。

该句英语原文开头 In 引导的介词短语中，有一 which 引导的定语从句，若作为修饰成分译成其先行词 years 的定语，则使汉语句子臃肿且不流畅，因此采用提出先译的方法。

从以上例句不难看出，英语长句包含的语法现象比较复杂，必须在充分理解其结构的基础上，先充分运用各种翻译技巧，把拆成的短句的内容译出，然后按汉语规范以及逻辑顺序，意义轻重的层次重新安排，才能使汉语译文通顺。准确地表达原文的内容。

Appendix IV The Mechanical Drawing in English

英文机械图样用语

由于图面的限制，英文图样上许多加工说明、技术条件都不是完整的句子，句中许多成分都已省略。这些图样用语只能按照我国图样上的习惯用法译成中文，很多情况只能是意思相符而文字不能对应。下面就几个具体问题做简要说明。

一、图样上的标题栏

Title	Drn		Appd	
	Chd		Date	

Title 名称

Drn=Drawn by 绘图

Chd=Checked by 校对

Appd=Approved by 审核

Date 日期

二、图样上的明细栏

3				
2				
1				
Part No.	Detail ref.	Name of part	Material	No. off
Scale		Projection	Drg. No.	
Finish		Name of Firm		

Part No. =Part number 零件序号

Detail ref. =Detail reference 零件图号

Name of part 零件名称

Material 材料

No. off=Number off 件数

Scale 比例

Projection 视图

Drg. no=Drawing number 图号

Finish 表面粗糙度

Name of Firm 公司名称

三、其他常见符号及图样用语

3-Φ10 holes equally speed	3-Φ10 均布
2-Φ6 drill with pc. #127 at assembly	2-Φ6 与#127 件配钻
1/8 sawcut	锯缝 1/8 英寸（宽）
2 req'd (required)	需用两件
2-M10 holes taped with #153 at assembly	2-M10 与#153 件钻攻螺纹
4-Φ10 drill spotfaceΦ16×2 deep	钻 4-Φ10，锪孔 Φ16 深 2
40-Φ8 holes each 20 apart	钻 40-Φ8，孔距 20
Bill of material	材料明细表
B-view	B 向视图
Cadmium(chromium，nickle) plating	镀镉（铬、镍）
Case –hardened to 40~45 HRC	表面淬火至 40~45 HRC
Chamfer both ends	两端倒角
Concentricity of ΦA in reference to ΦB to be within 0.02	ΦA 对 ΦB 的同心度允差为 0.02
C'bore(=counterbore)	（锪）平坑
C'sink(=countersink)	（锪）鱼眼坑
Crown to 1/32	（轮面车出）凸起 1 / 32 英寸
Dispatch No.	出厂号
Drawn to 250~300 HBS	回火到 250—300 HBS
Elevation	正视图
Finish Ra0.32μm unless otherwise specified	其余 Ra0.32μm
F.a.o (Finish all over)	全部加工
Inclination 1:100	斜度 1:100
Knurl	滚花
Legend	图例
Misalignment to be within 0.05	同轴度误差不超过 0.015
Neck 1/8 × 1/16	退刀槽 1/8 英寸宽×1/16 英寸深
To be normalized	须正火
Notes (or Remarks)	附注
Oil groove 1/8 × 1/16	油槽 1/8 英寸宽×1/16 英寸深
Optional parts	非标准件
Ovality of Φ25 B4 to be within 0.05	Φ25 B4 的圆度误差不超过 0.05
Pickled after peening (sand blast)	抛丸（喷砂）后酸洗
Psc rio.（piece no.)	件

Peen end of hand in position	手柄端部铆接固定
plan	平面图
Polish to mirror finish	镜面抛光
quench and tempered to 250～300 HBS	调质到 250～300 HBS
Rounds R5 unless otherwise noted	未注圆角 R5
Ream Φ20 for dowel pin	铰 Φ20 定位销孔
Runout of ΦA in reference to Φ to be within 0.05	ΦA 对轴线的径向跳动误差不超过 0.05
Section A-A	A-A（截面）
Serial No.	（机器）序号
Spot for set screw with pc．#1003 in position	与#1003 件配钻，并锪出定位螺钉浅窝
Superseded by drawing No．1135-A	本图样作废，由图号 1135-A 代替
Symmetrical position of slot in reference toΦto be within 0.05	槽对中心线的对称度误差不超过 0．05
Tap 4-M10 holes，equally spaced on Φ	攻螺纹 4-M10，各孔沿中心线均布
Taper 1:20	锥度 1:20
Taper to be within 0.05	锥度不超过 0.05
Technical specification (Tech. Sp.)	技术标准
Technical requirement (Tech. Req't)	技术要求

注：表中有个别用语的单位是英寸（已在表中注明）。这是英文习惯用法。1 英寸=25.4mm。

Appendix V Useful Words of Mechanical Engineering

机械工程常用词汇

3-Jaws indexing spacers 三爪、分割工具头

A

A.T.C.system 加工中心机刀库
acoustic emission inspection 声发射检测
age hardening 时效硬化
ageing 老化处理
alloyed tool steel 合金工具钢
aluminium alloy 铝合金
aluminium oxide 刚玉
aluminum continuous melting & holding furnaces 连续溶解保温炉
annealing 退火
anode effect 阳极效应
anodizing 阳极氧化处理
austempering 奥氏体等温淬火
austenite 奥斯田体/奥氏体

B

bainite 贝氏体
balancing equipment 平衡设备
ball bearing steel 滚动轴承钢
banded structure 条纹状组织
bayonet 卡口
bearing fittings 轴承配件
bearing processing equipment 轴承加工机
bearings 轴承
belt drive 带传动
bend test 弯曲试验
bending machines 弯曲机
blades 刀片
blades saw 锯片
bolts,screws & nuts 螺栓，螺帽及螺丝

boring heads 镗孔头
boring machines 镗床
boron carbide 碳化硼

C

cable making tools 造线机
carbide 炭化物
carbon and graphite material 碳和石墨材料
carbon tool steel 碳素工具钢
cast non-ferrous alloy 铸造有色合金
cast steel 铸钢
casting,aluminium 铸铝
casting,copper 铸铜
casting,gray iron 铸灰口铁
casting,malleable iron 可锻铸铁
casting steel 铸钢
cemented carbide 硬质合金
cementite 碳化铁
ceramics 陶瓷
chain drive 链传动
chamfer machines 倒角机
chemical analysis of material 材料化学分析
chemical plating 化学电镀
chucks 夹盘
clamping/holding systems 夹具/支持系统
CNC bending presses 电脑数控弯折机
CNC boring machines 电脑数控镗床
CNC drilling machines 电脑数控钻床
CNC EDM wire-cutting machines 电脑数控电火花线切削机
CNC electric discharge machines 电脑数控电火花机
CNC engraving machines 电脑数控雕刻机
CNC grinding machines 电脑数控磨床
CNC lathes 电脑数控车床
CNC machine tool fittings 电脑数控机床配件
CNC milling machine CNC 铣床
CNC milling machines 电脑数控铣床
CNC shearing machines 电脑数控剪切机

CNC toolings CNC	刀杆
CNC wire-cutting machines	电脑数控线切削机
composite material	复合材料
compressive test	压缩试验
conveying chains	输送链
coolers	冷却机
copper alloy	铜合金
copy lathe	仿形车床
copy milling machine	仿形铣床
copy shaping machine	仿形刨床
corrosion test	腐蚀试验
coupling	联轴器
creep test	蠕变试验
crimping tools	卷边工具
crusher	破碎机械
cubic boron nitride	立方氮化硼
cutters	刀具
cutting-off machines	切断机
cylindrical grinding machine	外圆磨床

D

dial snap gauge	卡规
diamond cutters	钻石刀具
diamond	金刚石
dicing saws	晶圆切割机
die casting dies	压铸冲模
die casting machines	压铸机
dies-progressive	连续冲模
disposable toolholder bits	舍弃式刀头
drawing machines	拔丝机
drilling machine	钻孔机
drilling machines bench	钻床工作台
drilling machines	钻床
drills	钻头
dryer	干燥器

E

easy-cutting steel	易切削钢

eddy current test 涡流检测
electric discharge machines(EDM) 电火花机
electric power tools 电动刀具
engineering plastics 工程塑料
engraving machine 雕刻机
engraving machines 雕刻机
etching machines 蚀刻机
evaporator 蒸发器

F

finishing machines 修整机
fixture 夹具
fluid machinery 流体机械
forging dies 锻模
foundry equipment 铸造设备

G

gas turbine 燃气透平
gaseous cyaniding 气体氧化法
gear cutting machines 齿轮切削机
gears 齿轮
globular cementite 球状碳化铁
gravity casting machines 重力铸造机
grinder bench 磨床工作台
grinding machines 磨床
grinding machines,centerless 无心磨床
grinding machines,cylindrical 外圆磨床
grinding machines,universal 万能磨床
grinding tools 磨削工具
grinding wheels 磨轮
general machining centers 通用加工中心

H

hardness test 硬度试验
heat preserving furnaces 保温炉
heat resistant steel 耐热钢
heating treatment funaces 熔热处理炉

high-speed drilling machines 高速钻床
high speed steel 高速钢
horizontal machine center 卧式加工制造中心
horizontal & vertical machining centers 卧式及立式加工中心
horizontal machining centers 卧式加工中心
hydraulic components 液压元件
hydraulic power tools 液压工具
hydraulic power units 液压动力元件
hydraulic rotary cylinders 液压回转缸

I

impact test 冲击试验
industrial robot 工业机器人
inside calipers 内卡钳
interferometer 干涉仪
internal cylindrical machine 内圆磨床

L

lapping machines 精研机
lapping machines,centerless 无心精研机
laser cutting 激光切割
laser engraving machines 激光雕刻机
lathe bench 车床工作台
lubricants 润滑液
lubrication Systems 润滑系统
lubricators 注油机

M

magnesium alloy 镁合金
magnetic particle test 磁粉探伤
magnetic tools 磁性工具
malleable cast iron 可锻铸铁
mechanical hand 机械手
milling machines 铣床
milling machines,bed type 床身式铣床
milling machines,duplicating 仿形铣床
milling machines,horizontal 卧式铣床

milling machines,turret vertical	六角立式铣床
milling machines,universal	万能铣床
milling machines,vertical & horizontal	立式及卧式铣床
milling machines,vertical	立式铣床
mining machinery	矿山机械
mixing machine	混合机械
mold & die components	模具单元
mold changing systems	换模系统
multi-spindle drilling machines	多轴钻床

N

nickel alloy	镍合金
nodular cast iron	球墨铸铁

O

optical metallographic examination	光学金相检验

P

penetrant test	渗透探伤
physical property parameter of material	材料物理性能参数
planer	龙门刨床
planing machines vertical	立式刨床
planing machines	刨床
pneumatic hydraulic clamps	气油压虎钳
pneumatic power tools	气动工具
powder metallurgic forming machines	粉末冶金成型机
powder metallurgy friction material	粉末冶金摩擦材料
powder metallurgy high speed steel	粉末冶金高速钢
powder metallurgy porous material	粉末冶金多孔材料
powder metallurgy structural parts	粉末冶金结构零件
powder metallurgy superalloy	粉末冶金高温合金
pulverizer and grinding mill	粉磨机械

Q

quenched and tempered steel	调质钢

R

radial drilling machines	摇臂钻床

rubber	橡胶

S

shafts	轴
shaper	牛头刨床
shear test	剪切试验
shearing machines	剪切机
sheet metal forming machines	金属板成型机
sheet metal working machines	金属板加工机
silicon carbide	碳化硅
slotting machines	插床
smelting machinery	冶炼机械
spindle	主轴
spring steel	弹簧钢
stainless steel	不锈钢
stamping parts	冲压机
straightening machines	矫直机
stress relaxation test	应力松弛试验
stress-rupture test	高温持久强度试验
surface analysis	表面分析
surface grinder	平面磨床
surface hardening steel	表面硬化钢
switches & buttons	开关及按钮

T

tapping machines	攻螺丝机
tensile test	拉伸试验
test for castability	铸造性能试验
test for forgeability	锻造性能试验
test for heat treatment processibility	热处理工艺性试验
test for machinability	切削加工性试验
titanium alloy	钛合金
torsion test	扭转试验
transmitted chains	传动链
tube bending machines	弯管机
turbine blade	透平叶片
turret lathe	转塔车床

U

universal tool grinding machine 万能工具磨床

V

vertical double-column type machining centers 立式双柱加工中心
vertical drilling machines 立式钻床
vertical hydraulic broaching machine 立式油压拉床
vertical machine center 立式加工制造中心
vises 虎钳

Z

wear resistant steel 耐磨钢
wear test 磨损试验
wheel dressers 砂轮修整器
wrenches 扳手

Appendix VI Glossary

总词汇表

A

a bewildering number of			一系列令人困惑的
a tug of war			拔河比赛
a waving flag			一面飘动的旗帜
abnormal	[æb'nɔːməl]	*a.*	异常的，反常的
aborted project			流产了的计划
accommodate	[ə'kɔmədeit]	*v.*	（使）适应
accumulate	[ə'kjuːmjuleit]	*vt./vi.*	堆积；积累
accuracy	['ækjurəsi]	*n.*	精确（性），准确（性）
acid cleaner			酸洗液
acronym	['ækrəˌnim]	*n.*	词头，只取首字母的缩略词
actuator	['æktjueitə]	*n.*	油缸，气缸，执行机构，传动装置
advent	['ædvənt]	*n.*	出现，到来
agency	['eidʒənsi]	*n.*	代理处，代理权
aggregate	['ægrigit]	*n.*	合计，聚集；
		a.	合计的，聚集的
agree with			同意
align	[ə'lain]	*vt.*	使成一直线；校正
alignment	[ə'lainmənt]	*n.*	对准，准线
alignment	[ə'lainmənt]	*n.*	成直线，对准，同轴度
allow for			考虑到，估计
alter	['ɔːltə]	*vt.*	改变，改动
analyze	['ænəlaiz]	*vt.*	分析，分解
angle	['æŋgl]	*n.*	角，角度
animate	['ænimeit]	*vt.*	使有生气，使活泼
		a.	栩栩如生的
anneal	[ə'niːl]	*vt.*	退火
anticlockwise	['æntiˌklɔkwaiz]	*a.*	逆时针的［地］
apply	[ə'plai]	*vt.*	应用，施加
appropriation	[əˌprəupri'eiʃən]	*n.*	据为己有，占有，拨款
arbitration	[ˌɑːbi'treiʃən]	*n.*	仲裁

arc welding			电弧焊
arc	[ɑːk]	*n.*	电弧，弧
architecture	[ˈɑːkitektʃə]	*n.*	体系结构；建筑学，建筑风格
are distinguished by			以……著名
arise from			由……而产生，起因于
armature	[ˈaːmətʃə]	*n.*	电枢
assembly	[əˈsembli]	*n.*	总成，组件
assume	[əˈsjuːm]	*vt.*	呈（某形式），假定，承担，接受
atmosphere	[ˈætməˌsfiə]	*n.*	大气（压），气氛，环境
attempt to (+inf.)			试图，企图
attractive	[əˈtræktiv]	*a.*	吸引人的，有魅力的
attribute M to N			认为 M 是由 N 引起的
audiovisual	[ˈɔːdiəuˈvizjuəl]	*n.*	视听设备
automate	[ˈɔːtəmeit]	*vt.*	使自动化
automatic tool changers			自动换刀架
available	[əˈveiləbl]	*a.*	可用的或可得到的
award	[əˈwɔːd]	*vt.*	授予，奖给；判给
axis	[ˈæksis]	*n.*	轴线，轴心

B

background	[ˈbækgraund]	*n.*	背景，后台
backlash	[ˈbæklæʃ]	*n.*	侧向间隙；后退
balance	[ˈbæləns]	*n.*	平衡
		vt.	使平衡
be available			可利用的
be defined as…			被定义为……
be directly proportional to			与……成正比
be equipped with			装备……
be exposed to			招致，与……相接触
be familiar with			熟悉
be known as			被称为
be subtracted from			从……减去
be population for…application			在……应用很广泛
be poured into			浇入
be responsible for			负责
bead	[biːd]	*n.*	水珠；[机]卷边；车轮圆缘；加强筋
bear an resemblance to			与……有相似之处

bed	[bed]	*n.*	床，床身
behavior	[bi'heivjə]	*n.*	行为，举止，表现，性质，状态
Belleville springs			蝶形弹簧（贝氏弹簧）
bilateral	[bi'heivjə]	*a.*	双向的
bismuth	['bizməθ]	*n.*	铋
boundary	['baundəri]	*n.*	界线，范围
box jig			箱式钻模，固定式钻模
braze	[breiz]	*vt./n.*	铜焊，硬钎焊
breed	[bri:d]	*n.*	品种，种类
brittle	['britl]	*a.*	碎的，易碎的
broaching machine			拉床
buffer	['bʌfə]	*n.*	缓冲器，减震器
		vt.	缓冲，减轻
bump	[bʌmp]	*vt./vi.*	撞倒；冲撞
		n.	碰撞，猛撞
bushing	['buʃiŋ]	*n.*	钻套，衬套

C

cadmium	['kædmiəm]	*n.*	镉
calculate	['kælkjuleit]	*vt./vi.*	计算，估计；打算，旨在
cam	[kæm]	*n.*	凸轮
cantilever-spring			半悬臂式（汽车）弹簧
capability	[ˌkeipə'biləti]	*n.*	性能，耐受力
capacity	[kə'pæsəti]	*n.*	容量，容积；才能，能力
carbide	['ka:bəid]	*n.*	碳化物
carbon	['kɑ:bən]	*n.*	碳
carriage	['kæridʒ]	*n.*	溜板，拖板
casting	['kɑ:stiŋ]	*n.*	铸件，铸造
category	['kætigəri]	*n.*	分类，种类
cease	[si:s]	*v.*	停止，结束；
		n.	停息
cement	[si'ment]	*vt.*	粘接
		n.	水泥
cementite	[si'mentəit]	*n.*	渗碳体，碳化铁
chip	[tʃip]	*n.*	片，板，切屑
chip conveyor			排屑输送机
chuck	[tʃʌk]	*n.*	卡盘，用（卡盘）夹紧

circularity	[ˌsəːkju'lærəti]	*n.*	圆度
cite	[sait]	*vt.*	引用，引证
clamp	[klæmp]	*n.*	夹具体；
		vt.	夹紧
clearance	['kliərəns]	*n.*	（公差中的）间隙，距离，容积
clutch	[klʌtʃ]	*n.*	离合器
coat	[kəut]	*vt.*	涂上
come in contact with			同……接触
comic	['kɔmik]	*n.*	连环漫画；喜剧的
commercially	[kə'məːʃəli]	*ad.*	商业上地，工业上地
commission	[kə'miʃən]	*n.*	授权，委托；委员会
commission	[kə'miʃən]	*n.*	佣金，回扣
commodity	[kə'mɔditi]	*n.*	商品，货物
communication	[kəˌmjuːni'keiʃən]	*n.*	交流，交际，通讯
compatible	[kəm'pætəbl]	*a.*	兼容的，可匹配的
component	[kəm'pəunənt]	*n.*	成分，组成部分，部件，元件
comprehend	[ˌkɔmpri'hend]	*vt.*	理解，了解
comprehensive	[ˌkɔmpri'hensiv]	*a.*	广泛的，综合的
compression	[kəm'preʃən] *n.*		压缩
compressive	[kəm'presiv]	*a.*	有压力的，压缩的
computation	[ˌkɔmpju'teiʃən]	*n.*	计算；估计；计算法；测定
computer integrated manufacturing system(CIMS)			计算机集成制造系统
concentricity	[ˌkɔnsən'trisəti]	*n.*	同轴度
concession	[kən'seʃən]	*n.*	承认，允许；妥协，让步；特许权
concretely	['kɔnkriːtli]	*ad.*	具体地
confine	['kɔn'fain]	*vt.*	限制；局限于；
		n.	界限，范围
construct	[kən'strʌkt]	*vt.*	修建，建立；构成，组成
contact	['kɔntækt]	*n./vt.*	（使）接触
contract	['kɔntrækt]	*vt./vi.*	缔结；订契约；
		n.	契约，合同
contrary	['kɔntrəri]	*a.*	相反的，相违的
conversion	[kən'vəːʃən]	*n.*	变换，转化
convert	[kən'vəːt]	*vt./vi.*	（使）转变，（使）转化
convey	[kən'vei]	*vt.*	运输；运送；表达，转达
conveyor	[kən'veiəː]	*n.*	搬运者，传达者，输送机
coolant	['kuːlənt]	*n.*	切削液，乳化液；润滑剂

cooperation	[kəuˌɔpə'reiʃən]	*n.*	合作
cope	[kəup]	*n.*	上箱
copying miller			仿形铣床
corporation	[ˌkɔ:pə'reiʃən]	*n.*	公司，社团
counter	['kauntə]	*n.*	计数器
counterbalance	[ˌkauntəˌbæləns]	*n.*	平衡
coupling	['kʌpliŋ]	*n.*	联轴器，连接
courtesy of			多亏（因为）有了……
crane	[krein]	*n.*	起重机，吊车，升降架，升降设备
crankshaft	['kræŋkʃɑ:ft]	*n.*	机轴；曲轴，曲柄轴
crash into			撞上，闯入
crisp	[krisp]	*a.*	脆的，鲜脆的
		n.	[英] 炸马铃薯片
criterion	[krai'tiəriən]	*n.*	依据，准则
critical	['kritikəl]	*a.*	决定性的，危急的；批评的，批判的
crosshatching	['krɔshætʃiŋ]	*n.*	交叉排线（法）；十字晕𣈶；双向影线
crucial	['kru:ʃəl]	*a.*	决定性的，紧要关头的
cst= centistoke	['sentistəuk]	*n.*	厘沲（动力粘度单位）
curve	[kə:v]	*n.*	曲线，弯曲；
		vt.	使弯曲
custom-built			客户定制
cut off			切掉，切断，关掉
cutter	['kʌtə]	*n.*	（切削）刀具
cylinder	['silində]	*n.*	液压缸

D

damper	['dæmpə]	*n.*	阻尼器，减震器；起抑制作用的因素
dash	[dæʃ]	*v.*	画线
dashed line			虚线
dead center			尾架顶尖
debris	['deibri:]	*n.*	废墟，残骸
debug	[di:'bʌg]	*vt.*	调试
decelerate	[di:'seləreit]	*vt./vi.*	（使）减速；降低速度，减速；慢化；制动
decode	[ˌdi:'kəudə]	*vt.*	译（码），解（码）
decoder	[di:'kəud]	*n.*	译码器
define	[di'fain]	*vt.*	解释，给……下定义
deflection	[di'flekʃən]	*n.*	（尤指击中某物后）突然转向，偏斜，偏离

delivery	[di'livəri]	*n.*	递送、交付
denote	[di'nəut]	*vt.*	指示，表示
deputy	['depjuti]	*n.*	副手，代理人，代表；议员，下院议员
deputy-headmaster			副校长
descriptive	[dis'kriptiv]	*a.*	描述的
detachable	[di'tætʃəbl]	*a.*	可分开的，可分离的
detect	[di'tekt]	*vt.*	发现，找到
determine	[di'tə:min]	*vt.*	决定，确定
deviation	[ˌdi:vi'eiʃən]	*n.*	偏差，误差
diamond	['daiəmənd]	*n.*	金刚石
differential	[ˌdifə'renʃəl]	*n.*	差异
dimension	[di'menʃən]	*n.*	尺寸，维数，量纲
direct	[di'rekt]	*a.*	正面的，正向的；
		vt.	指导，支配
disbursement	[dis'bɜ:smənt]	*n.*	支付款，支出额
disengage	['disin'geidʒ]	*vt.*	脱开，分离，解脱
dispatch	[dis'pætʃ]	*vt.*	派遣，快速处理
displacement	[dis'pleismənt]	*n.*	排液量
disposition	[dispə'ziʃən]	*n.*	安排，布置；支配；处理权
dissipate	['disipeit]	*vt./vi.*	驱散；消失；
		vt.	浪费
distinguished	[dis'tiŋgwiʃt]	*a.*	卓越的；著名的；受人尊敬的
disturbance	[dis'tə:bəns]	*n.*	动乱；干扰；侵犯
double throw switch			双掷开关
double-pole			双极（刀开关）
double-pole single throw			双刀单掷开关
dowel	['dauəl]	*n.*	定位销，销钉
downstream	['daun'stri:m]	*a.*	下游的
draft	[drɑ:ft]	*n.*	草稿，草案，草图；汇票
drag	[dræg]	*n.*	下箱；
		v.	拖，拉
drawing	['drɔ:iŋ]	*n.*	图
drill	[dril]	*n.*	钻头
		vt.	钻（孔）
drilling	['driliŋ]	*n.*	钻削
dry run			空运行
dullness	['dʌl'nis]	*n.*	钝化

duly	[dju:li]	*ad.*	正确地，适当地；按时地，准时地
duplicate	['dju:plikit]	*n.*	复制品
		a.	复制的
		vt.	复制
dwell	[dwel]	*vi.*	居留；居住，单居（at，in）
dyestuff	['daistʌf]	*n.*	染料

E

efficient	[i'fiʃ ənt]	*n.*	效率，功效
efficiently	[i'fiʃ əntli]	*ad.*	有效率地，有效地
elastic	[i'læstik]	*a.*	弹性的，有弹力的
electrode	[i'lektrəud]	*n.*	电极
electromechanical control			机电控制
electromechanical Department			机电系
electronic governor			电子调速器
electronic pathway			电子线路
eliminate	[i'limineit]	*vt.*	消除，排除；切断，分离
elliptical type spring			双弓式板簧
embrittle	[em'britl]	*v.*	使变脆
emerge	[i'mə:dʒ]	*vi.*	出现，形成
encoder	[in'kəudə]	*n.*	编码器
encompass	[in'kʌmpəs]	*v.*	包含或包括某事物
enterprise	['entəpraiz]	*n.*	事业，计划；企 [事] 业单位，公司
enunciate	[i'nʌnsieit]	*vt.*	（清晰地）发音；确切地说明
environment	[in'vaiərənmənt]	*n.*	环境，围绕，周围状况
equipment	[i'kwipmənt]	*n.*	设备；装备；配备；技能
establish	[is'tæbliʃ]	*vt.*	建立，成立；安置
evaporate	[i'væpəreit]	*v.*	（使）蒸发
evolve	[i'vɔlv]	*vt.*	（使）逐渐形成
except that			除……之外
exclusive	[iks'klu:siv]	*a.*	专用的；独家的
execute	['eksikju:t]	*vt.*	执行，实现；使生效
exhibition	[ˌeksi'biʃ ən]	*n.*	展览，展览会
extensive	[iks'tensiv]	*a.*	广泛的，广大的

F

fabric	['fæbrik]	*n.*	织物

fabricate	['fæbrikeit]	*vt.*	制作，装配，组合
facet	['fæsit]	*n.*	（宝石或首饰的）小平面，面
facing sand			复面砂
fasten	['fɑ:sən]	*vi.*	固定，紧固
face-helical			平面螺纹
fastening	['fɑ:səniŋ]	*n.*	紧固件
fatigue strength			疲劳强度
feasible	['fi:zəbl]	*a.*	可实行的，合理的；
feat	[fi:t]	*n.*	功绩
		a.	合适的，合身的（衣服）
feature	['fi:tʃə]	*n.*	特色
feed	[fi:d]	*vt./n.*	进给，送给
feeder	['fi:də]	*n.*	冒口，送料器
federate	['fedəreit]	*n.*	进给速率
ferrite	['ferait]	*n.*	铁素体
fiction	['fikʃən]	*n.*	虚构，杜撰
filament	['filəmənt]	*n.*	细丝，灯丝
filter out			过滤
Financial Bureau			财政局
Finite element analysis(FEA)			有限元分析
flatness	['flætnis]	*n.*	平面，平面度
flexible	['fleksibl]	*a.*	易弯的
flexible manufacturing system(FMS)			柔性制造系统
flip	[flip]	*vt.*	使翻转，掷
flowrate	['fləureit]	*n.*	流量
fluctuation	[ˌflʌktju'eiʃən]	*n.*	变化，波动
flush	[flʌʃ]	*a.*	齐平的；
		ad.	齐平地；
		vt.	使齐平；
flux	[flʌks]	*n.*	助熔剂，焊剂
flywheel	['flaiwi:l]	*n.*	飞轮
forge	[fɔ:dʒ]	*vt.*	锻造；
		n.	锻造车间；铁匠铺；熔铁炉
four-jaw independent chuck			四爪卡盘
frequence	['fri:kəns]	*n.*	频率
frictional	['frikʃənəl]	*a.*	摩擦的

G

geometry	[dʒi'ɔmitri]	*n.*	几何（学）
go unexplored			不被利用的
governor	['gʌvənə]	*n.*	操纵杆，控制器
granite	['grænit]	*n.*	花岗岩，花岗石
guarantee	[ˌgærən'tiː]	*vt.*	保证；担保
		n.	保证，保障；保证书；保用期

H

hall	[hɔːl]	*n.*	门厅
hardcopy	['hɑːdkɔpi]	*n.*	硬拷贝
hardware	['hɑːdwɛə]	*n.*	零件，附件，硬件
head-stock	['hedˌstɔk]	*n.*	头架，车床头，主轴箱，车头箱
helical	['helikəl]	*a.*	螺旋状的；螺旋线
hence	[hens]	*ad.*	然而，因此
hereafter	[hiər'ɑːftə]	*ad.*	今后，从此以后
hereby	['hiə'bai]	*ad.*	（用于公文件中的）以此方式；特此
hitch	[hitʃ]	*n.*	故障
hollow	['hɔləu]	*a.*	空心的
		n.	洞
hollow clamping cylinder			空心夹紧油缸
honing	['həuniŋ]	*n.*	珩磨
Hooke's law			虎克定律
hydraulic turbine			水力透平机
hype-eutectoid	[haip-juː'tektɔid]	*a.*	亚共析（的），亚共析体

I

identify	[ai'dentifai]	*v.*	识别
imbed	[im'bed]	*vt.*	埋置，把……嵌入
impact	['impækt]	*n.*	冲击，碰撞
impeller	['impelə]	*n.*	叶轮，转子
in a canned cycle			在一个封闭的周期内
in accordance with			按照
in case			万一
in depth	['in'depθ]	*a.*	深入的，彻底的
in direct proportion to			与……成正比

in the main			主要，大体上，总的来说
in-1ine			在线，在管线内
inactive	[in'æktiv]	*a.*	不活动的，不活跃的，停止的
inainhame	[in'æktiv]	*a.*	无生命的；无精打采的，单调的
incorporate	[in'kɔ:pəreit]	*vt.*	结合，使混合
indent	[in'dent]	*vt.*	订货，（向……）正式申请；
		n.	合同，国外订货单
index	['indeks]	*vt.*	记……号码；转换角度
indexing	['indeksiŋ]	*n.*	分度法，指标
indexing jig			回转式钻模
indicate	['indikeit]	*vt.*	指向
indicator	['indikeitə]	*n.*	指示物，指示器
indispensable	[ˌindis'pensəbl]	*a.*	不可缺少的，必需的
individual	[ˌindi'vidjuəl]	*a.*	独立的，个别的
Industrial Fair			工业博览会
inert	[i'nə:t]	*a.*	惰性的
inflame	[in'fleim]	*v.*	（使）燃烧
ingress	['ingres]	*n.*	进入
inherently	[in'hiərəntli]	*ad.*	天生地，本质地
in-process gaging			在线检测
installation	[ˌinstə'leiʃən]	*n.*	安装，设置；就职；装置，设备
installment	[in'stɔ:lmənt]	*n.*	部分；分期付款
instant	['instənt]	*a.*	立即的，直接的
institute	['institju:t]	*vt.*	建立，制定
		n.	协会，学会；学院
interchange	[ˌintə'tʃeindʒ]	*vt.*	交换
interface	['intəˌfeis]	*n.*	接口；界面
interference	[ˌintə'fiərəns]	*n.*	干扰，干涉，阻碍
interference fit			过盈配合，压配合
interference-free			无干扰
interior	[in'tiəriə]	*n./a.*	内部（的）
intermediate	[ˌintə'mi:djət]	*a.*	中间的；中级的
internally	[in'tənəli]	*ad.*	内部
invade	[in'veid]	*vt.*	拥入，占领
in the realm of			在……领域里
inventory	['inventəri]	*n.*	财产等的清单，详细目录，存货清单；
		vt.	把……编入目录

invest in			投资
investment	[in'vestmənt]	*n.*	投资
invoice	['invɔis]	*vt.*	开……的发票
is consists of			由……组成

J

jaw	[dʒɔ:]	*n.*	卡爪，虎钳牙
jig	[dʒig]	*n.*	夹具，钻模
jog feedrate override			点动进给倍率
join	[dʒɔin]	*vt.*	连接，结合
joint	[dʒɔint]	*n.*	接缝，接合处
joint-hinged			铰 [链] 接合，铰 [链] 接头
just about			几乎

K

key	[ki:]	*n.*	键，钥匙
knit	[nit]	*v.*	编织

L

labor cost			劳动力成本
lathe	[leið]	*n.*	车床
lead time			交货时间，交货期，生产周期
leaflet	['li:flit]	*n.*	传单，散页印刷品
leakage	['li:kidʒ]	*n.*	泄漏
legible	['ledʒəbl]	*a.*	清晰的，易读的
level switch			（信号）液位开关
linear	['liniə]	*a.*	线性的，直线的
linkage	['liŋkidʒ]	*n.*	连接；结合；联系；联动装置
literally	['litərəli]	*ad.*	严格地，字面上地
live center			主轴顶尖
load	[ləud]	*vt.*	装载；负荷，负载
locating	[ləu'keitiŋ]	*n.*	定位（法）
loosen	['lu:sən]	*vt./vi.*	解开，放松，松开，松弛
lubricating oil			润滑油
lubricity	[lju:'brisəti]	*n.*	润滑性能

M

machine centers			加工中心
machine tool			机床，工具机
machinist	[məʃi:nist]	*n.*	机械师，机械工人
magnitude	[ˈmægnitju:d]	*n.*	大小，积，量，长（度）；巨大；重要性
magnitude	[ˈmægnitju:d]	*n.*	大小，量
maintain	[menˈtein]	*vt.*	保持；继续；保养，维护；坚持；主张
maintenance	[ˈmeintənəns]	*n.*	维护，保持
manipulator	[məˈnipjuleitə]	*n.*	操作者，操纵者，操纵器
manual	[ˈmænjuəl]	*a.*	用手的，手工的
		n.	手册，指南
manuscript	[ˈmænjuskript]	*n.*	手稿，原稿，底稿
marine	[məˈri:n]	*a.*	海产的，海生的
		n.	海军陆战队士兵
martensite	[ˈma:tənzəit]	*n.*	马氏体
mate	[meit]	*v.*	配合，配成对；
		n.	配对物
memorandum	[ˌmeməˈrændəm]	*n.*	（备忘的）记录；非正式商业书信，便函
memory	[ˈmeməri]	*n.*	存储；存储器；记忆装置
merely	[ˈmiəli]	*ad.*	仅仅，只不过
metalwork	[ˈmetəlwə:k]	*n.*	金属加工（制造）
metrologist	[miˈtrɔlədʒist]	*n.*	计量师
metrology	[miˈtrɔlədʒi]	*n.*	计量学，计量制
microcomputer	[ˈmaikrəukəmˈpju:tə]	*n.*	微机
micrometer	[maiˈkrɔmitə]	*n.*	测微器，千分尺
microprocessor	[ˌmaikrəuˈprəusesə]	*n.*	微处理器
microstructure	[ˈmaikrəuˈstrʌktʃə]	*n.*	显微结构
mill	[mil]	*n.*	铣刀，铣床，铣
Milliamps(mA)	[miliˈæmps]	*n.*	毫安
milling	[ˈmiliŋ]	*n.*	铣（削），铣削法；铣出的齿边
milling machine			铣床
minus	[ˈmainəs]	*a.*	负的，减去的
		n.	负量，负号
mobile phone			移动电话
modify	[ˈmɔdifai]	*vt.*	修改
molybdenum	[məˈlibdinəm]	*n.*	钼

molybdenum wire			钼丝
monitor	['mɔnitə]	*n.*	监视器；检测器
		vt.	监视；检测
mould	[məuld]	*n.*	模型，铸型，压模
moulding box			砂箱
multifarious	[ˌmʌlti'fɛəriəs]	*a.*	许多的，多方面的；各式各样的
multimedia	['mʌlti'mi:djə]	*n.*	多媒体
multimeter	['mʌltiˌmi:tə]	*n.*	万用表
municipal	[mju:'nisipəl]	*a.*	市的，市政的
muting machine			特型铣床
mutual	['mju:tʃuəl]	*a.*	相互的，彼此的；共同的，共有的

N

negotiation	[niˌgəuʃi'eiʃən]	*n.*	协商，谈判
nominal	['nɔminəl]	*a.*	公称的，名义上的
non-elastic			非弹性的
notation	[nəu'teiʃən]	*n.*	符号，标志
nozzle	['nɔzl]	*n.*	管嘴，喷嘴

O

off-load			卸荷
opportunity	[ˌɔpə'tju:niti]	*n.*	机会
option	['ɔpʃən]	*n.*	选项
orifice	['ɔrifis]	*n.*	节流孔，小孔
original	[ə'ridʒənəl]	*a.*	最初的，原始的
overheat	[ˌəuvə'hi:t]	*vt.*	过热
overlap	['əuvə'læp]	*v.*	重叠，相交，（部分）一致
overload	['əuvə'ləud]	*n.*	过载
overload trip			超载脱扣
oxidation	[ɔksi'deiʃən]	*n.*	氧化
oxide coating			氧化膜

P

pallet	['pælit]	*n.*	棘爪，货盘
parity	['pæriti]	*n.*	同等，对等 [物] 宇称（性），奇偶性
parting operation			分离操作
parting sand			分型砂

patent	[ˈpeitənt]	*n.*	专利（权）
pattern	[ˈpætən]	*n.*	模型，试样，图案
pearlite	[ˈpəːlait]	*n.*	珠光体
perform	[pəˈfɔːm]	*vt./vi.*	执行；履行
performance	[pəˈfɔːməns]	*n.*	履行，执行
permanent	[ˈpəːmənənt]	*a.*	永久的，固定的，恒定的
perpendicularity	[ˌpəːˌpəndikjuˈlæriti]	*n.*	垂直度
pertaining to			适合
pick up			探测出
pin	[pin]	*n.*	销，钉
piping	[ˈpaipiŋ]	*n.*	管道
plastic	[ˈplæstik]	*a.*	可塑的，塑性的，塑料的
plate jig			盖板式钻模
plotter	[ˈplɔtə]	*n.*	密谋策划者；搞阴谋的人；描绘器，图形显示器，绘图器
plus	[plʌs]	*a.*	正的，略大的；正量
pneumatic	[njuːˈmætik]	*a.*	气动的，空气的
pneumatic control			气动控制
pocket	[ˈpɔkit]	*n.*	袋，口袋
		vt.	把……装入袋内
		a.	袖珍的；小型的
portion	[ˈpɔːʃən]	*n.*	部分，段
potentiometer	[pəˌtenʃiˈɔmitə]	*n.*	电位计，分压计
power shift gear			动力滑移齿轮
power-transmission-element			传递动力的零件
precede	[priːˈsiːd]	*vt./vi.*	在……之先[前]，领先于，在……之上；比……重要；在……前加上；为……加上引言（by，with）
precision	[priˈsiʒən]	*n.*	精确度，准确（性）
predict	[priˈdikt]	*v.*	预言
prefix	[ˈpriːfiks]	*n.*	〈语〉前缀
pressure relay			压力继电器
pretension	[priːˈtenʃən]	*n.*	预拉伸，预应力
process annealing			工序间退火
product quality			产品质量
productivity	[ˌprɔdʌkˈtivəti]	*n.*	生产率，生产力
profile	[ˈprəufail]	*n.*	轮廓，外形

profit	['prɔfit]	*n.*	利润，收益，赢利；益处，得益
proliferate	[prəu'lifəreit]	vt	繁殖，扩散
proportional	[prəu'pɔːʃənəl]	*a.*	成比例的
proprietary	[prəu'praiətəri]	*vt.*	先占有，先取
proximity switch			接近开关
pulley	['puli]	*n.*	皮带轮
pulsative	['pʌlsətiv]	*a.*	脉动的，跳动的
pump	[pʌmp]	*n.*	泵
		vt.	用泵抽吸扰.间歇地喷出
push button switch			按钮开关

Q

quality	['kwɔləti]	*n.*	质，质量；品质，特征，特性
quantity	['kwɔntəti]	*n.*	数目，数量
quotation	[kwəu'teiʃən]	*n.*	引用，引述；引文，；时价，报价

R

ram	[ræm]	*vt.*	锤击，夯紧；
		n.	伸杆，滑枕，夯
rapid traverse			快速进给，快速行程
ratio	['reiʃiəu]	*n.*	比，比率
reassemble	['riːə'sembl]	*vt.*	重新组合，重新装配
recess	[ri'ses]	*vt.*	开槽；隐藏，使……凹进去
recondition	['riːkən'diʃən]	*vt.*	再生，重磨
re-direction *n.*			改变方向
refine	[ri'fain]	*v.*	细化，改善，精炼
register	['redʒistə]	*vt./vi.*	记录；登记；注册
regulate	['regjuleit]	*vt.*	控制
relay	['riːlei]	*n.*	继电器
relay module			继电模块
release	[ri'liːs]	*vt.*	发表，释放
renovate	['renəuveit]	*vt.*	翻新；修复；整修
representation	[ˌreprizen'teiʃən]	*n.*	（总称）代表，代表制；代理
representative	[ˌrepri'zentətiv]	*n.*	代表，代理人
resizing	[ri'saiziŋ]	*n.*	尺寸再生
responsible	[ri'spɔnsəbl]	*a.*	有责任的，（应）负责任的
restriction	[ri'strikʃən]	*n.*	节流

restrictor	[ris'triktə]	*n.*	节流阀
resultant	[ri'zʌltənt]	*n.*	合力；
		v.	组合的，合成的
retain	[ri'tein]	*vt.*	保持，保留
reversal	[ri'və:səl]	*n.*	反向，反转，倒转；运气不好
revision	[ri'viʒən]	*n.*	修正，修改
rigid coupling			刚性联轴器
robot	['rəubɔt]	*n.*	机器人
roller	['rəulə]	*n.*	滚压机；滚杠，滚柱；定型卷夹
rotor	['rəutə]	*n.*	轮子，旋转器 [物] 旋度

S

sandwich-type machining			双面加工
sapphire	['sæfaiə]	*n.*	蓝宝石，蔚蓝色
sawing machine			锯床
schedule	['ʃədju:əl]	*n.*	时间表，日程安排表
science fiction			科学幻想
screw machine			车丝机
sculpt	[skʌlpt]	*vt.*	雕刻
seal	[si:l]	*n.*	密封垫
sectionalize	['sekʃənəlaiz]	*vt.*	分段，分布
sediment	['sedimənt]	*n.*	沉淀（物）
segment	['segmənt]	*n.*	部分，片段；瓣； [计] 程序段
selector switch			选择开关
sensor	['sensə]	*n.*	传感器
sequential	[si'kwenʃəl]	*a.*	按次序的，相继的，构成连续镜头的
set up			建立，产生，引起，安装
severity	[si'veriti]	*n.*	严格，严厉，恶劣
shaper	['ʃeipə]	*n.*	牛头刨床
shear	[ʃiə]	*vt./ n.*	剪力，切应变，剪床
shrinkage	['ʃrinkidʒ]	*n.*	收缩，缩水
sign	[sain]	*n.*	标记，符号
silicon	['silikən]	*n.*	[化] 硅
simulation	[ˌsimju'leiʃən]	*n.*	模仿；模拟
simultaneous	[ˌsiməl'teiniəs]	*a.*	同时发生的；同时存在的
single throw			单掷开关
slide	[slaid]	*v.*	滑动；

		n.	滑板，滑块
snapshot	['snæpʃɔt]	*n.*	快照
soak	[səuk]	*v./n.*	浸，泡
solder	['sɔldə]	*n.*	焊料
soldering	['sɔldəriŋ]	*n.*	锡焊，软钎焊
soldering copper			纯铜铬铁
solicit	[sə'lisit]	*vt./vi.*	恳求，请求，乞求
solidification	[ˌsɔlidifi'keiʃən]	*n.*	凝固，固化
spare part			备件
specification	[ˌspesifi'keiʃən]	*n.*	规定，技术要求，规范
specimen	['spesimin]	*n.*	样本，试样，试件
spelter	['speltə]	*n.*	硬钎焊料，锌铜焊料
spelter solder			硬焊料
sphericity	[sfe'risiti]	*n.*	球（形）度，成球形
spheroidal	['sfiərɔidl]	*a.*	类似球体的
spindle	['spindl]	*n.*	心轴，主轴
spray-painting			喷漆
sprinkle	['spriŋkl]	*n./v.*	洒，喷
sprocket	['sprɔkit]	*n.*	链轮
squareness	[skwεənis]	*n.*	垂直度，方（形）
stage	[steidʒ]	*n.*	阶段，步骤
stall	[stɔ:l]	*vt.*	停住，发生故障
standardize	['stændədaiz]	*vt.*	使标准化，使规格化
standardized	['stændəˌdaizd]	*a.*	标准化的
stearine	['sti:ərin]	*n.*	甘油，硬脂
step out			失步，不同步
stepper motor			步进电机
stipulate	['stipjuleit]	*vt.*	（尤指在协议或建议中）规定，约定
straightness	['streitnis]	*n.*	直线度
strain	[strein]	*n.*	应变，拉紧，张力，变形
strategy	['strætidʒi]	*n.*	战略，策略
stress	[stres]	*n.*	应力
strip	[strip]	*v.*	剥去
stylus	['stailəs]	*n.*	笔尖，唱针
sub-circuit	['sʌb'səkit]	*n.*	支路
subcritical annealing			亚临界退火
subject	['sʌbdʒikt]	*vt.*	使受到

subsequent	[ˈsʌbsikwənt]	*a.*	随后的，后来的
superior	[sjuːˈpiriə]	*a.*	（级别、地位）较高的；（品质、程度）优良的，较好的
supervision	[ˌsjuːpəˈviʒən]	*n.*	监督，管理
surpass	[səːˈpɑːs]	*vt.*	超过，优于
synchronize	[ˈsiŋkrənaiz]	*vt./vi.*	（使）同步；（使）同速进行
synthetic	[sinˈθetik]	*a.*	合成的，人工制造的

T

tail-stock	[ˈteilstɔk]	*n.*	尾架，尾座
take advantage of			利用
tapered key			斜键
technician	[tekˈniʃən]	*n.*	技术人员，专家；技巧好的人
technique	[tekˈniːk]	*n.*	技巧，手法
technology	[tekˈnɔlədʒi]	*n.*	科技（总称）；工艺；工业技术
temporarily	[ˈtempərərili]	*ad.*	临时
tendency to +inf .			……的倾向（趋势）
tensile	[ˈtensail]	*a.*	拉力的，抗拉的，能拉伸的
tension	[ˈtenʃən]	*n.*	张力，拉力
term	[təːm]	*n.*	术语；
		vt.	把……称为
terminate	[ˈtəːmineit]	*vt./vi.*	使终止；解除（契约等）
terminology	[ˌtəːmiˈnɔlədʒi]	*n.*	术语，专门名词
territory	[ˈteritəri]	*n.*	领域，范围
the sequence of operations			工序
the substitution of A for B			A 取代 B
theoretical	[ˌθiəˈretikəl]	*a.*	理论的
three jaw universal chuck			三爪万能卡盘
thumbwheel	[θʌmhwiːl]	*n.*	拨轮
tighten	[ˈtaitən]	*vt.*	使变紧
timer	[ˈtaimə]	*n.*	定时器，计时员
time-saving			省时的
to act on			作用于
to bring about			引起，产生，导致
to speak of			提到，谈到
tool post			刀座，刀架
transaction	[trænˈzækʃən]	*n.*	（一笔）交易；（一项）事务

transport	[træns'pɔ:t]	*vt.*	运送；流放
		n.	运输，运输工具
tremendous	[tri'mendəs]	*a.*	惊人的，非常的
triangular	[trai'æŋgjulə]	*a.*	三角形的
trigonometry	[trigə'nɔmitri]	*n.*	三角法
troubleshooting	['trʌbl'ʃu:tiŋ]	*n.*	发现并修理故障，故障检查
tumble	['tʌmbl]	*n.*	翻滚
tumble jig			翻转式钻模
turbine	['tə:bain]	*n.*	涡轮机
turn	[tə:n]	*vt.*	旋转，车削
turn out			生产，制造
turning	['tə:niŋ]	*n.*	车削
turret (=turret head)	['tʌrit]	*n.*	（机床刀具）转塔，六角（转）头
twin-turret			双塔刀架
turret lathe center			转塔式车削中心
typically	[`tipikəli]	*ad.*	典型地，具有代表性地

U

ultraviolet	['ʌltrə'vaiələt]	*a.*	紫外（线）的
undergo	[ˌʌndə'gəu]	*vt.*	经历，承受；遭受
undesirable	['ʌndi'zaiərəbl]	*a.*	不合需要的
undulating	['ʌndjuleitiŋ]	*a.*	波浪形的，起伏的
unexplored	[ˌʌnlik'splɔ:d]	*a.*	未被利用的，未开发的
uniform	['ju:nifɔ:m]	*n.*	制服
		a.	全都相同的
unilateral	['ju:ni'lætərəl]	*a.*	单向的
unload	['ʌn'ləud]	*v.*	卸载
unmanageable	[ʌn'mænidʒəbl]	*a.*	难管理的
upstream	['ʌp'stri:m]	*a.*	上游的

V

valve	[vælv]	*n.*	阀
variant	['vɛəriənt]	*a.*	不同的，各种各样的
variation	[ˌvɛəri'eiʃən]	*n.*	变化，变动
vaseline	['væzili:n]	*n.*	凡士林
vector	['vektə]	*n.*	矢量，向量
verticality	[ˌvə:ti'kæləti]	*n.*	垂直性，垂直状态

via	[ˈvaiə]	*prep.*	经过，经由
vibration	[vaiˈbreiʃ ən]	*n.*	振动
viscosity	[viˈskɔsəti]	*n.*	粘性
viscosity index			粘度指数
viscous	[ˈviskəs]	*a.*	粘性的
vitally	[ˈvaitəli]	*ad.*	非常
voltage	[ˈvəultidʒ]	*n.*	电压，伏特数
volumetric	[vɔljuˈmetrik]	*a.*	（测）容量的

W

warranty	[ˈwɔrənti]	*n.*	保证书，保单；授权
wastage	[ˈweistidʒ]	*n.*	损耗，损失
wear	[ˈwɛə]	*n./vi.*	磨损，损坏
welding	[ˈweldiŋ]	*n.*	焊接，熔接
whatnot	[hwɔtnɔt]	*n.*	类似的东西；诸如此类的东西
winding	[ˈwaindiŋ]	*n.*	线圈，绕组
wireframe			网线框架
wiring machine			金属丝接合机
wiring out			布线图
wobble	[ˈwɔbl]	*vi.*	摇晃，摇摆
woodruff key			半圆键
work handing			工件传送
workpiece	[ˈwə:kpi:s]	*n.*	工件
wrapping	[ˈræpiŋ]	*n.*	缠绕

Z

zinc chloride			氯化锌

Appendix VII Reference Translation

参考译文

第 1 课 力既有大小又有方向

也许解释一个力的最简单方法就是说它是推或拉。然而，当我们提及一个使物体产生运动的力时，如果我们想知道它所引起的结果，单纯说出它的大小是不够的。因此，如果有两个等同大小的拉力，它们产生的合力将取决于它们作用的方向。用 10 千克的力直接向上拉一个物体与用同等大小的力从一边拉同一物体，物体产生的位置变化是完全不同的。力是一个矢量，也就是它既有大小又有方向。为了说明任何一个力的效果，我们一定要既知道它的大小，也要知道它的方向。

通常两个力同时作用在一个物体上。在这种情况下，弄清这两个力的合力，即这两个合成而产生的作用，往往是有益的。如果两个分开的力作用于同一方向，则很容易找到其合力。两个力相加的大小就是合力的大小。

也有的情况是作用于同一个物体上的两个力的方向相反。如果两个人同时想要同一物体，并在相反的方向拉它，物体的运动方向总会朝着施加较大力的那个人的方向。拔河比赛就是这样两个力的例子。在这种情况下，为了确定合力的大小，必须从较大的力中减去较小的力。

有时，也许有两个以上的力同时作用于一个物体上。在这种情况下，只能通过具体地分析每个力的大小和它们作用的角度来得知它们产生的合力。因此，大小和方向是确定力所产生的作用的两个不可缺少的依据。

重量和质量

你知道重量是什么吗？重量是万有引力作用在物体上产生的。如果万有引力变化，则物体的重量也变化。而组成物体的物质多少，也就是物体的质量则不会发生变化。

如果一袋糖在地球上重 6 千克，在月球上会多重呢？在月球上，它重量将会是1千克，是在地球上的重量的 1/6。

在地球上，我们通常说重量和质量好像是一回事。我们用重量作为测量物体质量的一个方法。在地球上这是非常方便的：在加利福尼亚重量为 6 千克的糖，在夏威夷、加拿大或德国也将是大约 6 千克。这是因为在每个地方万有引力实际上都是一样的。

只要我们待在地球上，用重量来测量物体的质量还是很有效的。然而，现在人们已离开过地球了。突然，我们意识到重量和质量不是一回事!离开地球，万有引力就发生了变化。

随着万有引力的变化，重量也会变，可是物体的质量在宇宙的任何地方，无论在地球上，在月球上，在宇宙飞船上或是在火星上，它都是保持相同的。

你对为什么在月球上的引力是在地球上的 1/6 感到过奇怪吗？它的原因是这样的，物体的质量越大，它所受的引力越大，质量越小，则引力也越小。月亮的质量比地球小。由于月亮的质量比地球小得多，所以它的万有引力也比地球小得多。

记住质量和重量之间的区别是重要的。质量是与包含的物质的量相关的一个基本物理学概念，而重量是比质量更为复杂的一个概念，它不仅涉及物质的量，而且还和地球的万有引力有关。

第 2 课　机器人

不久前，我们只是在看一本连环画或一部像“星球大战”这样的电影时，才能看到机器人。然而，今天科学幻想正迅速地变成科学现实。在我们的日常生活中，我们开始感受到机器人的存在。这些机器人具有各种尺寸、形状和颜色。它们都有相同类型的“大脑”——嵌在成千上万的电路中的微小硅片。这样的硅片也用作微机的大脑。

工厂机器人：但是机器人可比微机能做的事情要多。它们不仅能“思考”，而且还能感知，做出反应，并且能改变它们周围的事物。

工业机器人可完成各种各样通常是枯燥，有时甚至危险的工作。这些工作包括装卸机械，喷漆和电弧焊。

机器人非常擅长做这些工作以至于到 1990 年止，仅在美国就可能有 10 000 到 20 000 的机器人努力地工作着。美国汽车工人联合会预言，到那时装配线上的工人数将会减少一半。

家庭机器人：机器人也正步入美国的家庭。尽管不像它们进入到工厂那样快。这些机器人不如“星球大战”中的那些机器人那么使人称心和能干。但是，它们的制造者声称：当今的家庭机器人能走路（实际上是滚动），能感受到它们前方的物品（有时也撞上它们），甚至能搬运物品（有时也会把物品掉在地上）。哎，人无完人嘛。

今天，我们也许会取笑家庭机器人，但是将来总有一天，它们的听觉和视觉也许比人类的更好。我们人类只能看到某些波长的光，听到某些频率的声音。那是因为我们的眼睛和耳朵都有局限性。然而，机器人不必有和我们一样的局限性。机器人还可以装上传感器，探测出人类无法感受到的无线电波或紫外线光。

工业机器人的应用

工业机器人是具有某种拟人化特征，通用、可编程的机器。它们在具有下列特征的场合中应用，是较为经济实用的。

1. 危险的工作环境。在对于人类操作者有潜在危险的工作条件下，或是工作地点很热或不舒适的情况下，就可选用工业机器人来完成这项工作。

2. 重复性工作。即使工作循环很长并包含着许多依次进行的分离动作，工业机器人也能完成，其条件是每个工作循环的动作程序不能变。

3. 重工件的移动。一些工业机器人可以举起几百千克的物体。

由工业机器人来完成的工作任务包含下列更典型的应用场合:

零件的搬运：许多各种各样把工件从一个位置移动到另一个位置的搬运工作。

机械的装卸：这些生产设备的类型包括冲压设备，锻压设备，模铸设备及大多数金属切削机床。

喷漆：将喷嘴连到机器手并对它编好程序，使其通过一系列顺序动作来完成喷漆操作。

焊接：包括点焊和连续焊。

装配：在简单的机械装配中，机器人完成的工作基本上是搬运动作的扩展。

第 3 课　计算机绘图的好处

用计算机完成绘图及设计任务的好处是令人难忘的：提高速度、提高准确性、减少硬拷贝存储空间及易于恢复信息、加强信息传输能力、改善传输质量和便于修改。

速度

工业用计算机能以平均每秒 3300 万次操作完成一项任务；新型计算机的速度更快。用敲竹杠，计算零件的变形量是一个重要功绩。当理论上的载荷力加到零件上时、通过计算机进行有限元分析或者在监视器上显示一个城市的整体规划时，这两者都是费时又计算时在的任务。AutoCAD 软件可根据需要多次复制所需模型的开关和几何尺寸，快速自动地进行剖面填充及尺寸标。

准确

AutoCAD 程序依靠操作系统及计算机平台每点具有 14 位的精度。这在用数学计算诸如一个圆的线段数、程序必须圆整线段数时是十分重要的。

存储

计算机能够在物理空间中存储上千幅图，这空间能够存储上百幅手工图。而且计算机能够很容易地搜索和找到一幅图，只要操作者拥有正确的文件名。

传输

由于计算机的数据是以电子形式存储，它能被送到各种位置。最明显的位置是监视器。计算机可以在屏幕上以不同的方式显示数据，如图形，并能方便地将数据转换成可读图形。这些数据也可被传送给绘图机，打印出常见的图纸，通过直接连接到计算机辅助制造机床或由电话线传到地球的任何地方。你可以不再冒损坏或丢失的危险去邮寄图纸，现在图纸可以通过电信网立即发送到目的地。

质量

计算机总是从最初生成的数据形式保存数据。它可以不顾疲劳的不断重复同一个数据输出。线型将总是鲜明和清晰的，具有一致的线宽，而文本也总是清晰明了的。计算机不会改变输出质量，因为计算机不会像人那样因周末的郊游或深夜观看娱乐节目而疲劳。

修改

计算机以某种便于修改的形式存储数据并且不断地提供反馈给用户。某些图形一旦画成，它就不必再画，因为物体可以被复制、延伸、改变尺寸，并且在不重画的情况下，可以多种形式加以修改。

除了最初购买 CAD 工作站的花费，CAD 的唯一缺点也是很小的因为它很容易克服。由于图形是以电子格式存储而不是纸介质格式，所以有可能会容易地删除绘图文件。这就是为什么强调要培养自己一个好的绘图习惯以避免意外地删除绘图文件。

计算机辅助设计

计算机辅助设计给了设计者去尝试几个可行的解决方案的能力。通常还需要某些形式的设计分析计算，而为了这一任务已经编写了许多程序。计算机为设计者所建议的各种结构设计的分析和为最终设计准备正式绘图提供了强有力的工具。

在二维绘图领域中，计算机方法能够提供比传统的纸和笔的方法更有意义、更大成本节约的优点，但是一个 CAD 系统并不仅仅是一个电子绘图板。计算机绘图系统可以使设计者设计出既快又准确的图形，并且很容易修改。当涉及重复性工作时，会戏剧性的产生复制产品，因为标准图形只要一次构建成功，就可以从图库中取出。剪切和粘贴技术作为节约劳动力的辅助工具被使用。当几个分项目设计人员从事同一个工程时，要建立中心数据库，使得由某一个人绘制的细节图可以很容易地合并到其他不同的装配图中。中心数据也可以作为标准参考零件库使用。

有限元是一项成熟的应力分析技术，它多被土木工程和机械工程所采用。它由将结构划分成有限个小单元所组成，计算每一个单元之间的作用力。如果被分割的单元足够小，就能对一个结构或实体的内部应力获得一个好的估计。这些计算机技术惯用于大型结构物的设计，诸如船体、桥梁、飞机机身和海面油井平台。汽车工业也使用类似的方法来设计和制造车身。

第 4 课　水切割

毫无疑问水有很多种用途，但你曾经想过用水作为一种液体刀具吗？

最近实验表明和电剧或激光机床一样，喷射的水流真的能够切割金属——铝、花岗岩和几乎所有的其他的材料。这项技术的发现是一个名叫莫亨·维杰的博士，他是印度科学家，加拿大国家研究理事会理事，他用水的射流来切削，工具刃口是高压水流。它能产生 150 千瓦的能量，喷射的水流能迅速地切割大多数材料而不留下任何残留物，对被切割物没有任何影响。

“水刀的工业用途是广泛的”维杰博士说，“尽管水刀在我们周围已经超过十年了，提来高压水泵的发展使这些刀具成为可能，比以前更经济可行”，他说。

他们已经广泛用于坚硬的清洁工作（就像近海的石油钻井敲打海洋生物），这种水切割在采矿工业中也逐渐开始使用。在建造业，当建筑物被拆除时，在一些国家正在使用的喷射切割机，通过具体切片进行处理特别是废墟的处理。

但水刀也可以处理需要更多技巧的工作。准确地切割皮草，铝，壁板，橡胶，以及其他材料的精密仪器已经被开发出来，他说。仪器的喷嘴是由人造蓝宝石组成的，如同一个小玻璃珠测量直径小于 0.076 毫米。

维杰博士说，从这种喷嘴喷射出的水流可以像刀刃一样切割大部分金属材料，却没有在机械加工中遇到的许多问题。他说在喷射的水流中没有刃口变钝的现象。

维杰说“一个这样的精密仪器在制造业中有不断增长的需求”。“前景是好的，他们已经有不少的客户，特别是在清洁行业，”他补充说。

开关和保险丝

电源开关常常安放在房门附近的墙上。在房间里，两条导线和室内的灯泡相通，其中的一条导线通向开关。开关能够使这条线断开，那么电灯就会熄灭。开关也能把这条电线的两部分再连上，那么电灯就又亮了。

开关能控制许多不同的东西。小开关可以控制电灯和收音机，因为这些不需要大电流。大开关控制电炉。其他开关可以控制电动机。

优质开关通断灵活，它们必须瞬间将电流切断。如果它们通断的慢，就会产生电火花。电火花能穿越电线两端之间的空间。这是很不安全的，并会使开关变热。非常大的开关有时被放置在油里。火花不能轻易地穿越油，因此开关变得更加安全。

强大的电流会使电线变热。如果电线非常细，即使小电流也会使它变热。电灯中发生的就是这种现象。房间里的电线被某种绝缘体包着。电流不能透过绝缘体流出来，因此电流决不会从一条导线直接流到另一条导线上。但是在旧导线上的绝缘体经常会破裂，那时两条导线内的铜丝就会接触上。如果发生这种情况，可能会产生很大的电流，导线就会变得很热，房屋就有可能着火。

保险丝可以阻止这种麻烦的产生。保险丝只是容易熔化的导线。它被固定在保险盒内。保险盒是由一些不能燃烧的材料制成。强大的电流会使保险丝变热，然后使它熔断。

我们说保险丝“爆”了。导线断了，就没有电流可流动了。因此房子就不会着火；但是由于没有电流，所有的电灯和电炉子也都熄灭了。

当保险丝烧断时，一定是出问题了。我们必须首先找出原因。也许是两根导线接触了。我们必须用新的某种绝缘体把它们包上。然后我们还需找到烧断的保险丝并把它修理好。

当保险丝烧断时，一些人会很生气。因此他们在保险盒里放上一个粗铜丝！当然粗铜丝不会轻易熔断，如果电流突然增大，没有什么能阻止它，粗导线很容易传送电流。

那么房子里的导线也许会变得很热，房子就可能着火。房子里的一些人也许逃出去，他们可能失去生命。因此最好一直使用适当的保险丝。这样将会使得房子里的每个人和每样物品都安全。

第 5 课　多媒体在我们的时代（1）

尽管它的潜力巨大，今天的多媒体，互联网的革命性的机器，与流产的项目有不幸的相似之处。和其他沟通渠道的类型一样，如移动电话，几乎没有在图像里（保留下来）。但是这次，有了 MPFEG-4 这项本月才发布的革命性的通讯标准，这一大好时机就不会白白溜走了（也叫做“M-Peg”）。

总部设在日内瓦的标准化组织（ISO），运动图像专家组 2（MPEG）在 5 年内开发的标准，探索每一个数字环境的可能性。录制好的图像及声音和计算机生成的同时并存；一种新的声音语言以极低的数据速率保证产生的光盘一样的音质，而且多的内容甚至可以根据传输速率和品质进行自我调节。

由 MPEG-4 取得的最大进展可能是观众和听众的需要不再是被动的。在今天 “互动中的视听系统的” 的高度只是用户开始停止正在进行的录像的能力。MPEG-4 是完全不同的：它允许用户进行交互场景内的物体，无论是来自所谓的真实来源，如移动视频，或从合成来源，如计算机，计算机辅助设计输出或电脑产生的漫画。内容作者可以让用户有权修改或删去场面，添加或重新定位对象，或改变对象的行为，例如，在设置框中单击它可以旋转。

也许最迫切需要的 MPEG-4 是防御性的。它在互联网上提供的工具，可以创建统一（和最高质量）的音频和视频编码器和解码器，以应对可能会变成一个无法控制的专有格式纠纷。

例如，用户必须选择不同的视频格式，如 QuickTime（苹果公司，总部位于加州库比提诺 Cupertino），AVI（来自微软公司，位于华盛顿州雷德蒙），和 Real 视频（来自 Real Networks 公司，位于华盛顿西雅图）以及一些令人困惑的音频格式。

多媒体在我们的时代（2）

在 MPEG-4 的所有的新的和有用的特性中，最有趣的也许是它能够将图像和计算机生成的形状建立起一一对应的关系。当形状被做成动画，合成和真实之间的差距可以相当有效地弥合。原则上，任何网孔（目前的 2-D，下一版标准 3-D）可能有它映射到任何图像。少许使用网眼畸变的参数能让静止图像建立起动态的感觉。例如，一个飘动的旗帜。对于更高级的影响，移动视频图像也可以映射到网格。

预先定义的面孔是特别有趣的网格。这是独立运动剧目和一些共同的情感状态的计算模型。

采用 MPEG-4 的文本到语音的界面可以用栩栩如生的面孔生成一个化身——一个数字化的，随时可用来制作替身的人或别的合成物。

脸部的外观可能留给解码器或完成，自定义面部模型可能被下载。网线框架的脸模型也许有若干的表面，甚至人拍的快照也是如此，既然面孔生来是三维的，因此需要一种特别的快照。任何模型上特征，例如嘴唇，眼睛等可以通过与说话同步的特别指令使之栩栩如生。

第 6 课　公差和配合

虽然对于现代工业来说标准化的测量是必不可少的，或许更重要的是显示一个零件的尺寸的设计规格。零件尺寸的这些方面控制着它的特性，和/或零件上的位置或相对于其他零件的位置。虽然如此，零件可以进行互换，并相互配对，形成完整的程序集。本课的目的是介绍公差与配合的基本术语。

极限和配合

因为加工某一个零件到精确的尺寸是不可能，设计者必须指定一个可接受的尺寸范围，将仍然允许零件安装和发挥应有的作用。零件实际零件尺寸必须在可能得到的最大和最小的极限尺寸范围内。

最大极限尺寸和最小极限尺寸的差就是公差，是一个零件尺寸变公化的总量。图纸上的公差经常通过指定一个极限或用加减符号来表示（如图 6-1 所示）。随着加减公差，当加减公差在名义尺寸（真实的理论尺寸）之上和之下时，它叫双边尺寸（对称）。

公差怎样影响零件尺寸的配合

当两个零件配合或在装配中互换，公差尤为重要。看看下面的例子（如图 6-2 所示）。轴必须适合轴承孔，并能够自由地转。轴的直径指定为$1.000^{+0.001}_{-0.001}$。这意味着轴的最大极限是 1.001，最小为 0.999。那么公差是 0.002，对称公差。

轴承孔的最大极限尺寸是 1.001，最小极限尺寸是 0.999。公差还是 0.002。由一个加工车间加工的轴会和另外一个车间使用指定公差加工的轴承相配合吗？如果轴被加工成最大极限尺寸 1.001 而轴承被镗到最小极限尺寸 0.999，两个零件都符合公差要求，但是不能互相配合，因为轴比孔大 0.002。但轴承孔如果以单边公差$1.002^{+0.002}_{-0.000}$来指定，零件就会根据要求配合上。即使轴被做成最大极限尺寸 1.001，轴承孔被加工成最小极限尺寸 1.002，它仍能相互配合。虽然机械师通常不与建立公差和限制有关的规定，你可以通过在这个例子中讨论的过渡公差，很容易地看到如何配合的问题。

配合

配合是指相互配合的两个零件间隙的数量或间隙的量。配合范围可以从相配零件之间存在一定间隙量的间隙配合，变化至要用压力迫使零件装在一起的过盈配合。间隙配合的范围可以从几英寸的百万分之一，如将是一个球或滚动轴承的零部件，到一个速度非常低的驱动，或者控制杆的应用的一个由几千分之一英寸间隙。

机械师非常关心过盈配合，在这种情况下，两个零件通过机械或液压机床被装配在一起。然后相关的摩擦力就会使两个零件保持在一起，不用额外的硬件如键或螺母副。过盈配合时的公差非常关键，如果相配合尺寸相差过大，零件很容易在进行加压配合的过程中被损坏。此外，零件在某种程度上变形。

结果会导致破坏，机械黏合，或在零件被压到一起后要求进行二次操作来校正尺寸，如手工铰孔或珩磨。

尺寸测量

机械师主要考虑长度的测量；也就是在两个点之间直线的距离。长度是定义大部分物体的尺寸单位。宽度和尝试只是长度的另一个名称。机械师测量长度是以基本的线性单位如英寸、毫米和先进的光的波长的测量单位。此外，机械师有时需要测量一个表面和另一个表面的关系，即俗称斜度。和斜度密切相关的方形是真正的垂直度偏离测量方法。一个机械师会以角度测量的基本单位，度，分，秒和弧度来测量角度。

除了长度和角度测量之外，一个机械师也需要测量表面粗糙度，同轴度，直线度和平面度。他或她有时也会接触圆度，球度和直线度。然而，这些更专业的测量技术有不少是在实验室检查员或实验室计量师的领域里，出现在一般的加工车间工作里的很少。

第7课　联轴器，键，轴和弹簧

联轴器是用于连接两个轴。例如，一个联轴器是用来连接一个电机轴和一个机床的轴或出于实际原因，水力透平机和发电机相连接，也用于分段连接一个长轴等。由于这类用途的联轴器其结合状态只是在修理或一般维修时才脱开，故称做固定联轴器。这些需要轴定期脱离的应用被称为离合器。固定联轴器分为两组，刚性联轴器，弹性联轴器。

键是用来防止轴和如齿轮，滑轮，链轮，凸轮，杠杆，飞轮，叶轮等机械零件之间的相对运动。有无数种用于各种设计要求的键（其中有些已标准化）。最常用的键有方键，锥形键，半圆键。

轴是一个旋转轴或固定的轴，通常是圆截面，如齿轮，皮带轮，飞轮，曲柄，链轮及其他动力传动元件被安装在上面。轴可以承受弯曲、拉伸、压缩或扭转载荷，作用的载荷既可以是单一的，也可以是复合的。当他们被结合起来，人们可以期望发现静态和疲劳的强度是很重要的设计考虑，因为一个轴可能同时承受到作用在它上面的静态压力，完全相反的压力，重复的压力。单词“轴”包括许多变化，如轴，主轴。轴是一个轴，无论是静止或旋转，不会受到扭转载荷的影响。一个短的旋转轴常常被叫做主轴。

机械弹簧用机器使力，以提供灵活性，并存储吸收能量。一般来说，弹簧可以被分为钢丝弹簧或平板弹簧，虽然有在这些界限有些变化。钢丝弹簧包括螺旋弹簧，圆形，方形，或特殊截面弹簧钢丝，用以抵制拉伸，压缩或扭转载荷。平板弹簧包括悬臂和椭圆形，时钟类型的弹簧和平板弹簧通常被叫做蝶形弹簧。

应力和应变

当材料受载荷作用时，在材料的内部会产生一个平衡力，这种内部作用力叫做应力。通常认为应力类型有拉伸应力，压缩应力和剪切应力。当材料处于应力状态下时，它的尺寸将会产生变化。拉伸应力会使材料的长度变长，而压缩应力将会缩短材料的长度。拉伸应力和压缩应力叫做正应力。由应力引起的尺寸变化叫做应变。

在弹性状态下，当材料受到应力时，材料内部所产生的应变会在应力去除时立即完全消除。某些材料在很高的应力下仍显示弹性，而其他材料即使有的话也只是具有极少的弹性。1678 年，虎克发表了虎克定律：应变与引起应变的应力成正比。虎克定律对于大多数材料在某种限度内都适用。

图 7-1 是一种金属在拉应力下的力与材料伸展关系曲线图。从曲线的第一段 OA 可以看出试样的伸长量与加在这个试样上的载荷大小成正比，可见，应变与应力成正比。虎克定律不适用超出 A 点以外的范围。在 OA 范围内材料状态是弹性的。超出 A 点材料完全弹性的伸展停止了，产生了一些永久应变。非弹性的永久应变叫塑性应变。A 点就是弹性极限。

第 8 课 普通碳素钢的退火和正火

工序间退火是指在惰性气体中，把经过冷加工的低碳钢（带钢、钢板和线材）加热到 550~600℃，也就是其下临界温度以下，所以，工序间退火又叫："在临界温度以下退火。"接下来的冷却速度并不重要，但是要避免钢和空气接触以防止钢被氧化。工序间退火比完全退火要便宜，因为后者是在更高的温度即在上临界温度以上来完成的。

完全退火是使亚共析钢成为最软状态的热处理方法；其显微结构得到完全细化，达到很高的塑性。完全退火是把钢加热到其上临界温度以上大约 30℃，然后慢慢地冷却（例如放在炉子里）。

完全退火通常用于使热加工亚共析钢和铸铁软化并使其颗粒细化。浸泡时间依据零件的厚度（例如：每厘米可用 20 分钟），热处理的温度随含碳量的不同而不同。如下所示：

碳	百分比	0.1	0.2	0.3	0.5	0.7	0.8
温度	摄氏度	900	860	830	810	780	770

正火是对低、中碳钢（即含碳量少于 0.6%的材料）进行的热处理。对于材料而言处于

最软状态（即经完全退火后的性能）不能符合需要的时候，用正火可使材料达到最佳机械性能的组合。

正火是把钢加热到其上临界温度以上约 30℃（也就是和完全退火的加热温度一样），但是接下来要在静止的空气中冷却。更快的冷却的速度（和完全退火相比），使珠光体细化，铁素体颗粒变小，使钢的硬度和强度有所提高。然而，在正火钢中实际获得的性能会随着零件截面厚度不同而不同，大的正火零件也许与那些小零件经完全退火后性能相类似。

普通碳素钢的淬火和回火

含碳量低于 0.3%的钢不能有效地被硬化，而含碳量约 0.8%的钢可获得最高硬度。含碳量超过 0.8%时，在淬火结构中残留的奥氏体有增加趋势，此奥氏体会抵消掉马氏体所提高的硬度，因此，最后的硬度与含碳量为 0.8%的钢所达到的硬度几乎一样。

亚共析钢的淬火是加热到其上临界温度以上 30~50℃，在这个温度上保持一段时间（每厘米厚约 20 分钟），接下来在水中淬火。然而，过共析钢不按上面的规则处理。如果过共析钢在其 Ac3 温度以上淬火，那么游离渗碳体将会在奥氏体颗粒边界沉淀下来，这会使钢脆化。处理这些钢的第一步是通过热加工（例如：锻造），来确保游离渗碳体作为微小颗粒散布在结构中。然后把钢加热到其下临界温度以上约 30℃，保持此温度一段时间后再淬火使钢变硬。这种热处理产生一种渗碳体散布在以马氏体为基体中的球状颗粒显微结构。

回火：淬硬的钢可通过将其加热到 200~700℃范围内进行回火。这种处理将会去除材料在淬火过程中所产生的内应力，去除部分或全部硬度，并增加材料的韧性。

第 9 课　软钎焊和硬钎焊

将金属连接在一起的方法很多，选用哪种方法要取决于金属的类别和所要求的接缝强度。

软钎焊能使薄的钢件、铜件或黄铜件获得合乎要求的接缝，但软钎焊的接缝强度比硬钎焊、铆焊或焊接的接缝强度低得多。这些接合方法（硬钎焊、铆焊或焊接等）通常用于高强度的永久接合。软钎焊是靠施加熔融状态的第三种金属使两种金属连接在一起的焊接方法。焊料由锡、铅组成，而加入铋和镉是为了降低焊料的熔点。钎焊的重要工序之一是将需要焊接的接缝表面洗擦干净，这一工序可用某种酸洗液进行。虽然通过清理操作，氧化物被除去，但清洗完毕之后，会立即产生新的氧化膜，从而阻碍了焊料与金属件表面的连接。助焊剂是用来去除氧化物和防止需要焊接的金属表面的氧化，使焊料能自由地流动并与金属件连接。氧化锌在钎焊绝大多数铁金属和非金属时是最好的助焊剂；钎焊铝时，用硬脂酸和凡士林作为助焊剂。钎焊用的纯铜烙铁是连接在一钢条上的纯铜块，钢条上有手柄。纯铜烙铁做成不同的长度，形状和重量。钎焊的质量在很大程度上取决于纯铜烙铁的形状和尺寸。只有在接缝表面吸收足够热量后，使焊料有一段时间保持熔融状态，这样才能将两部分焊牢。

在某些场合下，可能有必要采用熔点高的硬焊料来连接金属表面。这种钎焊方法称硬钎焊。

黏结剂

用黏合剂黏结金属零件是一个迅速发展的领域，它几乎影响着各种各样的产品的设计。用黏合剂黏结有许多优点。它不像用螺钉和铆钉连接那样需要孔（孔会降低零件的强度）。它不像焊接那样需要很高的温度而使零件产生扭曲和残余应力。当接缝承受载荷时，应力扩散到很大面积，在接触边缘仅有较小的应力集中。这样通常可允许使用更薄的构件，从而减轻重量。用黏合剂黏结可形成光滑完整的外表面以达到良好的外观，更容易磨光，并减少流体摩擦（在有流动的液体或气体中应用，像飞机机翼或直升机旋翼桨叶）。几乎任何固体材料都能用适当的黏合剂来黏合。当黏合不相近的金属时，黏合层可有效地作为绝缘层来阻止电流流动。黏合材料的柔韧性可用来弥补构件间热胀的差异。这种柔韧性也可用来吸收冲击载荷，而且，黏合剂黏合可产生阻尼以减少振动和声音的传递。

在消极的一面，黏合剂比机械连接更容易受温度影响。大多数普遍使用的黏合剂局限于-129~260℃范围内。黏合剂在温度变化下，性能有很大不同，当选择用于特殊应用的黏合剂时必须考虑这一点。黏合处的检查、重新装配和修理都是不实际的。并且，一些黏合剂的长期耐用性也是令人置疑的。

第 10 课　砂型铸造

砂型铸造生产的第一步是设计并制作一个合适的模型。铸造模型一般由硬木做成，考虑到金属液在凝固及冷却过程中所产生的收缩，模型的尺寸要大于最终铸件的尺寸。

生产铸件的砂型是在砂箱中做出的。为了能在造型后取出模型，砂型由两个或更多部分组成。在由两部分组成的砂型中，砂箱的上半部分叫上箱，下半部分叫下箱。将下砂箱放置在厚实的平板上，并将下半模型安放在适当的位置上。在模型上撒上面砂，然后往砂箱中填满型砂，并在模型周围将型砂夯实。紧砂作业完成后，除去多余的型砂，使表面平整并与砂箱的周边齐平。此时可将下箱翻转过来，将上箱放在下箱上。将上半模型放在准确的位置上，用定位销将上、下两半模型对准定位。这时要往铸型内撒上薄薄一层干燥的分型砂，用来防止在上箱造型时，上、下两砂箱粘连在一起。向上箱内填入型砂，并像制作下箱一样，将上箱内的型砂夯实造型。上箱紧砂后，去除顶面多余的砂子，然后小心地将两砂箱分开。细心地将模型从上、下砂箱中取出。再将上箱放到下箱上面，重新装配好铸型以待使用。液体金属可经由冒口平稳地注入铸型中。

待注入砂型内的金属完全凝固后，将砂型打破，取出铸件。

锻 造

锻造有两种类型：冲锻和压锻。前者载荷由撞击锤来提供，变形在很短时间内产生。而压力机锻造则是逐渐施加压力使金属变形，力的作用时间相对较长。90%以上的锻造过程都是在加热状态下进行的。

冲锻可以细分为两种主要类型：

a）自由锻造

b）落锤锻造

自由锻造无疑是最古老的锻造类型，但现在已不普遍应用。使工件变形的撞击力是由铁匠用锤子手工施加的。金属件要在锻炉中被加热，达到适当温度时，将其放置在铁砧上。当金属被锤打时，要用合适的钳子将其夹紧。最容易锻造的金属是低、中碳钢，大多数的自由锻件都是由这些金属制成的。高碳钢和合金钢很难锻造并需要加倍小心。大多数有色金属能够成功地被锻造。

落锤锻造是自由锻造的现代等同物，它用机械或蒸汽锤取代了铁匠那有限的打击力。落锤锻造是用撞锤代替了自由锻造中的锤子，并用手工操纵把金属放在铁砧上来完成锻造的。产品的质量很大程度上依靠锻工的技能。闭模锻造应用的较为广泛，它是用模具代替了撞锤和铁砧。图 10-1 说明了冲锻的工作原理。

压锻：冲锻通常是用机械压力，而压锻则需要液压动力。最大的锻件几乎都是在大液压机上生产出的。这些液压机具有垂直移动的压头，它可以在相当大的压力作用下慢慢地向下移动。因此这种机器所需的设备也更大，图 10-2 显示这样一个锻造机。典型的液压机锻造能力在 6000 到 10，000 吨范围内。在这样的锻压机中，可以轻松地对重量达 100 吨的锻件进行操作，并且由这一技术可生产出最高质量的产品。

第 11 课　车　床

机床是金属切割的机器。最工业用机床重要的是车床，钻床和铣床。其他的金属切削机床没有前三种广泛用于金属加工中。

车床是用来从圆形工件表面上切除金属的机床，工件安装在车床的两顶尖之间，并绕顶尖轴线旋转（图 11-1）。车床车削工件时，车刀与工件的旋转轴线平行移动或者与工件的旋转轴线交一斜角移动，将工件表面的金属切除。刀具的这种运动叫进给。刀具装夹在刀架上，刀架安装在溜板箱上。溜板箱沿着刀具所需的方向进给。车工可以手动进刀，也可以借助专门的齿轮组实现自动进刀。

车床上最大的零件是床身，主轴箱安装在上面，尾座安装在床身的另一端。床身的上面有溜板箱和尾座滑动的导轨。

车削中心安装两个轴，一个（主轴顶尖）安装在主轴箱的主轴上，而另一个（尾座顶尖）安装在尾座的主轴上。

车床的夹盘用于装夹工件，也就是夹紧它以便在车削工件时不至于因它的旋转而产生振动。如果工件是回转类零件，它可以被安装在所谓的三爪万能卡盘上，可以通过转动螺栓使三爪万能卡盘的三个爪同时向中心移动。但是如果工件不是十分圆，可以使用四爪单动卡盘。

在车削不同材料不同直径的工件时，车床必须以不同的速度运行。装入床头箱内的齿轮系统能使车床以不同的速度运转。

车床在车削工件前，它的顶尖要对准，即两个顶尖的轴线必须在一条直线上。

可以通过试切来实现车床的校准，然后用千分尺来测量试切件的两端。

不是所有的工件都被安装在车床的两顶尖间。短工件车削时可以不使用尾座顶尖，只是把工件正确地装夹在主轴箱的主轴上。

切削工具

为了在变化的恶劣条件下切削不不同中的金属。金属切削工具必须拥有许多不同的特性。为了满足这些特性，必须用来同的材料来生产刀具。

刀具的最重要的性能是它的热硬性耐磨性和冲击强度。

当刀具切削时，由于摩擦和挤压的作用，使刀具切削刃的温度很高。当被加热到足够高的温度时，所有的刀具都会失去硬度。当刀具由于热而软化时，它的前后刀面的边缘就会磨损或破损。不同的刀具材料在不同的温度推动失去硬度。因此，在选择刀具材料时，刀具的硬度和它的热硬性非常重要。

如果刀具的边缘和刀具能抵抗磨损的能力就是刀具的耐磨性。刀具的硬度提高它的耐磨性就会增加。为了防止振动承受冲击，刀具也必须具有较高的强度。刀具的强度不是总是和硬度成比例。一些最硬的刀具材料缺少强度，因为它们太脆了。

制作刀具的大部分材料可以按下面的分类：

1. 碳素工具钢
2. 高速钢
3. 铸造合金
4. 硬质合金
5. 陶瓷
6. 金刚石

在制造一个零件或产品中，刀具寿命或刀具需要重磨之前加工的零件数是非常重要的成本因素。在刚有磨钝的迹象时就重磨刀具。如果这时不重磨，它就会很快破损。

为了检测换刀时间，大部分现代的机床都有能够显示在加工工操作期间所用马力的显示器。当刀具磨钝了，显示器上就会显示这项操作就会需要更多地马力。当发生这一现象时，该工具应立即翻新（重磨或换刀）。

第12课　机床的液压系统

现在，液压系统在机床中得到了广泛的应用。主要用于主运动和进给运动的驱动，控制变速机构，制动机构和夹紧机构及工作循环的自动控制等。液压系统成为磨床、牛头刨床、仿形铣床及拉床等机床的主要驱动类型。

液压系统的应用之所以广泛是由于它们具有能提供很大范围的无级变速，使移动的机床构件平稳换向，自动过载保护及容易润滑等优点。液压系统控制的机床占地面积小，并且它们的零部件很容易被标准化。液压系统的缺点是液体流经密封垫和缝隙时产生泄漏，气体进入液体及温度和时间对液体性能的影响等等。液压系统的能量损耗包括：由于液体泄漏造成的流量损耗，由于压力下降造成的压力损耗及由于接触表面的摩擦造成的机械损耗。液压系统的总效率为：

$$\eta = \eta_v \eta_h \eta_m$$

其中$\eta_v \eta_h \eta_m$分别是流量效率，压力效率和机械效率。

液压系统的正常功能 很大程度上依靠所用的工作液的类型。这种液体应该是足够黏的而且是均匀的；它应该具有良好的润滑性和防止机械腐蚀的性能；它应该在温度、压力、速度和运动方向的变化下仍保持其原有性能。此工作液不应该易氧化或逐渐形成沉淀、蒸发或燃烧。矿物油和它们的混合物最能满足这些要求。

在油的选择及比较上所用的主要性能指标是粘度指数，它显示了油在温度变化下黏性的变化。粘度指数越高，油的质量越好，精炼度也越高。粘度指数为90的油最适用于液压系统。

压力和流量控制

只要原动机（通常是电动机）驱动泵，液压能源就会产生，由阻力产生的液体压力使泵工作。因此，在油路非循环期，如果泵中流体不停止或关闭负载（重新循环）回到油箱，液压系统受到损害。非动作期间使所有的驱动器停止动作，或者到达行程或工序的终点，或在工序延时期间。

为了避免液压系统破坏，功率损失，液压液体过热，工序设计者在泵中液体非工作期间使用了许多的灵巧的设计系统以控制最大系统压力。

在液压系统中，压力控制阀用来控制油缸驱动力（驱动力=压力×面积），并选择及确定机器工作时的油压。压力控制主要用于执行下面的系统功能。

1. 为了限制液压回路或子回路中的最大系统压力，会提供过载保护。

2. 为了提供重新确定泵中液体流回油箱的方向，系统压力必须保持（系统卸载）。

3. 为了提供重新确定泵中液体流回油箱的方向，系统压力不必保持（系统卸载）。

4. 为了提供在选择压力水平抗力（抗衡力量流体）。

5. 为了提供一个在选定的压力水平流体流动的路径选择（压力顺序）。

6. 为了减少主回路的压力水平到子回路中较低的压力。

压力控制阀常常很难鉴别，主要有很多叙述性强的名字应用到它们。在回路中阀的功能通常成为它名字的基础。阀的名称常常用于完成上面提到的系统名称，因此分别给出下面的名字:

1. 溢流阀;
2. 卸荷溢流阀;
3. 卸载阀;
4. 背压阀和抽动阀;
5. 顺序阀;
6. 减压阀。

• 要液压系统中流体控制阀用于控制流体从系统的一部分到另一部分的速率。流体控制完成下面的一个或多个功能:

• 限制线性驱动器和液压马达的最大速度（流速/活塞面积=活塞速度）;

• 它的最大功率可通过控制子电路流向他们（功率=流量 × 压力）;

• 按比例分成或调节泵的流量电路的各个分支。

在液压系统中部分封闭的节流孔和流量控制阀会使泵流量受阻。这一阻力将节流孔进口压力提高至溢流阀的调定压力，油泵多余油通过阀回到油箱。(图 12-1)

为了了解流程控制设备的功能和操作，必须理解的各种因素决定通过节流孔口流量或限流（Q）的各种因素。这些因素是:

• 节流孔的横截面积（2 平方毫米）;

• 节流孔的形状 （圆形，方形，三角形）;

• 限制的长度;

• 通过节流孔的压差 （ΔP）;

• 流速（厘斯（黏度单位），取决于温度）。

这样控制给定节流阀的流速的规律可以被近似的定义为 $Q2 \propto \Delta P$。这意味着，任何压力变化时，或节流口的出口改变压差ΔP，因此通过节流孔来控制流速。不论是由系统安全阀或由变量泵压力控制器，流量压力控制阀的进口通常保持不变。因此，压力差（ΔP）变化只引起由出口造成的压力波动，结果驱动器的负载变化。

第 13 课 控制装置的类型

工业中常用的几种控制装置是为了以下一些控制要求：

➢ 机械控制

- 气动控制
- 机电控制
- 电子控制
- 计算机控制
- 可编程逻辑控制

机械控制有凸轮和调速器。尽管它们曾用于对非常复杂机器的控制、也比较经济，但现在它们仅仅用于简单的固定循环控制中。一些自动机床，如攻螺纹机床，仍旧使用基于凸轮的控制。机械控制的缺点是装置制造较困难而且容易磨损。

气动控制对于某些应用仍很流行。它利用压缩空气、阀门及天关构成简单的控制逻辑，但它的速度相对较慢。由于采用标准件构成控制逻辑，因此它比一个机械控制装置更易于加工制造。气动控制元件同样易于磨损。

正像机械控制那样，机电控制也使用开关、继电器、定时器、计数器等构成控制逻辑，因为采用了电流来控制，所以它更快，更灵活。使用机电控制的控制器称为继电器装置。

除了将机电控制装置中的机电控制元件用触点开关代替外，电子控制类似于机电控制、控制速度更快更可靠。

计算机控制是最通用的控制系统。其控制逻辑是使用软件将其程序化后存入计算机内存中。它不仅用于机床及制造系统控制，而且也可用于数据通讯。具有庞大计算量的非常复杂的控制方法也能被程序化。首先要解决与外界的连接。在控制电路内部计算机使用低电压（5~12V）和小电流（几毫安），机床的外部主电路则需要高电压（24，110 或 220V）和大电流（以 A 计量），接口不仅要进行不同中电压的转换，而且必须对车间中通常存在的电噪声加以过滤。这种接口对不同应用来说也是必须是用户定做的。

可编程逻辑控制器

为了利用那些控制器的优势，消除弊端，可编程逻辑控制器（PLC）应运而生，一个 PLC 就能代替整个继电器控制装置，它亿用梯形图（梯形图是标准化的电路）编程。由于 PLC 的编程灵活性逐渐增强，既可使用高级语言也可使用低级语言。PLC 不仅具有计算机的灵活性，同时也具有与处理过程及其他装置连接的界面标准简易的特点。在工业上，从单一设备到复杂的制造设备都广泛 PLC 控制。

可编程逻辑控制器（PLC）于 1968 年首次使用，用来替代一个硬接线的继电器控制板。最初目的是替代机械开关装置（继电模块）。然而，自从 1968 年以来，PLC 的功能逐渐代替了继电器控制板，现代 PLC 具有更多的功能。其用途从单一过程控制延伸到整个制造系统的控制和监控。

可编程逻辑控制器也可用于高速数字化处理、高速数字化通信以及高级计算机语言的支持方面，当然也可用于基本的过程控制（图 13-1）。

PLC 在尺寸和功率上不尽相同，一个大型 PLC 可以有高达 10000 个输入/输出结点；并且具有前面讨论过的所有功能。PLC 有连接 PC 机和其他通讯设备的扩展槽，在很多场合下，一个小的 PLC 就足够了。图 13-2 所示为一个小型 PLC，它有 16 个输入/输出结点及一个标准的 RS-232 串行通信口。PLC 的速度正在不断提高，甚至低端的 PLC 也能在高速下运用。每千字节 1 微秒至 2 微秒的内存速度是很普遍的。

第 14 课 数控编程

零件编程

在任何数控系统中，零件编程员是非常重要的。在获得零件图后，零件编程员决定加工顺序、不同加工的速度和进给量，以及所需各种位移量的大小。因此，编程员熟悉各种加工和所用机床，这一点非常重要。他要能在几何和三角学基础上进行各种运算。

编程所需数据资料

为了给零件手工编程的准备好草稿，编程员需要收集与零件加工相关的资料。这些资料如下：

机床说明书

各种工具说明书

工件材料说明书

速度和进度表

EIA/ISO 代码

在纸带上编码时遵循 EIA 代码或 ISO 代码。数控机床通常用来处理这两种信息。如今，大多使用 ISO 代码。

在程序中，一部分完整的信息称为程序段，在穿孔带上表示程序块有三种类型：

（1）固定顺序格式

（2）字地址格式

（3）标号格式

以下是在编程中用的字母地址：

N 操作顺序号地址

G 准备功能地址

X、Y、Z、A、B、C……尺寸地址

S 主轴转速字

F 进给度地址

T 刀具地址

M 辅助功能地址

绝对方式和增量方式准备功能

准备功能指令 G90 和 G91 分别用来指定其后程序段中的数据是绝对方式（相对于一个共用数据）或者是增量方式（相对于当前位置）。G90 指令可由 G91 指令取消；反之亦然。如，M03 意思是主轴顺时针转动，而 M04 是主轴逆时针转动。

准备功能

准备功能信息是由以 G 开头后面加操作数字代码的形式给出，由控制单元控制机床操作。比如，G81 说明是钻孔指令。进行加工操作的参数必须跟在其后。字母 G……不能对机床进行操作，除非加上所有的相关信息，这就是下面要进行的工作。

绝对和增量编程方式准备功能

准备功能 G90 和 G91 用于指定下面段分别是数据是绝对方式（相对于坐标原点）还是增量方式（相对于当前坐标）。G90 可以被 G91 取消，反之亦然。

辅助功能指令

当要执行一些操作时，可能希望启动主轴并使其顺时针方向旋转或逆时针方向旋转。实现这样指令的字在专业术语中称为辅助功能指令。同样，切削液的开和关的指令也属于此类。这些指令和工件的尺寸无关，但进行加工时却要执行。当一些接受辅助功能指令时，机床就立即作出反应。这种指令是字母 M 后跟所需的数字代码组成的。例如，M03 意思是主轴时针转动，而 M04 是主轴逆时针转动。

数控机床的坐标系

在一个数控系统中每个运动轴都配备一个单独的驱动源，以此来代替传统机床上的手轮。驱动源可以是一个直流电机，一个步进电机或一个液压传动装置。选择何种驱动源主要是根据机床的精度要求。

刀具与工件之间的相对运动是通过机床工作台的运动获得。运动的三个主坐标轴是指 x、y 和 z 轴。z 轴与 x、y 轴都垂直，主要是为使用右手坐标系，如图 14-1 所示。刀具远离工件的移动方向为 z 轴的正方向。现详细说明如下：

1．z 轴

（1）在工件旋转的机床中，如车床，z 轴平行于主轴、并且正方向是刀具远离工件的运动方向（图 14-1）。

（2）在刀具旋转的机床中，如铣床或钻床，z 轴垂直于工件，其正方向也是刀具远离工件的运动方向（图 14-2）。

（3）其他机床上，如冲床、刨床或剪断机，z 轴垂直于工件，其正方向是刀具和工件距离增加的方向（图 14-3）。

2．x 轴

（1）车床的 x 轴是刀具运动方向，正方向是刀具远离工件的方向。

（2）在卧式铣床上，x 轴平行于工作台。

（3）在立式铣床上，正 x 轴方向是当程序员面向机床时，指向右边的方向。

3．y 轴

y 轴是标准笛卡儿坐标系中剩下的轴。

第 15 课 夹具种类

夹具是指确保在正确位置钻孔、铰孔、攻丝的一种装置。

以下介绍四种常用的夹具种类：

箱式夹具

箱式夹具是一种能够装夹箱体零件的特殊的夹具（图 15-1）。夹具的底座（夹具体）用于支撑夹具的侧壁，通常也用于定位并夹紧工件。箱式平具的侧壁在对钻模板提供支撑的同时，也可以对工件进行夹紧和定位。夹具的顶端装有一个或几个相对定位面（或点）精确定位的钻套。这种夹具刚性好，精度高，因此可以应用于许多加工场合。然而，固定钻模板在装卸每个零件时费时。从箱体内排除切屑也很困难，会定期地延缓操作时间。

滚筒夹具

当给定的工件需要在几个面上钻孔，可以考虑使用滚筒夹具。滚筒夹具是箱式平具的变形，在夹具的一个或几个面有钻孔衬套。在小批量生产中，工件被放在滚筒夹具中并夹紧。然后，通过从一边翻转到另一面，在夹具内每个钻套置于在钻削主轴中。滚筒夹具的主要优点是：（1）由于一次定位并夹紧，减少了孔与孔之间的位置差，（2）一个夹具可以代替多个夹具，（3）处理工作量少，使加工时间缩短。

回转式夹具

回转式夹具，无论是卧式还是立式的，在工业上具有标准设计，适用于钻削按圆周排列的孔系（图 15-2）。工件在一个钻套中被定位并夹紧。用来确定工件高度和位置钻套的位置是可以调整的。这种调整使得用一个钻套来加工一个或几个相似零件的孔成为可能。和第一孔的相对位置可能通过分度头来确定。分度头被安装在特殊的分度盘上，这种分度头可以实现特殊的或不常见的分度。

盖板式夹具

盖板式夹具是因为它的要结构为板式而得名的。所有的夹具附件都被安装在这个板上。这种夹具的敞开式结构适合于形状不规则的工件的装卸。

钻套类型和应用

无肩固定钻套 这种无肩固定钻套在许多小批量的夹具生产中使用。衬套压入套盘，直到它与板的顶部齐平。无头可以减少间隙，允许在紧密结合的中心放置两个或多个衬套。

有肩固定钻套 有肩固定钻套类似于无肩固定钻套，除了在顶端有头部和肩部外。当有较高的轴向切削力时期望使用这种钻套。肩可以防止衬套被套筒板推动。

固定可换钻套 当夹具的生产周期超过一个衬套的正常磨损寿命，可以选择固定可换钻套。

这种钻套用于钻套衬里和锁紧螺钉压紧配合。钻套滑入衬里，并通过锁紧螺钉放在合适的位置。当钻套被磨损后，它很容易地被用同批的产品替代。

快换钻套 快换钻套也用于压接式衬里。当在一个孔上使用一个夹具完成不止一项操作时，选择这种类型的钻套。在这种情况下，首先使用一个钻套钻孔，然后那个钻套被移走并换一个可容纳铰刀的规模较大的钻套。在这种方式下，可以在同一夹具中钻孔和铰孔。钻铰刀都将具有相同的衬套，让他们完美地和衬里配合。

钻套用衬套 当使用固定或滑动可换衬套，无肩的和有肩的钻套用衬套都被永久地压入夹具衬套盘中以防止它磨损。当使用的轴向载荷最小时，使用无肩衬套。当轴向切削载荷压力过大时，使用有肩衬里。

钻削典型的沉头孔使用衬套板，以便允许衬里肩齐平地安装。

第 16 课 HTM125600 车铣中心

HTM125600 车铣中心采用双刀架配备，五轴联运，具有重型机床的承载能力，主要用于电机转子，气化转子，轧辊、曲轴等精度高、工序多、形状复杂的回转体的机械加工。该机床可用中小批量，多品种的生产。节省工艺装备、缩短生产准备周期、保证零件加工质量、提高产生率。关键件选用国际知名厂家的产品，保证机床的精度和可靠性。

机床的结构特点：

底座采用高强度的铸铁铸造，整体箱式结构；床身后面装有意大利 LICAT m=8 斜齿齿条，用于立柱的驱动；

床头箱润滑采用恒温油润滑，前轴承外部配有油冷却循环装置；

主电机选用大功率的直流电机；

尾座由上下两部分组成，配有与工件重量一一相关推力显示；

立柱采用侧挂式结构，Z 轴进给采用主从驱动机构，消除反向间隙；

采用双驱动，极大地提高了运动的平稳性，配有换刀机械手、刀库，BLUM 刀具检测装置；

操纵台从机床下部悬出，可沿 Z 轴方向拖动；

配置西门子 840D 数控系统。

主要参数：

项目	单位	备注
最大切削长度	mm	6000
最大切削直径	mm	Φ1250
顶尖间的最大重量	kg	30000
主轴转速范围	r/min	1-200
主电机输出功率	kW	75（直流 500-2000rpm）
花盘直径	mm	Φ1250（手动四爪）
花盘最大扭矩	kN.m	35

C 轴最大扭矩	N.m	1200
单刀最大切削力	k.N	55
X1/X2 轴行程	mm	1330/790
Y1 轴行程	mm	-300—+540（考虑换刀）
Y2 轴行程	mm	±190
Z 轴行程	mm	8130
B 轴行程		-90°—+180°
A 轴行程		0°—+90°
X1/Y1 轴快速移动速度与进给速率	mm/min	0-15000/0-12000
X2/Y2 轴快速移动速度与进给速率	mm/min	0-15000/0-12000
Z 轴快速移动速度与进给速率	mm/min	0—15000
B 轴最高转速	r/min	30
C 轴最高转速	r/min	20
尾座套筒直径/行程	mm	Φ300/200
尾座快移速度	mm/min	3500
尾座套筒移动速度	mm/min	660
中心架支承范围（可依用户需求定型）	mm	Φ150—Φ500
镗铣主轴功率	kW	52
镗铣主轴速度 档 1/档 2（max）	r/min	180/3150
镗铣主轴扭矩 档 1/档 2（max）	N.m	2400/157
机床重量	Kg	80000
机床外形 （长×宽×高）	mm	17020×7252×4707

数控机床的维修和故障诊断

FANUC 系统的部件被装在可拆卸的模块中。机箱内有四个模块，即：带接口的计算机、驱动板（每台步进电机一块）、电源板和变压器。变压器采用新开发的体积小，高效率和低噪音的 R 型结构。开关电源是专为无干扰操作而设计的。计算机上有 2 层印刷电路板，以确保高可靠性；每个轴上都装有单独的驱动板，所有的驱动器中可以互换的。这种柔性结构使维修方便，维修时只要换上备用件即可。制造商提供备件以及使不工作的部件板恢复工作，服务快捷，价格合理。最常见的麻烦，可能发生的系统是逐步淘汰，步进电机，并采取以下措施解决可能有帮助。最常见的故障是步进电机失调，下面的措施对故障检查非常有效：

1. 检查从电源板所有电压的值是否正确；
2. 切换到手动模式，以脉冲驱动步进电机，并且用手动触摸来检查普通电机电枢。如果电枢节拍正确，进给失步可能由于松动的紧固件，紧固件应改装和拧紧，否则，(电枢不正确的步进)，该系统的运作必须受到进一步的检查；

3. 去掉底盘盖。在正常或异常工作电机的驱动印刷电路板电机的信号输入插座（XS-9和 XS-10））的插头互换，然后就像在第 2 项中所描述的那样以手动方式再次检查两个电机。如果异常的电机现在正常运转，则故障可能在印刷电路板的器上；否则，它们可能在计算机中失效；

4. 和正确的电压相比较，检查印刷电路板电源输入插座电压（参考接线图)。当没有发现电压故障，检查和比较电路元件，主要是功率晶体管，并用万用表在线测量。有异常参数的元件已经遭到破坏；

5. 如果在电压是正确的，另一种发现并修理故障的方式是换一个好用的印刷电路板驱动器不正常工作的步进电机；

6. 一般来说，尺寸小的偏差是由于机械故障，而大的偏差可能是由于系统电路故障或电动机减震器中松动的紧固件；

7. 当在高速空运行时失步，应检查减速齿轮箱；

8. 当在所有功能模块单独检查中都没有找到故障，而整个系统工作不稳定，应仔细检查连接电缆的焊接缺陷；

9. 当这种令人费解的显示器故障或者键盘缺陷发生在大型机板上，切断的控制单元底盘主要来源，检查插入的IC芯片，以确保连接牢固、合理。

我们的制造商，提供各种售后的服务，以解决在应用程序的问题。请与我们联系。我们准备支持和保证这一体系的有效运行。

第 17 课　计算机辅助制造

计算机辅助制造（CAM）是 1949 年在麻省理工学院随着数控的发展而出现的。由美国空军倡导的这项技术，是计算机技术控制铣削加工的第一次应用。

标准的数控机床极大地减少了加工单一零件和完成零件整个生产过程所需要的加工时间，但整个加工仍然费时。必须为零件准备纸带，编辑程序将导致生成一个新纸带，每次加工完零件后，纸带必须倒回。考虑到这些，机床生产厂家把计算机引入现有的数控机床，计算机数控便出现了。

计算机的引入极大地增加了机床的适应性，零件加工程序运行于计算机存储器中，从而取代了须重绕的纸带。在机器上任何程序修正和编辑都可以做，修改后也能存储。

随着机床生产厂家不断地提高它们的机床效率，计算机上编程微处理器的能力也极大地增强了，采用了很多节省时间的装置，用于切削加工的时间增长了，停机时间减少了。有些机床具备自动换刀、零件自动装卸、切屑自动传输、自动监控刀具磨损、在线检测和机器人等功能——这就产生了现在的加工中心。

在加工和处理生产中的数据方面，CAM 使用了全部的先进技术去自动执行。CAM 的工具包括计算机技术、计算机辅助工程及机器人技术。CAM 使用所有的这些技术把设计过程和自动加工机床、材料处理设备及控制系统连接起来。没有计算机这个工业中最重要的工具，美国的生产率将陷入严重的困境。计算机帮助人们提高产量，做没有计算机人们就不能做的事情。

CAM 将一个工厂所有主要的职能联结起来。将制造或生产运营和工艺设计、生产计划、材料处理、报表控制、产品检验、机器控制和维修联系在一起，形成一个完整的加工系统。

一个 CAM 系统一般包括三个主要的部分：

制造：控制机床、材料处理设备的实际操作及检测等，用以制造需要的零件。

工程：涉及设计和工程行为的工艺，用以确保零件设计合理，达到所要求的功能。

管理：类似计划、报表控制、劳力、制造成本及所有需要的数据信息，以管理整个工厂。

CAM 提高了机床的生产率，增强了机床的功能。在采用数控和 CAM 以前，大多数机床的加工时间只占总时间的 5%。现有的自动加工系统其加工时间占总时间的 70%。我们的目标是要使它们的切削时间尽可能接近总时间的全部。

CAM 有用的菜单和参数

1. UG 的主菜单及功能

文件:	新建，打开，关闭，保存，仅保存保存工作部件，另存为，全部保存，保存书签，选项，打印，绘图，发送到打包文件，导入，导出，实用工具，属性，最近打开的部件，退出
编辑:	撤销列表，重做，剪切，复制，复制显示，粘贴，选择性粘贴，删除，选择，对象显示，显示和隐藏，变换，属性，曲线，特征
视图:	刷新，操作，透视，方位，布局，可视化，摄像机，信息窗口，当前对话框，显示资源条
插入:	草图，基准/点，曲线，来自曲线集的曲线，来自体的曲线，设计特征，关联复制，组合体，修剪，偏置/缩放，细节特征，网格特征，网格曲面，扫掠，小平面体，直接建模
格式:	图层设置，在视图中可见，图层类别，移动至图层，WCS，引用集，组，特征分组
工具:	表达式，电子表格，材料属性，更新，重用库，定制，制图标准，操作记录，用户自定义特征，部件族，定义可变形部件
装配:	关联控制，设置工作部件
信息:	对象，点，表达式，产品制造信息，部件，装配，其他
分析:	测量距离，测量角度，最小半径，几何属性，测量体，截面惯性，检查几何体，强度向导，简单干涉，装配间隙，内容积计算器，单位：千克 · 毫米

首选项:	对象，用户界面，资源板，选择，可视化，可视化性能，3D 输入设备，工作平面，建模，草图，装配，注释，产品制造信息，Teamcenter 集成，NX 基本环境，JT
窗口:	新建窗口，层叠，横向平铺，纵向平铺，route_logic_model1.part 更多
帮助:	

2. 零件特征

特征	特征操作
草图	拔模体
拉伸	边倒圆
回转	面倒圆
扫掠	软倒圆
沿引导线扫掠	抽壳
管道	螺纹
孔	镜像特征
凸台	镜像体
腔体	缝合
凸垫	补片体
凸起	包裹几何体
偏置凸起	偏置面
键槽	比例体
开槽	凸起片体
三角形加强筋	拆分体
用户定义特征	分割面
抽取几何体	孔
引用几何体	修剪体
曲线成片体	连结面
有界平面	实体特征
加厚	求和
片体到实体助理	求差
基准平面	求交
基准轴	装配切割
基准 CSYS	提升体
块	
圆柱	
圆锥	
球	
球形拐角	

第 18 课 计算机集成制造

计算机集成制造（CIM）是用于描述最现代的制造方法的术语。虽然它包括计算机数控（CNC）、计算机辅助设计与制造（CAD/CAM）、机器人技术和及时生产（JIT）等许多不同的先进制造技术，CIM 与其说是一种新的技术，还不如说是一个新的概念。现在计算机集成制造是一个全新的制造方式，或是一种新的经营方式。

为了理解 CIM 的概念，有必要将现代制造和传统制造进行比较。现代制造包括了把原材料转换成成品、把产品投向市场和进行售后服务所必需的一切活动和过程。这些活动包括：

（1）确定产品需求；

（2）设计满足需求的产品；

（3）获取制造产品所需要的原材料；

（4）采用合适的方法把原材料转换成成品：

（5）把产品推向市场；

（6）维护产品以确保产品在现场使用性能正常。

这种广义的、现代的制造观可以与受到了限制太多的传统的制造观进行一个比较，后者几乎完全集中于产品的转变过程。旧的方法把为制造而进行的市场调研、开发和设计这些产品转变前的单元以及产品销售与维护这样的产品转变后的单元分割开来。换句话说，在旧的方法中，仅仅将在车间发生的生产过程认为是制造。这种传统的将整个概念分割成许多独立的专用单元的方式并没有随着自动化的出现而发生根本性的改变。当独立的单元自身实现自动化（例如产品设计时采用计算机辅助绘图和计算机辅助设计及在加工中采用计算机数字控制）后，它们仍然是相互分离的。单靠自动化不能导致这些“自动化岛”的集成。

有了 CIM，不仅各个要素可以实现自动化，而且所有的“自动化岛”之间都能连接即集成起来。集成意味着系统能够提供完全和即时的信息共享。在现代制造中，集成是借助于计算机实现的。因此，CIM 现在可以被定义为利用计算机实现所有的要素之间的完全集成。

制造业在最终完全实现 CIM 的方向正在取得进展。如果实现了 CIM，完全集成化的制造公司将从中得到以下利益：

（1）提高产品质量；

（2）缩短交货时间；

（3）降低直接的劳动成本；

（4）缩短产品开发时间；

（5）减少库存；

（6）提高整个生产率；

（7）提高设计质量。

柔性制造系统

这里介绍的单个的制造系统可以结合起来成为一个单一的大规模的系统，在这个大系统中，零件的制造是借助于一台中心计算机来进行控制的。这样一种生产系统的优势在于其高度的适应性，这种高度的适应性就依据省力省时的原则制造出新的产品，因此，这个系统就称为柔性制造系统。

美国现有的 FMS 通常由加工中心组成，它们与各种类型的机床协调动作，都处于一台中央计算机（主机）的控制之下。工件放在托盘上，在位于地板下的牵引索或其他机构的驱动下，被传递到系统内的各个地方。这些 FMS 限制了操作者的人工处理并能够更容易地重新编程来满足新的加工需求。

未来的 FMS 将包含许多制造单元，每个单元包括一台机器人，该机器人同时服务于若干台 CNC 机床或其他像测量机、焊机、电火花加工机床等独立的系统。这些制造单元沿着一个中心传输系统（例如传送带）布置，各种不同的工件和零件均通过它传送。零件的生产需要制造单元的不同组合来完成。在许多情况下，每个给定的加工步骤都可以在不同的加工单元上完成。当一个特定的工件随着传送带靠近所需的加工单元时，相应的机器人就会拿下工件并送入到单元中的 CNC 机床。在单元里加工完成后，机器人再把半成品或成品放回到传送带上。半成品将在传送带上继续移动，直到接近下一个加工单元以便继续加工，相应的机器人再把半成品放到机床上，这个过程沿传送带不断重复进行，直到在整个传送路线上只有成品在移动。这时，零件就可以送到自动检测站，接着从 FMS 上卸下来。制造单元之间的协调以及传送带上的零件流的控制是在中央计算机的监控下完成的。

FMS 的优点包括以下几点：

（1）提高了生产率；

（2）缩短了新产品的准备时间；

（3）减少了工厂内的零件库存；

（4）节省了劳动力成本；

（5）提高了产品质量；

（6）把熟练的工人吸引到制造业中来（因为工厂的工作向来被认为是又枯燥又脏）；

（7）提高了操作者的安全性。

像操作者的私人工具、手套等的减少会带来一些附加的经济上的节省。其他节省则是当公司由于使用柔性自动化系统而扩大生产时，并不需要扩大像贮藏室、沐浴和食堂等一些占用工厂宝贵使用空间的设施。

第 19　课机电产品介绍与谈判签约

地点：上海工业博览会 一 数控机床展示台现场。

人物：某数控机床制造公司销售代表周先生。

买方代表：某学院负责教务的副校长徐先生、机电部主任蒋先生、科研部主任史先生。

周：　您好，欢迎参观我们的产品，您对哪台设备最感兴趣？

蒋：　我对贵公司的 SV—1000 加工中心感兴趣，请递给我一份产品样本说明书好吗？

周：　好的。能知道您的贵姓大名吗？

蒋：　我叫蒋忠理，这是我的名片。这是我们的徐副校长，这位是我校科研部主任史先生。

周：　这是我的名片，谢谢您的光临。蒋先生，您也对加工中心感兴趣？

蒋：　是的，我校是一所集机电、商务、外语于一体的综合性重点高等技术学院，设有机电一体化和工业技术外语等专业，学院有数控实训中心，CAD/CAM 实验室。今年在市教委和财政局支持下，将在设备方面作进一步的投资。

周：　噢，我明白啦!您们买数控机床主要是用于教学，对吧？

蒋：　是的，除了教学培训以外，我们还将利用这些设备从事科研和生产。因此，我们对数控设备要求很高，必须满足以下条件：

1）技术先进；

2）功能齐全；

3）精度更高，以保证满足教学科研与生产的要求。

周：　没问题，我们公司创始于 1943 年，具有悠久的历史和丰富的制造经验，她以高质量和优越的售后服务赢得了众多用户的称赞。产品远销世界各地。从展品上，您们可以看到其功能和技术精度指标优于其他同类产品；刀库有 16 把刀，能快速自动换刀；工作台行程范围较大，完全可以胜任常规模具的加工。该型号加工中心的性能价格比较高，最适合于您们这类学校和中型企业。

史：　除了保证样本上所列出的结构功能、技术精度以外，能否加配第四轴，实现 X、Y、Z、B 四轴联动？

蒋：　在您的加工中心上，还须有能支持 CAD/CAM 通讯并由 DNC（直接数字控制）完成复杂曲面加工的 RS—232 通讯接口。

徐：　另外，是否请您配备适合于该加工中心的一些附件（如刀柄、刀具和工具小车等），行吗？

周：　行，没问题。

徐：　那就请您给我们报个价吧。

周：　您们要订购几台数控机床？

史：　一台。

周：　让我算一下，人民币 56 万。

徐：　您的报价过高了。

周：　考虑到质量，我认为我们的报价是合理的。

蒋： 周先生，您知道学校教育经费不多，这次难得争取到市教委和财政局的拨款来改造数控实训室，要买的设备还很多，经费很紧。希望您从支持教育事业的角度，给学校一个最优惠的价格，这是其一。其二，学校是播种子的地方，如果贵公司能进一步让利，那么我们每年培养出的几百名毕业生将来都是贵公司的潜在用户。希望贵公司从长远利益出发，予以考虑。

周： 今天碰到三位谈判高手了（笑）。顺便我想问一下，您们怎样付款？

徐： 我们将分期付款。

周： 签约首付30%，提货时付清怎样？

徐： 按我们的惯例，提货时付60%，还有10%余款待试用三个月后付清。

蒋： 你们的售后服务怎么样？

周： 一年包修期内实行三包，过后跟踪服务。噢，刚才听蒋先生说，好像你们还要买什么数控设备？

蒋： 是的，我们还要买线切割、电火花等。

周： 对啊，线切割、电火花，我们也可以代理啊。

徐： 周先生，这台加工中心就50万吧。这笔生意做好后再谈别的设备。

周： 我恐怕做不下来，我想你们总不能让我们公司亏本买卖。我看这样，53万，这是我方的最低报价，不能再让了。其实，已无利可言了。就算是做个广告吧。

徐： 包括运费，怎么样？

周： 唉……好吧。

史： 你们最快的交货期多长？

周： 两个月吧。

徐： 如果您答应提前15天交货，我们可以接受你方的报价。

周： 请稍等，让我与我方制造部经理协商一下。

徐先生，刚才我就此事与杨经理商谈，他同意您提前15天交货的要求。

蒋： 周先生，在这台加工中心装配期间，我们能否到贵厂实地学习一下您们的技术人员如何对该设备测试和调整各项精度指标的。

周： 行。别客气，你们是这方面的行家，欢迎来工厂实地指导。请放心，我们将用计算机—激光测量反馈系统去测试和调整该机床，以确保各项精度指标满足要求。

史： 好，到时请电话通知我们。

周： 行，下面能否就购买加工中心的有关事项签一份合同及备忘录？

徐： 好，祝我们合作愉快！

数控系统的面板

可以得到下面的面板

7.2″单色 LCD/MDI 面板（见图 19-1）

14″彩色 CTR/MDI 面板（见图 19-2）

MDI 面板上键的位置 （见图 19-3）

MDI 面板上键的详细说明

1. 复位键

按此键可以使 CNC 复位，消除报警等。

2. 帮助键

按此键用来显示如何操作机床，如 MDI 键的操作。可在 CNC 发生报警时提供报警的详细信息（帮助功能）。

3. 软件

根据其使用场合，软键有各种功能。软件的功能显示在 CRT 屏幕的底部。

4. 地址和数字键

按这些键可以输入字母，数字以及其他字符。

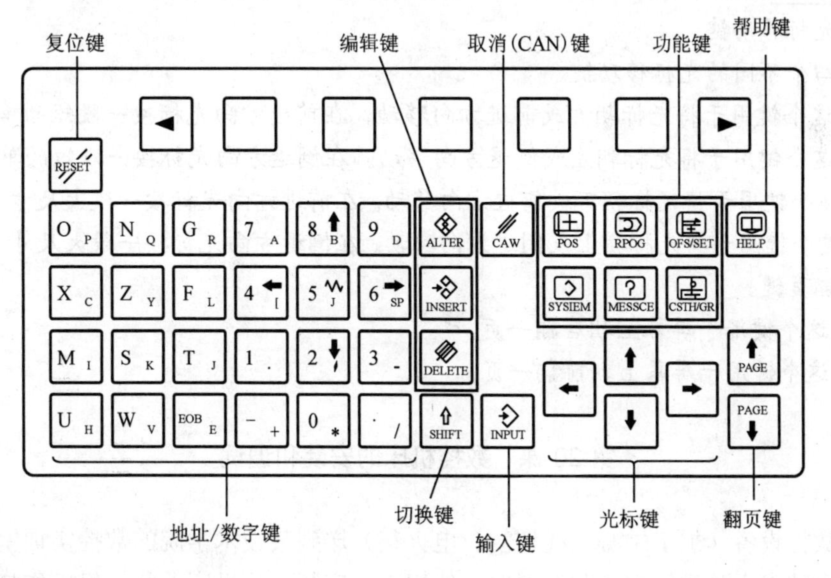

5. 换档键

有些键的顶部有两个字符。按 SHIFT 键来选择字符。当一个特殊的字符^N 在屏幕上显示时，表示键面右下角的字符 Q 可以输入。

6. 输入键

当按了地址键和数字键后，数据被输入到缓冲器，并在 CRT 屏幕上显示出来。为了把键入到输入缓冲器中的数据拷贝到寄存器，按INPUT键。这个键相当于软件的INPUT键，按此二键是一样的。

7. 取消键

按此键可以删除已输入法到键的输入缓冲器的最后一个字符或符号。

当显示缓冲器数据为：

>N001 × 100Z___ 时，按CAN键，则字符Z被取消，并显示：>N001 × 100

8. 程序编辑键

当编辑程序时按这些键。

ALTER：替换

INSERT：插入

DELETE：删除

9. 功能键

按这些键用于切换各种功能功能显示画面。

POS：按此键显示位置画面

PROG：按此键显示程序画面

OFS/SET：按此键显示刀偏/设定（SETTING）画面

SYSTEM：按此键显示系统画面

MESSAGE：按此键显示信息画面

CSTM/GR：按此键显示用户宏画面（会话式宏画面）或显示图形画面

10. 光标移动键

这是四个不同的光标移动键。

←：这个键用于将光标朝右或前进方向移动。在前进方向光标按一段短的单位移动。

→：这个键用于将光标朝左或倒退方向移动。在倒退方向光标按一段短的单位移动。

↓：这个键用于将光标朝下或前进方向移动。在前进方向光标按一段大尺寸单位移动。

↑：这个键用于将光标朝上或倒退方向移动。在倒退方向光标按一段大尺寸单位移动。

11. 翻页键

⇞：这个键用于屏幕上朝后翻一页。

⇟：这个键用于屏幕上朝前翻一页。

第20课　数控机床的安装和调试

一批数控设备（加工中心、线切割、电火花）送到某技术学院的数控实训室。某些设备是由厂方技术人员进行安装和调试的。他们正在安装数控机床并就如何操作与维护这些新机床面对用户进行培训。

地点：学院数控实训室

人物：厂方工程师：周先生、张先生、李先生。

校方技术人员：蒋先生、史先生、由小姐

蒋：周先生、张先生、李先生，你们好！
我们已为这次安装准备好了吊车和搬运工具。让我们讨论一下如何安装这些机床以及如何培训我们。

周：我方负责设备的安装与调试。你们可以分几个组去做下面的事：
1）按照设备装箱单进行清点和验收。
2）配合我们工程师一起对设备进行安装。
3）在工程师对设备进行调试时，按出厂精度指标逐项验收。
蒋先生，您看行吗？

蒋：行，您考虑得很周到，我同意您所说的。

周：蒋先生，为了节约时间，三台设备分组进行，好吗？

蒋 好，我和周先生验收加工中心。史先生和李先生验收电火花，由小姐与张先生验收线切割。

（加工中心调试现场）

蒋：周先生，首先，让我们按照出厂精度对加工中心各项指标复验一下，好吗？

周：好，让我们开始。由于运输途中颠簸原因，原始精度会有一些变化，所以我们现应对它们重新调整。

蒋：好，现在各项几何精度都已达标。下面我想设计一个零件，在该机床上加工一下，好吗？

周：这得要专门的试件和工具。

蒋：这些我已经准备好了。

周：哇！够复杂的了，有铣面、铣台阶、铣凹槽、钻孔、攻丝，还有曲面等。看来今天我们得经受一场考试了（笑）。既考机器又考人。

蒋：那不是我们的意图，我们还不熟悉新设备。我想了解一下该设备的实际加工能力，以便我们今后承揽加工业务时，做到心中有底。

周：好，让我们开始。

蒋：周先生，你在机床这一边做好准备，我在另一边向您 NC 程序，该机床的传送波特率为多少？

周：4800

蒋：准备，开始！

周：好，机床正在开始加工试件了！刀具在刀库顺利地换刀，铣面、铣凹槽、钻孔、攻丝，所有加工都顺利！

蒋：让我们测量一下完工的试件。噢，精度基本达到要求。您不介意补充加工试件中的几个尺寸吧？

周：行，调整好刀补值后，我们将完成加工再测试件。

蒋：好，现在尺寸和精度都满足要求了，验收通过，谢谢您！

（电火花调试现场）

李：史先生，首先，让我们测试机床工作台面的平面度和移动时的直线度，然后，测试主轴对工作台的垂直度。以上几项指标都在出厂规定的精度范围内。

史：接下来，能否对两种加工状态（粗、精加工）进行现场试验？

李：行。

史：您是怎样保证加工精度的？

李：第一，保证电极本身的精度；第二，在安装时要保证电极对工作台的垂直度；第三，合理选择电加工参数。比如：电压、电流的大小，脉冲的宽度、间隙，频率等，这些要靠长期经验的积累。

史：谢谢！

（线切割调试现场）

由：张先生，线切割加工应注意哪些事项？

张：第一，上钼丝避免叠丝；第二，紧丝时保证钼丝松紧适当，不宜过紧，否则容易断丝。

由：如何提高线切割加工精度？

张：第一，要注意钼丝的松紧与进给速度间的协调；第二，要注意钼丝的垂直度（试用电极矫正其垂直度）；第三，根据不同的材料选择适当的加工参数，这要靠经验积累，当然也有经验数据库可供参考。

由：谢谢您！

安　装

1. 开箱

开箱，必须先检查装货单，以确保所需系统正确的配置。

必须根据其种类，数量及外观逐项检查所有的零件，附件及发售的系统的备件，以排除混乱，错误包装，短缺和损失。

必须进一步检查正确类型的控制单元底座，良好的机械紧固和所有部件可靠的电气连接，如印刷电路板的开关和钥匙，变压器等（参考控制单元装配图和线路图）。

2. 安装

控制单元机箱安全地安装在机床上，其位置使操作者操作方便。如图 20-1 所示悬臂支架可能也是相当有帮助的。在某些系统中，电源变压器驱动电路被装在一个单独的机箱，它也应固定牢固。

步进电机安装在机床的进给机构中。

3. 供电

根据装配和接线图连接电机驱动器，步进电机和主电源给控制单元底盘供电。“Befor”主要电源打开之前，功率放大器负载按钮必须设置为“OFF”。打开主电源开关，控制单元就会正常工作。在这个瞬间，风扇鼓风机必须正常工作，因为鼓风机禁止控制单元在未经强制通风时工作。然后打开负载按钮，因为这个控制单元，驱动器，和步进电机可以通过手工操作测试负载按钮。当手动操作检查验证的所有零部件的良好的性能，一个简单的PMP应该有所准备，并被输入到系统中以检查的各种功能。如果此功能检查证实，该系统现在可以为综合调试电机驱动器。

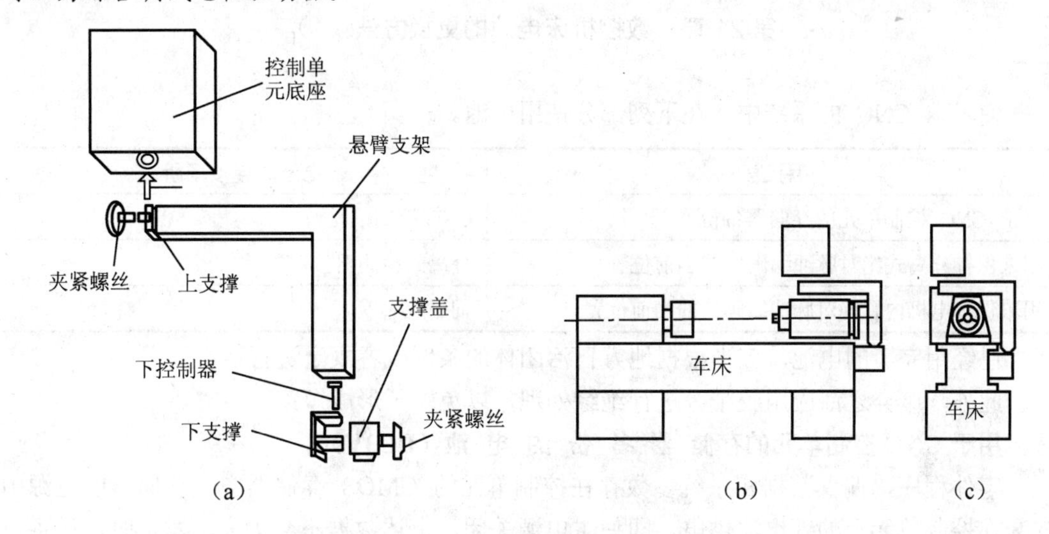

图 20-1 控制底盘的安装

(a) 安装支架 (b) 安装-I (c) 安装-II

4. 注意事项

(1) 测试时如果发现电机的旋转方向与所设定的方向相反，可将连接驱动板和步进电机的电线接头交换。

注：一定要同时交换两个接头，由于两对中任何一个都会引起功率晶体管损坏。

(2) 系统中的IC芯片必须防止手指触摸，当通电时严禁插拔。当维修保养时焊接是必要的，系统的所有电源必须首先切断，所有的在计算机主机和外围设备的插座都应断开。为避免损坏时，在焊接电路元件的瞬间，烙铁的电源必须立即切断，芯片引脚应与电烙铁余热焊接。

(3) 当步进电机静态锁定，可能会出现轻的高频振动声音，这是一个正常现象，无须进一步关注。

(4) 当由站立一段长时间，功率放大器必须关掉，以减少电力消耗和零件损耗。出于同样的原因，长期的持续快速进给超过 4000 毫米/分钟也不合理，因为它可能会给功率晶体管带来损害。

(5) 一旦系统的主电源被关闭，系统在 10 秒内不能重新上电；同样禁止不当操作或频繁开关电源，所有这些将导致在电脑和零部件的损害的缺陷。

(6) VMOS 高功率晶体管的特点是由系统严格规定的，因此，所有的晶体管，禁止其他类型的替代品。

(7) 当插座的插头连接或断开时，主电源必须切断以确保该系统和操作人员的安全。

当配合时，我们必须小心，以确保正确的方向和稳定的插入，以避免连接件的损坏。

（8）该控制单元机箱框架为基础，因此用户必须确保主电源的正确连接，以防止底座被通电，因为底座通电会导致严重的危害。

第21课 数控机床电池的更换方法（1）

使用本 CNC 的系统中，在下列部分使用电池。

用途	电池的连接场所
用于 CNC 控制单元的存储器备份	CNC 控制单元
用来保持分离式绝对脉冲编码器的当前位置	分离式检测器接口单元
用来保持电机内置绝对脉冲编码器的当前位置	伺服放大器

已经用完了的电池，应当根据地方自治团体的条例或者规定进行适当处理。

此外，废弃之前应用胶带等进行绝缘处理，以免端子形成短路。

用于 CNC 控制单元的存储器备份的电池（DC3V）

零件程序，偏置数据和系统参数存在控制单元的 CMOS 存储器中。存储器的电源由安装在控制单元上的锂电池供电。即使主电源关闭，上述数据不会丢失。发货时，后备电池装在控制单元上。后备电池可用一年。

当电池的电压变低，LCD 屏幕上闪烁显示报警信息“BAT”，电池报警信号输出到 PMC。当显示警告后，要尽早更换电池。通常，可以在第一次发出报警信息的 1—2 周内更换，但这要取决于系统的配置。

如果电池的电压进一步降低，存储的内容将会丢失。在这种状态下给控制单元通电，由于存储内容丢失，将引起系统报警 935（ECC 报警）。此时在更换电池后，应对存储器全清并重新输入数据。

因此，FANUC 公司建议用户不管是否出现电池报警，每年定期地更换一次电池。

在更换电池时，务须在接通控制单元的电源的状态下进行。如果在断开电源的状态下拆下用于存储器备份的电池，存储器中的数据有可能丢失，这一点需要引起注意。此外，如前所述，控制单元使用锂电池。应遵守下列注意事项。

〈警告〉

电池的不正确安装可能会引起爆炸。

请不要使用非指定电池（指定电池 A02B-0200-K102）。

电池的使用方法有两种：使用内置在 CNC 控制单元中的锂电池的方法，和在外部安装电池盒使用市面出售的碱性干电池（一号）的方法（见图 21-1）。

〈注意〉

出厂时标准配置为锂电池。

使用锂电池时的电池更换方法

1. 请使用锂电池（备货图号：A02B-0200-K102）。
2. 通过控制单元的电源（30 秒左右）。
3. 断开控制单元的电源。
4. 先拆下连接器，然后从电池盒中取出电池。

电池盒，若是无插槽的单元位于单元的上部右边，若是带有插槽的单元则在上部靠中（夹在两风扇之间）位置。

5. 更换电池，连接上连接器。

〈注意〉

从3到5的步骤应在10分钟内完成。请注意，如果电池脱开的时间太长，存储器中的内容将会丢失。

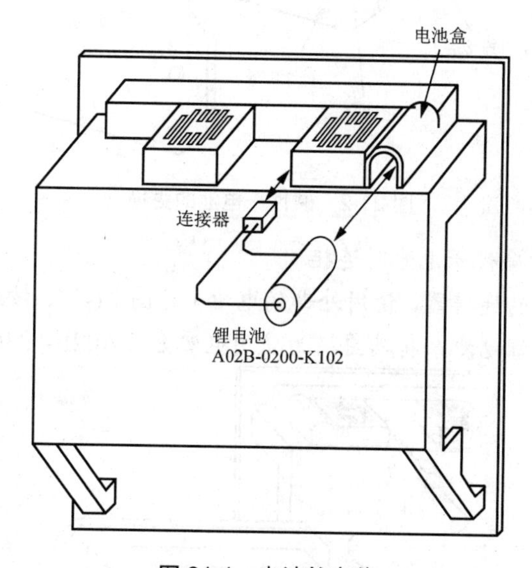

图 21-1 电池的安装

〈警告〉

电池的不正确安装可能会引起爆炸。

请不要使用非指定电池（指定电池 A02B-0200-K102）。

数控机床电池的更换方法（2）

使用市面出售的碱性干电池（一号）时的电池更换方法（见图 21-2）

1. 请使用市面上出售的碱性干电池（一号）。
2. 接通控制单元的电源（30 秒左右）。

3. 断开控制单元的电源。

4. 取下电池盒的盖子。

5. 更换电池，要注意电池的极性。

6．安装电池盒的盖子。

〈警告〉

在进行更换作业时，请按照与上面所述的锂电池的更换方法相同的方法予以更换。

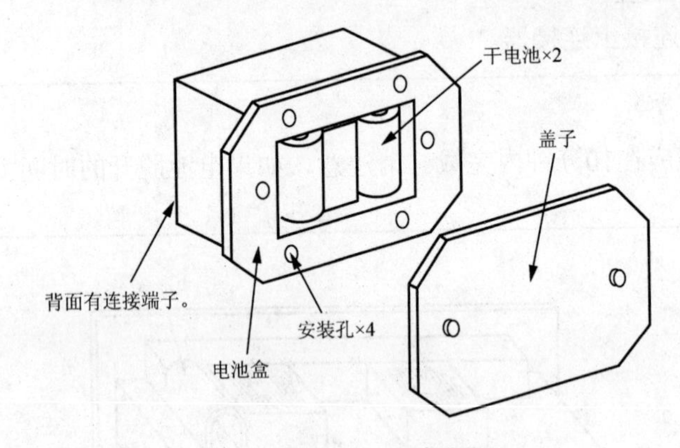

图 21-2　碱性干电池的更换

使用普通 D 型尺寸碱性干电池时连接

使用连接有锂电池的连接器，使用外部的电池（见图 21-3）。按照上面所述的电池的更换方法，从标准安装的锂电池，将其更换为使用电池盒（A02B-0236-C281）的外部电池。

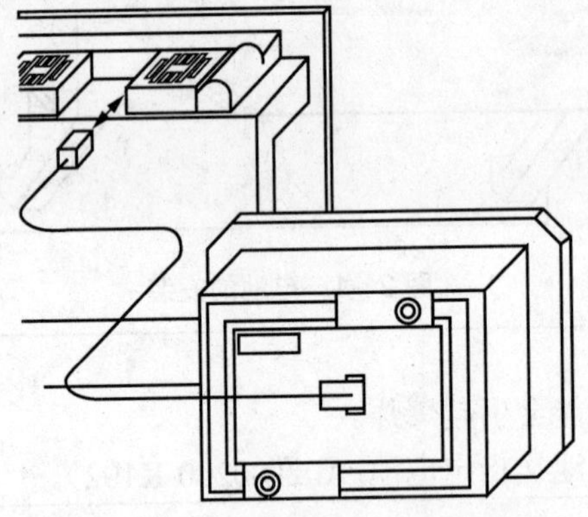

图 21-3　碱性干电池时连接

〈注意〉

1. 电池盒（A02B-0236-C281）的安装位置，应设置在即使在控制单元的电源处在接通状态下也可以进行电池更换作业的场所。

2. 本电池线缆的连接器部分采用简单嵌合的方式，应将距离连接器 50cm 之内的线缆部分在不会产生拉伸的状态下固定起来，以避免线缆的自重和线缆的拉伸等引起连接器的脱落。

第22课 自动运行

用编程程序运行 CNC 机床称为自动运行。

本课叙述以下种类的自动运行：

存储器运行

执行存储在 CNC 存储器中的程序的运行

MDI 运行

执行由 MDI 面板输入的程序运行

DNC 运行

从输入/输出设备读入程序使系统运行

程序再启动

从一个中间点重新启动程序进行自动运行

作业调度功能

通过执行存储在外部输入/输出设备（手持文件盒）的程序进行作业的调度

子程序调用功能

在存储器运行时，调用和执行存在外部输入/输出（手持文件盒）设备中子程序的功能

手动插入功能

在自动运行执行过程中，执行手动操作的功能

镜像功能

在自动运行过程中，允许沿着一个轴的镜像移动的功能

手动干预和返回

从自动运行过程中手动干预的起始位置重新启动自动运行的功能

利用存储卡进行 DNC 操作

自动运行存储在存储卡中的程序。

存储器运行

程序事先存储到存储器中。当选择了这些程序中的一个并按下机床操作。

面板上的循环启动按钮后，启动自动运行，并且循环启动 LED 点亮。

在自动运行中，机床操作面板上的 RESET 进给暂停按钮被按下后，自动运行被临时中止。当再次按下循环启动按钮后，自动运行又重新进行。

下述步骤只是一个范例。实际的操作，请见机床制造厂商提供的相关说明书。

存储器运行的步骤

步骤

1．按下存储器方式选择键。

2．从存储的程序中选择一个程序。其步骤如下：

（1）按下 PROG 键以显示程序屏幕。

（2）按下地址键 O 。

（3）使用数字键输入程序号。

（4）按下 [O SRH] 软键。

3．按下操作面板上的循环启动按钮。启动自动运行，并且循环启动 LED 闪亮。当自动运行结束时，指示灯熄灭。

4．要在中途停止或者取消存储器运行，请按以下步骤进行。

（1）停止存储器运行。

按下机床操作面板上的进给暂停按钮。进给暂停指示灯（LED）亮，并且循环启动指示灯熄灭。机床响应如下：

（i）当机床移动时，进给减速直到停止。

（ii）当程序在停刀状态时，停刀状态中止。

（iii）当执行 M，S 或 T 时，执行完毕后运行停止。

当进给暂停指示灯亮时，按下机床操作面板上的循环启动按钮会重新启动机床的自动运行。

（2）终止存储器运行。

按下 MDI 面板上的 RESET 键。

自动运行被终止，并进入复位状态。当在机床移动过程中，执行复位操作时，机床会减速直到停止。

详细说明

存储器运行

在存储器运行启动后，系统的运行如下：

（1）从指定程序中读取一段指令。

（2）这一段指令被译码。

（3）启动执行该段指令。

（4）读取下一段指令。

（5）执行缓冲，即指令被译码以便能够被立即执行。

（6）前段程序执行后，立即启动下一段程序的执行。这是因为执行缓冲的缘故。

（7）此后，存储器运行按照（4）到（6）重复进行。

超精加工

20 世纪 60 年代开始，用于计算机，电子，核能部件及国防应用的精密制造的需求越来越多。一些例子包括光学反射镜，电脑内存磁盘，以及复印机硒鼓。表面光洁度要求以数万纳米（10^{-9} 米或 0.001 μm）范围内，精度范围在微米和亚微米内形成。

由于应用的超精密加工刀具几乎完全是单晶金刚石，这一过程也被称为金刚石切削。

金刚石工具有一个半径边缘小到几纳米抛光切割。金刚石的磨损可能是一个重大的问题，最近的进展包括低温金刚石切削，其中工具系统是由液态氮冷却至约-120℃温度。

有记载的用于超精密加工工件材料包括铜合金，铝合金，银，电解镍，红外材料和塑料（丙烯酸树脂）。所涉及的切削深度是在纳米范围内。在此范围内，硬脆材料产生连续芯片（该过程称为韧性切削）；更深的切削，产生不连续的芯片。

加工工具这些应用是建立具有非常高的高精度，机械，主轴和工件的设备高刚度。这些超精密机床，其中一部分是由低的热膨胀和尺寸稳定性好的结构材料组成，位于一个无尘环境（即）干净的房间，温度控制在1度左右。

无论是内部来源以及从外部来源的机床，例如在同一层楼附近的机床，也尽可能避免振动。激光计量用于进给和位置控制，以及具有高度先进的计算机控制系统和热性能和几何误差补偿功能配备的机床中。

第23课　程序检查（1）

下面的功能用于在实际加工之前的工作检查，检查机床是否按编好的加工程序进行工作。

1. 机床锁住和辅助功能锁住
2. 进给速度倍率
3. 快速移动倍率
4. 空运行
5. 单段运行

机床锁住和辅助功能锁住

要想不移动刀具而显示其位置的变化，使用机床锁住功能。

有两种类型的机床锁住：所有轴的锁住（停止沿所有轴的运动），和指定轴的机床锁住（这种锁住仅停止沿指定轴的运动）（见图23-1）。另外，辅助功能的锁住，禁止执行M，S和T指令，是和机床锁住功能一起使用检查程序是否编制正确。

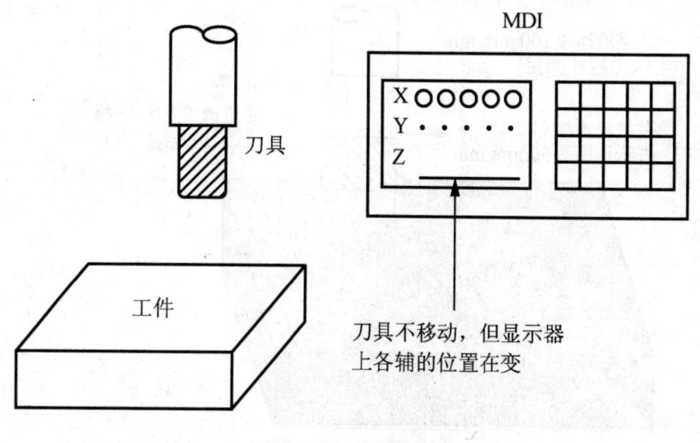

图23-1　机床锁住

机床锁住

按下机床操作面板上的机床锁住开关。刀具不再移动，但是显示器上沿每一轴运动的位移在变化，就像刀具在运动一样。

有些机床的每个轴都有机床锁住功能。在这种机床上，按下机床锁住开关，选择将要锁住的轴。有关机床锁住的功能，请见由机床制造厂提供的说明书。

〈警告〉

机床坐标系和工件坐标系之间的位置关系在机床锁住前后有可能不一样。在这种情况下，用坐标设置指令或者执行手动参考点返回来指定工件坐标系。

辅助功能锁住

按下机床操作者面板上的辅助功能锁住开关，M，S,T 和 B 代码被禁止输出并且不能执行。请见由机床制造厂提供的说明书。

限制

机床锁住情况下的 M,S,T,B 指令

在机床锁住的状态下，可以执行 M,S,T 和 B 指令。

机床锁住情况下的参考点返回

当机床锁住状态下，发出 G27,G28 或者 G30 指令时，指令被接受，但刀具并不移动到参考点，并且参考点返回指示灯也不亮。

辅助功能锁住时，没有锁住的 M 代码

M00,M01,M02,M30,M98,M99 和 M198（调用子程序）指令即使在辅助功 能锁住的状态下也能执行。调用子程序的 M 代码（参数 No.6071 到 6079）和调用宏程序的 M 代码（参数 No.6080 到 6089）也可以执行。

进给倍率

编程的进给速度可以通过倍率旋钮进行选择，按照一定的百分数增加或者减少。这个特点可以用于检查程序。例如，如果程序中指定了 100mm/min 的进给速度，并将倍率开关打到 50%，则刀具的移动速度变为 50mm/min（见图 23-2）。

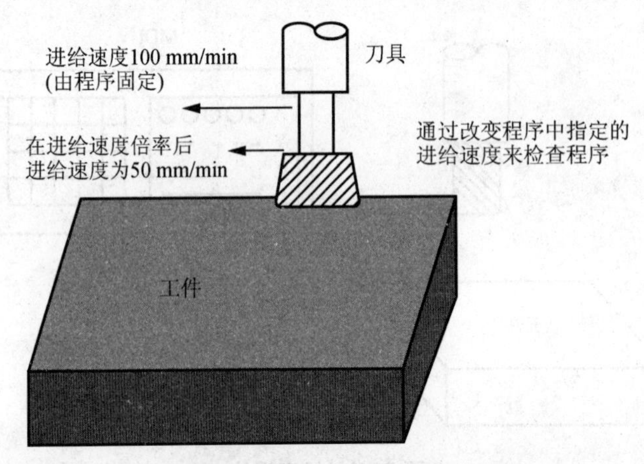

图 23-2 进给速度倍率

进给速度倍率的执行步骤

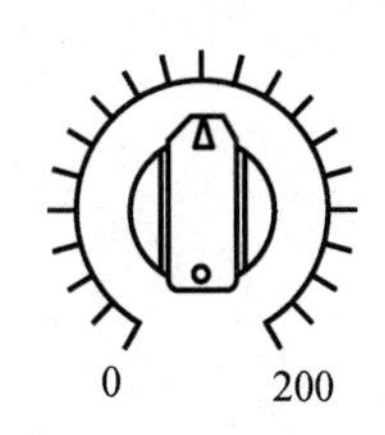

手动进给速度倍率

在自动运行之前或者期间，将机床操作面板上的进给速度倍率的旋钮转到想要的百分数。

在有些机床上，一个波段开关用于进给速度倍率和 JOG 进给速度倍率。请参阅由机床制造者提供的说明书。

限制

倍率范围

倍率范围从 0 到 254%。不同的机床，倍率范围不同，取决于机床的规格。

螺纹加工时的倍率

加工螺纹时进给倍率被忽略。进给速度不变，保持为程序中的指定值。

程序检查（2）

快速移动倍率

快速移动时，可以指定 4 级不同的倍率（F0,25%,50%,和 100%）（见图 23-3）。F0 由参数设定（No.1421）

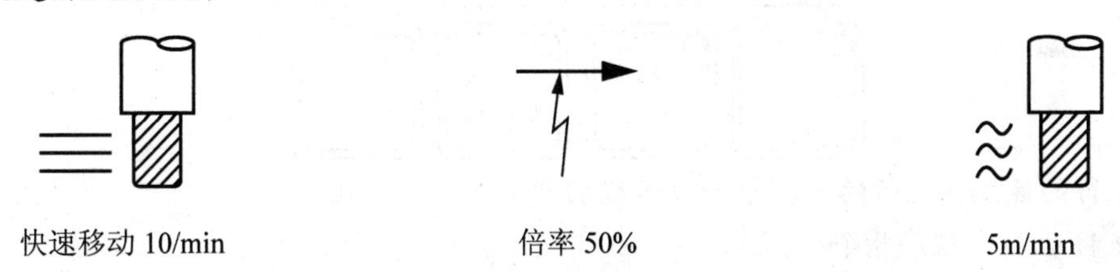

图 23-3 快速移动倍率

在快速移动时用快速移动倍率开关选择 4 种移动速度的一种。请见由机床制造者提供的说明书。

CNC 有以下几种快速移动。快速移动倍率可用于其中的任何一种。

1. 通过 G00 的快速移动
2. 在固定循环过程中的快速移动
3. 在指令 G27,G28,G29,G30 和 G53 中的快速移动
4. 手动快速移动
5. 手动参考点返回中的快速移动

空运行（见图 23-4）

刀具按参数指定的速度移动，而与程序中指令的进给速度无关。该功能用来在机床不装工件时检查刀具的运动。

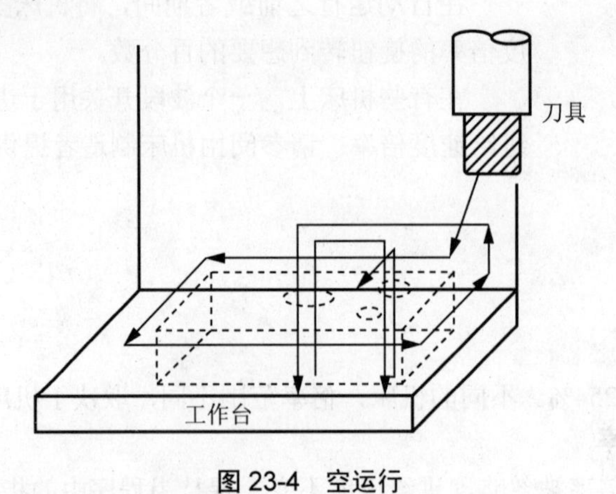

图 23-4 空运行

空运行的操作步骤

在自动运行期间，按下机床操作面板上的空运行开关。

刀具按参数中指定的速度移动。快速移动开关也可以用来更改机床的移动速度。

有关空运行的情况，请见由机床制造者提供的说明书。

详细说明

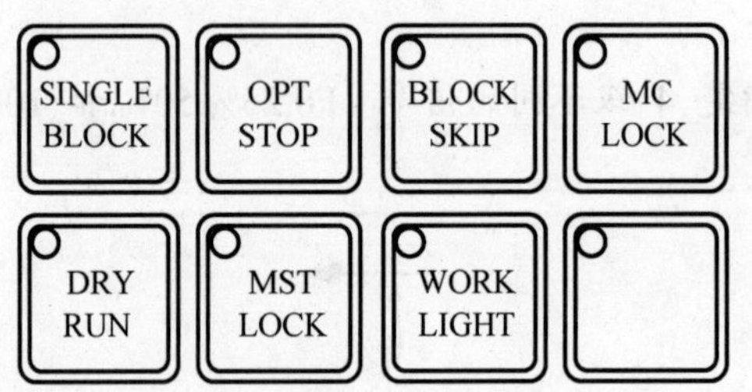

空运行的速度空运行的速度根据快速移动开关和参数变化如下表：

快速移动	程序指令	
按钮	快速移动	进给
开	快速移动速度	空运行速度×JVmax *2）
关	空运行速度×JV，或者快速移动速度	空运行速度×JV *2）

最大切削进给速度…………由参数 No.1422 设置

快速移动速度…………………由参数 No.1420 设置

空运行速度……………………由参数 No.1410 设置

JV：JOG 进给倍率

*1 当参数 RDR（No.1401#6）为 1 时为空运行速度×JV。当 RDR 为 0 时，为快速移动速度。

*2. 制在最大的快速移动速度

JVmax：JOG 进给速度倍率的最大值

单程序段

按下单程序段方式开关进入单程序段工作方式。在单程序段方式中按下循环启动按钮后，刀具在执行完程序中的一段程序后停止。通过单段方式的一段一段地执行程序，仔细检查程序。

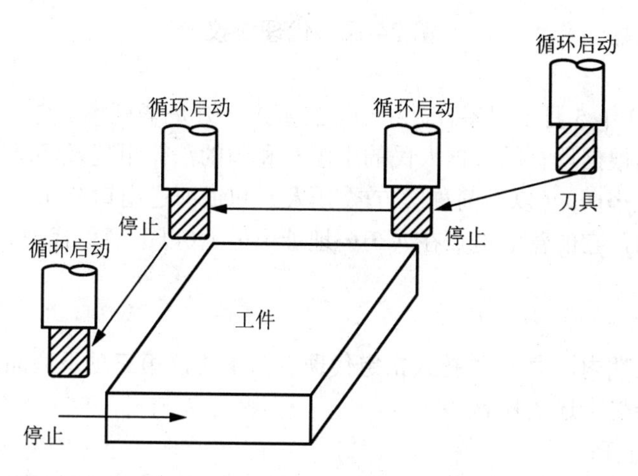

图 23-5（a） 单程序段方式

单段方式执行步骤

1. 按下机床操作面板上的单段程序执行开关。程序在执行完当前段后停止。
2. 按下循环启动按钮执行下一段程序。刀具在该段程序执行完毕后停止。

有关单程序段的执行，请见由机床制造者提供的说明书。

详细说明

参考点返回和单程序段的执行

如果采用了 G28 和 G30，单段程序的执行功能在中间点有效。

固定循环中的单程序段的执行

在固定循环中，单程序段的停止点是下图所示的 1，2 和 6 点。当单段方式在点 1 或者 2 后停止时，进给暂停的 LED 点亮。

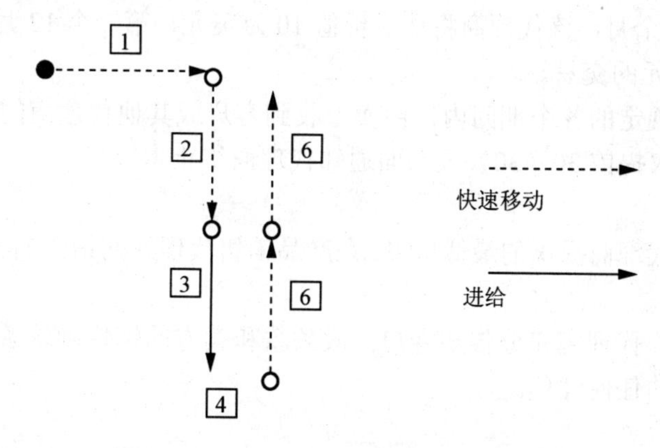

图 23-5（b） 在固定循环中的单段运行

子程序调用和单程序段的执行

在有 M98P_；.M99 或者 G65 的程序段中，单程序段停止不执行。但是，当程序段中有 M98P_或者 M99 指令且有 O,N,P,L 之外的地址时可以执行单段停止。

第 24 课　代理协议

本协议于 2009 年 5 月 1 日签订并生效。当事人一方是华夏华工进出口总公司，简称华夏化工，该公司是根据现有的根据人民的中国共和国的法律组建及活动的，其主要营业地点位于（……地址……）（以下简称卖方/委托人）和银河进出口公司，该公司是根据美国现有的法律组建的，它的营业地点在（……地址……）（以下简称代理）。特此双方达成协议如下：

1. 约定：

本协议在有效期内，卖方/委托人指定代理者为本协议第三项下商品的独家代理。代理商同意并接受并接受上述委托。

2. 代理商的责任：

代理商应严格遵守任何和给予卖方代理（不时）所有指示，不得作出任何陈述，保证，合同，协议或作出任何约束卖方的行为。卖方不对任何及所有行为或在超出或违背这些指示的代理商失败行为负责。

3. 商品/产品展示：

协议中的产品应该由代理商染色，产品的商标是“钻石”（以下简称的产品）。

4. 地区

根据本协议所涵盖的地区，应明确限于美国（以下简称境内）。

5. 专用权

在本批审议专用权，卖方（委托人）不得直接或间接不通过代理商而通过其他渠道在该地区销售产品；代理商不得在本地区销售，分销或促销任何具有竞争性的或类似产品，不得索取和接受在该产品范围外的任何订单。

6. 最小交易

在协议的头 12 个月，该代理商将达成价值 10 万美元，第二个 12 月 14 万美元和第三个 12 个月 20 万美元的交易。

倘若在本协议规定的各个期间内，由卖方收到客户或其他代理商的总额少于上述规定的数额，卖方应有权提前 30（30）天书面通知代理商终止本协议。

7. 销售价格

卖方应不时给代理商提供的最低价格，在产品销售代理期间销售的各自的条款及条件。

8. 订单

在招揽订单中，代理应充分告知客户一般条款和卖方的销售确认条件。代理商应立即分派商收到或拒绝的任何订单。

9. 费用

和产品销售有关的所有费用与支出都应入代理商的账户。

10. 佣金

卖方应给代理商支付的佣金第一个 12 个月为 3%，第二个 12 个月为 4%和第三个 12 个月为由代理商和由卖方获得的订单的产品净发票售价的 5%。这种佣金的支付条件是卖家收到的款项后，每 6（6）个月支付一次。佣金的支付均应当通过银行转账的方式。

11. 市场报告

该代理须每月向卖方报告关于其库存，市场情况和其他活动。

12. 促销

卖方应提供一份足够数量的免费的宣传材料，如文字的，目录，传单和诸如此类的东西。卖方和代理将共同制定一项推广计划和时间表。代理应认真贯彻落实促销计划，并就推广活动的反馈意见的影响做必要的报告。

13. 期限

本协定在双方签署后生效。至少在条款期限的前 3 个月，卖家和代理时应进行相互磋商对本协议进行更新。如果双方同意本协议的更新后，本协议修正后将延长三年。

14. 不可抗力

由于不可抗力导致失败或延迟履行的全部或部分责任，任何一方都要对其负责，不可抗力指天灾，政府命令或任何限制或不能在本协议订立之时预测的事情和其他协议双方无法控制、避免或克服的事情。但是，因不可抗力事件的影响的一方，应尽快以书面告知另一方。

15. 贸易条款和政府法

根据本协定的贸易条款应根据 2000 年制定的国际条款来解释，协议应根据人民的中国共和国的法律管辖的所有事宜中。

16. 仲裁

本协议履行过程中的所有争议都应通过友好协商解决。如果不能达成和解，那么案件应提交中国经济贸易仲裁委员会应用委员会的规则进行仲裁。该仲裁裁决是终局的，适用于双方。仲裁费用应由败诉方承担，除非委员会另有奖励。

关于签名：本协定一式两份，双方签署后立即生效；双方各持一份副本。

华夏华工进出口总公司　　　　银河进出口公司

卖方签字：_______在北京　　　　买方签字：______在北京

阅读理解

货物出口合同

编　号：______________________________

签约地：______________________________

日　期：______________________________

卖　方：______________________________

地　址：______________________________

电　话：________________ 传真：________________

电子邮箱：______________________________

买　方：______________________________

地　址：______________________________

电　话：________________传真：________________

电子邮箱：______________________________

买卖双方经协商同意按下列条款成交：

1. 货物名称、规格和质量：

2. 数量：

3. 单价及价格条款：

（除非另有规定，“FOB”、“CFR”和“CIF”均应依照国际商会制定的《2007年国际贸易术语解释通则》（INCOTERMS 2007）办理。）

4. 总价：

5. 允许溢价：______%。

6. 装运期限：

收到可以转船及分批装运之信用证______天内装运。

7. 付款条件：

买方须于____前将保兑的、不可撤销的、可转让的、可分割的即期付款信用证开到卖方，该信用证的有效期延至装运期后____天在中国到期，并必须注明允许分批装运和转船。

买方未在规定的时间内开出信用证，卖方有权发出通知取消本合同，或接受买方对本合同未执行的全部或部分，或对因此遭受的损失提出索赔。

8. 包装：

9. 保险：

按发票金额的______%投保______险，由______负责投保。

10. 品质/数量异议：

如买方提出索赔，凡属品质异议须于货到目的口岸之日起30天内提出，凡属数量异议须于货到目的口岸之日起15天内提出，对所装货物所提任何异议于保险公司、轮船公司、其他有关运输机构或邮递机构所负责者，卖方不负任何责任。

11.由于发生人力不可抗拒的原因，致使本合约不能履行，部分或全部商品延误交货，卖方概不负责。本合同所指的不可抗力系指不可干预、不能避免且不能克服的客观情况。

12. 仲裁：

因凡本合同引起的或与本合同有关的任何争议，如果协商不能解决，应提交中国国际经济贸易仲裁委员会深圳分会。按照申请仲裁时该会当时施行的仲裁规则进行仲裁。仲裁裁决是终局的，对双方均有约束力。

13. 通知：

所有通知用______文写成，并按照如下地址用传真/电子邮件/快件送达给各方。如果地址有变更，一方应在变更后______日内书面通知另一方。

14. 本合同为中英文两种文本，两种文本具有同等效力。本合同一式______份。自双方签字（盖章）之日起生效。

卖方签字：______　　　　　　　　买方签字：______

参 考 文 献

[1] John. V,B. Introduction to engineering materials. Second Edition. London: MACMILLAN PRESS, 1983.
[2] Mark A. Curtis.Tool Design for Manufacturing. New Yorl: McGraw-Hill, 1982.
[3] 管俊杰. 机械工程专业英语[M]. 北京：机械工业出版社，1999.
[4] 董建国. 机械专业英语[M]. 西安：西安电子科技大学出版社，2004.
[5] 杨春生. 机电技术专业英语[M]. 北京：电子工业出版社，2000.
[6] 蒋忠理. 机电与数控专业英语[M]. 北京：机械工业出版社，2005.
[7] 黄海. 数控应用专业英语[M]. 西安：西安电子科技大学出版社，2005.
[8] 刘瑛，罗学科，朱运利. 数控技术专业英语[M]. 北京：人民邮电出版社，2004.
[9] 沈阳机床集团产品说明书.